THE STRONGER WOMEN GET, THE MORE MEN LOVE FOOTBALL

Sexism and the American Culture of Sports

MARIAH BURTON NELSON

AVON BOOKS ◆ NEW YORK

ɪne cartoon on page xi is by Tim Eagan, copyright © 1988. It first appeared in *The Main Event*. Excerpt from Pearl Cleage's *Deals with the Devil: and Other Reasons to Riot,* copyright © 1993. Reprinted by permission of Random House. Excerpt from bell hooks's *Talking Back: Thinking Feminist, Thinking Black,* copyright © 1989. Reprinted by permission of South End Press. Excerpt from *M. Butterfly* by David Henry Hwang. Copyright © 1986, 1987, 1988 by David Henry Hwang. Used by permission of Dutton Signet, a division of Penguin Books USA, Inc. Excerpt from "Paper Matches" by Paulette Jiles from *Blackwater,* copyright © 1988. Reprinted by permission of Random House. Excerpt from *Water Dancer,* copyright © 1982 by Jenifer Levin. Reprinted by permission of Harvey Klinger, Inc. Excerpt from *Taller Women: A Cautionary Tale,* copyright © 1992 by Lawrence Naumoff. Reprinted by permission of Harcourt Brace & Company. Excerpt from "Phantasia for Elvira Shatayev" reprinted from *The Dream of a Common Language: Poems 1974-1977,* by Adrienne Rich, by permission of the author and W. W. Norton & Company, Inc. Copyright © 1978 by W.W. Norton & Company, Inc. Excerpt from *The Beauty Myth* by Naomi Wolf, copyright © 1990 by Naomi Wolf. Used by permission of William Morrow & Company, Inc.

AVON BOOKS
A division of
The Hearst Corporation
1350 Avenue of the Americas
New York, New York 10019

Copyright © 1994 by Mariah Burton Nelson
Inside cover author photo by Betsy Webster/Salty-Web Studios
Published by arrangement with Harcourt Brace & Company
Library of Congress Catalog Card Number: 93-44358
ISBN: 0-380-72527-4

The Harcourt Brace edition contains the following Library of Congress Cataloging in Publication Data:

Nelson, Mariah Burton.
 The stronger women get, the more men love football: sexism and the American culture of sports / by Mariah Burton Nelson.—1st ed.
    p.   cm.
Includes bibliographical references and index.
1. Sports—Psychological aspects.   2. Sex role—United States.
3. Sports—Social aspects—United States.   I. Title.
GV706.4.N45   1993
796'.01—dc20 93-44358

First Avon Books Trade Printing: August 1995

To Katherine

Contents

Acknowledgments

EXPLAINING THIS book to my brother Peter, I said, "Nowadays, women can and do compete with men on an equal basis almost everywhere—business, government, science, academia, art, and even in many sports. Football is one of the few remaining arenas in which male muscle matters."

"Thank God for football," said Peter wryly.

I'm grateful to Peter and to all of my family members, friends, and colleagues who, throughout my process of writing this book, responded to my ideas with interest, insight, and—just when I needed it—humor.

My good friends Dave Epperson and George Selleck helped me conceive of this book during a brainstorming session. Soon afterward, numerous friends, colleagues, acquaintances, and strangers offered stories, articles, academic papers, and ideas. Knowing that many people were eagerly anticipating the book and taking the time to clip newspaper articles and discuss it with their friends proved to be a great source of support for me during the essentially solitary activities of research and writing.

That support began with Felicia Eth, my agent, who wisely rejected several bad book ideas preceding this one, then made herself consistently available with encouragement and good advice. My editor, Alane Mason, understood this book from the outset and paid careful attention both to the big picture and to the details long after I'd lost perspective. I came to think of Felicia and Alane as kind coaches who believed in me and pushed me to excel, even when I became tired and discouraged. The book was greatly enhanced by their efforts.

I thank the experts who graciously served as informal consultants in history (Allida Black), sexual abuse (Cordelia Anderson), the physiology of gender (Alison Carlson and Angela Pattatucci), and sports journalism (Johnette Howard).

I thank those who sent articles, especially Carol Nagy Jacklin, Michael Messner, Kitty Porterfield, Anne Bolin, Celia Brackenridge, Rebecca Carpenter, Jay Coakley, Lauren Cux, Carol Galbraith, Linda Gebroe, Jane Gottesman, Chris Grant, Jackson Katz, Wendy Neely, Susan Reifer, Margie Shuer, Linda Stern, Linda Stoick, and Michele Sullivan.

I thank those who read a draft of the entire manuscript and offered valuable feedback: Katie Gekker, Donna Lopiano, Sarah Burton Nelson, Carol Nelson Shepherd, Dave Epperson, Ellie Smeal, Nancy Kass, and Ellen Wessel. I'm also thankful to Ann Bauleke and Sue Schaffer for reading individual chapters.

I'm especially grateful to the hundreds of scholars, writers, administrators, coaches, and athletes who are quoted in these pages. In particular I thank Susan Birrell for asking, What counts as sport?; Susan Greendorfer for asserting that female athleticism is a political act; Mary Jo Kane and Lisa Disch for their perspective on female journalists' power; and Michael Messner and Don Sabo for writing extensively on men, masculinity, and sport. I also thank Sally Edwards for asking me, during a lecture in Oregon, to talk about women, sports, and power. Here, at last, is my answer.

Most essentially, I'd like to thank my parents, Sarah and Arthur Nelson, for their lifelong, loving support. I also thank their partners, Bernie Makowsky and Linda Brock-Nelson, for their interest and input. Lastly, I thank my siblings, Carol Nelson Shepherd, Peter Martin Nelson, and Bill Henwood, who, despite our many heated discussions about this book, are still able to laugh when, during each Christmas vacation, the sisters work out at the gym while the brothers stay home and watch football.

1

We Don't Like Football, Do We?

I F Y O U grew up female in America, you heard this: Sports are unfeminine. And this: Girls who play sports are tomboys or lesbians. You got this message: Real women don't spend their free time sliding feet-first into home plate or smacking their fists into soft leather gloves.

So you didn't play or you did play and either way you didn't quite fit. You didn't fit in your body—didn't learn to live there, breathe there, feel dynamic and capable. Or maybe you fell madly, passionately in love with sports but didn't quite fit in society, never saw yourself—basketball player, cyclist, golfer—reflected in movies, billboards, magazines.

Or you took a middle ground, shying away at first but then later sprinting toward aerobics and weight lifting and in-line skating, relishing your increasing endurance and grace and strength. Even then, though, you sensed that something was wrong: all the ads and articles seemed to focus on weight loss and beauty. While those may have inspired you to get fit in the first place, there are more important things, you now know, than how you looked. No one seemed to be talking about pride, pleasure, power, possibility.

If you grew up male in America, you heard this: Boys who *don't* play sports are sissies or faggots. And this: Don't throw like a girl. You got this message: Sports are a male initiation rite, as fundamental and natural as shaving and deep voices—a prerequisite, somehow, to becoming an American man. So you played football or soccer or baseball and felt competent, strong, and bonded with your male buddies. Or you didn't play and risked ridicule.

Whether we were inspired by Babe Ruth or Babe Didrikson or neither, and whether we played kickball with our brothers or sisters or both, all of us, female and male, learned to associate sports prowess and sports privilege with masculinity. Even if the best athlete in the neighborhood was a girl, we learned from newspapers, television, and from our own parents' prejudices that batting, catching, throwing, and jumping are not neutral, human activities, but somehow more naturally a male domain. Insidiously, our culture's reverence for men's professional sports and its silence about women's athletic accomplishments shaped, defined, and limited how we felt about ourselves as women and men.

• • •

You may remember. There was a time not too long ago when women in bright tights did not run along highways, bike paths, forest trails. Now they do. "Horses make a landscape look more beautiful," the Sioux medicine man Lame Deer (and, later, Alice Walker) said. You may harbor a similar feeling about this endless stream of rainbow runners: Women make a landscape look more beautiful.

You may have noticed that boys are no longer the only ones shooting baskets in public parks. One girl often joins the boys now, her hair dark with sweat, her body alert as a squirrel's. Maybe they don't pass her the ball. Maybe she grabs it anyway, squeezes mightily through the barricade of bodies, leaps skyward, feet flying.

Or she teams with other girls. Gyms fill these days with the rowdy sounds of women hard at play: basketballs seized by calloused hands, sneakers squealing like shocked mice. The players' high, urgent voices resonate, too—"Here!" "Go!"—and right then nothing exists for them except the ball, the shifting constellation of women, the chance to be fluid, smooth, alive.

What does this mean? What does it mean that everywhere, women are running, shooting baskets, getting sweaty and exhausted and euphoric? What changes when a woman becomes an athlete?

Everything.

On playing fields and in gyms across America, women are engaged in a contest with higher stakes than trophies or ribbons or even prize money. Through women's play, and through their huddles behind the scenes, they are deciding who American women will be. Not just what games they will play, but what role they will play in this still-young nation. Not only what their bodies will look like, but what their bodies can do.

• • •

One recent Sunday my young niece, Teagan, walked past the family room, where her father and brother were watching football on television. Her father's big fist punched the air. Her little brother's small fist made the same gesture. "Touchdown!" yelled her father in his big booming voice. "Touchdown!" yelled Alex in his small child's voice. They did not notice Teagan.

Teagan entered the kitchen, where her mother was preparing dinner. "Mommy," she said, "we don't like football, do we?"

We don't like football, do we?

Oh, some women do. Some of us appreciate the balletic dance between passer and receiver or the impressive speed, skill, or strength of individual athletes. We enjoy rooting for the home team, feeling in tune with a community. We find that by watching—even a few minutes here and there—we can better converse with men at work. Or we take to the fields ourselves, enjoying autumn games of flag football with our friends.

"I happen to love football," says Jamie Zimron, a San Francisco therapist and aikido teacher. "When I'm watching it, I block out all the crashing and violence that goes on. I look at the team play: the timing, the beauty of the quarterback going back and the receiver making the cutting motion, reaching out his hands, taking it in." Quarterback Joe Montana, Zimron's favorite player, "is not a big macho man," she says. "He's humble and understated, with presence, vision, grace, and ease. He doesn't force things, doesn't hurry, doesn't get rattled. When he plays, magic happens."

Carol Galbraith, a Washington, D.C., writer and lawyer, enjoys playing. "What I love is being a tight end. As a kid, I never got to play. It was a very male sport, the kind you're excluded from, and that made it more attractive. I like seeing the ball into my hands and hauling ass and scoring."

But we're also troubled by football. Jamie Zimron is bothered by the high injury rate. "I read in the paper the next day about the torn ligaments, destroyed knees, concussions, broken ankles, separated shoulders." And the steroid use: "It's insane. Sort of like the nuclear arms race: The other team's doing it, so I've got to, even if it's totally toxic and fatal."

Galbraith refuses to watch men play. She refers to football players as "grunty slobs" whose larger-than-life portrayals serve as a "constant reminder that males are bigger than females and that violence is a male province." Men's large bodies and their displays of aggression "are supposed to trigger all this fear and respect," she says. "It's a show of force. A veiled threat in a way."

Many women are angry at football, basketball, baseball, boxing, ice hockey, wrestling, soccer—sports that I call the manly sports; sports that men use to define masculinity. Many women hate the veiled threat. Many resent the time their husbands, fathers, or brothers spend screaming at the tube, slapping raucous high-fives, indulging in loud emotional outbursts that seem misplaced and out of proportion to the drama at hand. Women often feel alienated from their male co-workers when they spend so much time talking sports. Most women lack the nostalgic reference points—Little League did not admit girls until 1973—and the ability to identify with hulks.

Many mothers don't want their sons to play—or want them to play but not get injured, and that omnipresent fear of injury clouds all enthusiasm. They're uncomfortable when coaches call their sons wimps or sissies. Women don't want sissy sons, but women don't want the opposite either: brutal sons who grow inured to their own pain or to the pain of others.

Women seem to intuit that football and other manly sports hurt women. There's something about the way certain games are played and the way they're worshiped that's injurious to women's mental and physical health. When Patricia Bowman testified that William Kennedy Smith "tackled" her on the lawn, we cringed. When Desiree Washington testified that boxer Mike Tyson "pinned" her to the bed, then raped her, we were furious but not surprised. When a new "sports bar" opens in New

York and it features topless dancers, we understand that this seems natural to the bar's owner and its enthusiastic patrons. We sense a connection: there's something about male sports privilege that contributes to the sexual objectification and abuse of women. Given how pervasive and what cultural icons men's sports are, that's a scary thought.

• • •

"Who's your team?" a man asks a boy he has just met in a doctor's office.

"The Atlanta Braves," the boy replies.

"Good choice," says the man. Actually, almost any men's pro or college team would suffice. The important thing is to "have" a team, love a team, follow a team. To identify with successful manly athletes is to feel successful and manly oneself, to feel a part of the dominant male culture. Millions of men affirm their manliness and manly ties by betting on sports, discussing sports, arguing over sports, agonizing over decisions such as, Should I root for Baltimore, where I grew up, or Cleveland, where I live now? These men argue over whether Pete Rose should be admitted into the Hall of Fame. They can become irritable for an entire day if "their" team loses.

To women, this can sound silly, but many men take manly sports seriously. The games become symbolic struggles, passion plays reenacted daily to define, affirm, and celebrate manliness. The games offer men a chance to admire huge bodies, "aggressive play" and "very physical teams," to gossip over who did what and in what year, to compete over statistics: "When did the Boston Red Sox win their last World Series?" "Who scored the most points in a single NBA game?" When discussing sports, men reminisce about their own high school sports "careers." They imagine that they themselves somehow "just missed" becoming famous athletes.

Few men take no interest in the World Series, the Super Bowl, the Final Four, or the latest boxing match. Of those who do abstain from the daily sports dialogue, some have failed at youth sports and retain an antagonism for the arena that injured their egos or their bodies. "I was big, slow, and clumsy," recalls Brent LaFever, a facilities manager from Winston-Salem, North Carolina. "Now I hate watching sports. They're so barbaric. When people come to visit, my wife and I don't let them turn on the television. Often they leave."

Other men develop an antipathy for sports because they did play and didn't like what they saw of the manly sport culture: the cutthroat competition, the cruel coaches, the required "toughness." Numerous men were humiliated by coaches who insisted on "making a man out of them" but ignored the sensitive boys that they were.

Regardless of his reasons, the grown man who pays no attention to male sporting dramas must be, it seems to me, among the most secure and confident of all men, because he relinquishes a daily opportunity to identify with the culture's primary male heroes and in the process risks censure or at least estrangement from other men. Yet even a man who steers clear of the daily barrage of sports events, sports pages, sports television, and sports talk radio shows will often devise ways to fake it. In response to overtures such as, "How 'bout those Redskins!" he may utter an ambiguous, noncommittal exclamation, such as, "They've got quite a quarterback!" Rare is the man who not only opts out of the manly sports system but also criticizes it—who, in response to "How 'bout those Redskins!" will say, "I hate football. It's racist, sexist, and far too violent for me."

Sport has been called the last bastion of male domination. Unfortunately, there are others—Congress, for instance. But sport constitutes the only large cultural institution where men and women are (sometimes) justifiably segregated according to gender. It is one of the few remaining endeavors where male muscle matters.

Women have always been strong. We have carried water, harvested crops, birthed and raised children. Women do two-thirds of the world's work, according to New Zealand economist Marilyn Waring. But as women in the late twentieth century gain increasing economic, political, and athletic strength, many men cling to manly sports as a symbol of "natural" male dominance. The stronger women get, the more enthusiastically male fans, players, coaches, and owners seem to be embracing a particular form of masculinity: toughness, aggression, denial of emotion, and a persistent denigration of all that's considered female. Attitudes learned on the playing fields, or by watching sports on television, leach into the soil of everyday life, where many men view women and treat women with disdain. They call baseball the national pastime—which, in a diverse society, "unites us all." But baseball, football, and other manly sports do not unite Americans. They unite American men in a celebration of male victory. By pointing to men's greater size and strength and by imbuing those qualities with meaning (dominance, conquest), many men justify to themselves a two-tiered gender system with men on top. As University of Iowa sports sociologist Susan Birrell has noted, "It's a short leap from seeing men as physically superior to seeing men as superior, period."[1]

Sports are an escape, men often say. One wonders what they are escaping from. Men who *must* watch The Game seem to me to be escaping from women's demands for freedom, equality, and simple attention—as well as from housework, child-care, and other family responsibilities.

Manly sports are more than a refuge from the reality of women's liberation. By creating a world where masculinity is equated with violence, where male bonding is based on the illusion of male supremacy, and where all of the visible women are cheerleaders, manly sports set the stage for violence against women. When we begin to understand how male coaches and players speak and think about women and masculinity, it ceases to be surprising that college football and basketball players gang-rape women in numbers equaled only by fraternity brothers.[2] Or that male basketball and football players are reported to police for sexual assault 38 percent more often than their male college peers.[3] Or that football and basketball players are more likely to engage in sexually aggressive behaviors (including everything from whistling and unwanted touching to attempted rape) than their peers, including those who play other sports.[4]

"It's just a game," former commissioner Fay Vincent used to say about baseball. But baseball and other manly sports are more than games. They constitute a culture—the dominant culture in America today. Manly sports comprise a world where men are in charge and women are irrelevant at best. Where assaults that would be illegal off the field become an accepted, even celebrated part of "play" and replay. Where big men wearing tight pants embrace each other, openly loving men and male power. Where "girls" flash their underwear.

Sports offer a pre-civil rights world where white men, as owners, coaches, and umpires, still rule. Within a sports arena, a man can express racist, sexist, and homophobic attitudes not tolerated in many other parts of society. The public denigration of women (and minority men) has become such a mainstay of the American sporting experience that when *Sports Illustrated* took an "unscientific" poll of fans in 1988, "everyone who had ever been a spectator of any kind had, at one time or another, experienced the bellowing of obscenities, racial or religious epithets [and] abusive sexual remarks to women in the vicinity."[5]

• • •

Most women, by contrast, don't really "have" a team. They don't ask little girls, Who's your team? Women don't indoctrinate girls into a world of statistics and heroes and athletic history. Few women crave violent entertainment. "In a boxing match, women tend to identify with the loser," says writer Joyce Carol Oates, author of *On Boxing* as well as several dozen other books.[6]

Women often ignore women's sports, not taking seriously their daughters' or even their own athletic passions, not noticing the link between physical strength and personal power, or between female team bonding and female political clout. Without thinking about it, many women attend high school football games but never drop by to see how the girls' basketball team is faring.

Feminists have tried to reduce sexual violence in all its forms: child sexual abuse, sexual harassment at work, battering and rape by husbands and "lovers," rape by strangers, and the glorification of rape through pornography. Women have tried to empower women through jobs, education, health care, politics, and therapy. For the most part, women haven't paid attention to sports. Women tend to ignore the sports section of the newspaper and to avoid living rooms and bars and college dormitories where men gather ritually, as if to worship the televised game.

Women—and fair-minded men—need to pay attention. We live in a country in which the manly sports culture is so pervasive we may fail to recognize the symbolic messages we all receive about men, women, love, sex, and power. We need to take sports seriously—not the scores or the statistics, but the process. Not to focus on who wins, but on who's losing. Who loses when a community spends millions of dollars in tax revenue to construct a new stadium and only men get to play in it, and only men get to work there?

Who loses when football and baseball so dominate the public discourse that they eclipse all mention of female volleyball players, gymnasts, basketball players, swimmers?

Who loses when coaches teach boys that the worst possible insult is to be called "pussy" or "cunt"?

Who loses when rape jokes comprise an accepted part of the game?

Sport is a women's issue because on playing fields, male athletes learn to talk about and think about women and women's bodies with contempt. It's a women's issue because male athletes have disproportionately high rates of sexual assaults on women—including female athletes. It's a women's issue because the media itself cheers for men's sports and rarely covers women's, thereby reinforcing the notion that men are naturally more athletic. It's a women's issue because of the veiled threat, this homage paid to bulky, brutal bodies. And it's a women's issue because female sport participation empowers women, thereby inexorably changing everything.

2

Feminism and Football: Then and Now

[Martha:] "The more I helped Bob and the more patient I was and the more I put up with, and the more strength I provided for both of us, the more he seemed to resent it, and the angrier he got at me. I never understood that."

[Lydia:] "Well, you just said it. And you know what it is. They like us weak, I swear they do."

—Lawrence Naumoff, <u>Taller Women</u>

PICTURE THIS: A group of college women challenge their male peers to a game—a football game. Not necessarily a friendly game. A serious, competitive, grass-stained game, a game in which the man who runs with the football runs scared. The women, fueled by more than simple strength and speed—fueled perhaps by a "we're mad as hell and not going to take it anymore" anger—gain the advantage. They chase the man, tackle him.

Imagine how he feels as he lies in the mud, pinned to the earth by a pile of weighty women. Imagine the smiles on the women's faces. Imagine their celebratory dance.

This is the image Charles Dana Gibson brought to mind in 1896 when he published a drawing entitled, *The Coming Game: Yale versus Vassar.* Both colleges were single-sex at the time. Both women and men were streaming onto playing fields to enjoy newly invented or newly organized sports. In Gibson's illustration, five fierce women chase the football-carrying man. Wearing bloomers and vests, their long hair heaped on top of their heads, the women—who are larger than the man—run with clenched fists. They have already knocked one hapless male player to the ground. They do not stop to pick him up. It is clear from the women's focused faces and from the ball carrier's terrified stare that they will soon tackle him, too.

The Coming Game was political satire. Gibson did not expect college women to compete against men in football. But satire points out truths: in this case, an actual fear on the part of many men that women's growing athleticism somehow threatened not only men and men's sports but the very nature of things: men on top.

• • •

A century later, some men support and encourage female athletes. Some fathers throw baseballs to their daughters even if they also have sons. But many men are again interpreting women's increasing strength as a threat, a harbinger of the demise of men, masculinity, or male privilege. If women become free to engage in athletic activity as they see fit, what else might they do? How strong might they become? Might they gang up (five women versus two men) and in some sense tackle men? Might women begin to win at games men have defined as exclusively male? Might they challenge men's exclusive right to those games and to "masculine" qualities such as aggressiveness? Who would win this Coming Game?

Perhaps the fearful are correct. After all, Yale and Vassar have become coed, as have most other institutions. Women are now competing with and against men in almost every conceivable vocation and avocation. Women *are* gaining economic, social, and political power.

But while colleges, Congress, corporations, and other American institutions become painstakingly integrated, football clings to its all-male status, resisting women's attempts at participation whether as players, coaches, administrators, or reporters. Football is male, masculinity, manliness. So when women demand the right to play, control, judge, report on, or change football—and other manly sports—their struggle is not just about equal access to fitness and fatlessness. It's about redefining men and women. It's about power.

First-wave feminists—and their opponents—seemed to understand this connection between male athletic privilege and female power. In 1913, after ten years of active agitation for voting rights, Christabel Pankhurst and her British comrades in the Women's Social and Political Union snuck onto golf courses late at night. Using razor blades, they inscribed on the greens their heartfelt messages. "Votes for Women," they wrote, and "Votes Before Sport," and the ultimate threat, "No Votes, No Golf."

They had tried other tactics, from peaceful demonstrating to civil disobedience. They had become increasingly militant, staging hunger strikes, stoning police, smashing store windows, and setting empty buildings afire. Now they attacked true sanctuaries of male privilege: golf courses.

I like to envision the women hitching their long skirts as they quietly carved guerrilla artwork on cropped golf greens under a starry sky. Armed with packets of sharp blades, they must have grinned with glee at the thought of the first foursome of male golfers trying to putt their balls across the bumpy engravings.

Many of these women had never trod on golf courses before—not necessarily because they lacked the class privilege to afford such diversions, but because many courses in *fin-de-siècle* England and America were closed to women altogether, or closed to women during prime playing times. Thus the golf theater promised an audience of men not yet converted to the equal-rights cause. Surely this will get their attention, the women must have thought.

They were right. At a time when much feminist activity was being dismissed by the press as "not of public interest," *Golfing* magazine could not overlook this grave trespass onto sacred male turf. The editor complained, pleading that "golfers are not very keen politicians."[1]

The suffragettes responded, "Perhaps they will be now."[1]

The women were right to link feminist gains and masculinist games. Sports contests, so often described as battles between men, in fact reflect an essential struggle between men and women, especially when women are excluded from the actual play. By defining certain sports as male, and by linking maleness to muscular might, men attempt to erect a seemingly biologically determined supremacy.

Women counter by sprinting past, spraying unladylike sweat in their wake. They sue, demanding equal opportunities in high school and college sports programs. And they somehow find ways to take the war out of sports, hugging their opponents as if they were friends.[2]

The female challenge to men's sports is not just, "We want to play, too." We want to play in a neither ladylike nor manlike fashion. We want men to relinquish their treehouse mentality—No Girls Allowed—but we also want them to stop using sports to justify brutish behavior. To stop using sports to define maleness and thus femaleness.

Who will win, Team Macho or Team Feminism? Force or finesse? Archaic masculine–feminine straitjackets or more enlightened views of human possibility? This is the Coming Game. For women, it's a fun game when we're winning—which can mean something as simple as joining a previously all-men's team without ridicule. For women, it's a deadly game when we're losing—which can mean being beaten, sometimes literally, or having men "score" on us against our will. It's a game that began during the first wave of feminism, and the first wave of athletic backlash, one hundred years ago.

• • •

During the first American feminist movement, which spanned from 1848 to 1920, women agitated for what Elizabeth Cady Stanton called self-sovereignty. First they helped abolish slavery, then, buoyed by that success, they demanded the vote for all women. They demanded birth control and abortion. They insisted on dress reform, divorce reform, married women's property rights, prohibition of alcohol and prostitution, educational opportunities, and economic power. They demanded entry into the military and government. They advocated job training, equal wages, labor unions, cooperative child-care and kitchens, and child custody rights for mothers. And they demanded sports for women and girls.[3]

The bicycle in particular caught the attention of middle- and upper-class women. Seated on the newly designed bikes (including brakes!), women of the 1890s became free to tour the countryside and to escape chaperones, who often perceived themselves to be too old to learn to ride. Sidesaddle was the required form of horseback riding for women in that era, but bicycles required all riders to sit astride, a task nearly impossible to accomplish in corsets and petticoats. Thus thousands of eager female cyclists risked public censure by wearing the infinitely more comfortable bloomers.

As sports became standardized, with recorded times and measured courses, women demonstrated great passion for the sporting life. It was in the late 1800s that the first American women's championships in archery, golf, and tennis were held. The first intercollegiate women's basketball game, between Stanford University and the University of California, Berkeley, took place on April 4, 1896, the same month the first modern, all-male Olympic games were held in Athens. James Naismith had invented basketball just five years earlier, and had proclaimed it an ideal sport for women. The first college women's game featured Naismith's original nine-player, one-point-per-basket format. Because public female sweat was deemed indelicate, men were not allowed to watch, but five hundred boisterous women packed the stands of San Francisco's Armory Hall. "The fighting was hard and the playing was good," the *San Francisco Examiner* reported. "The girls jumped, scrambled, and fell over one another on the floor, but they didn't mind it. They were up quick as a flash, chasing after the ball again."[4]

Stanford won, 2 – 1.

Throughout the first years of this century, the popularity of women's basketball (and the scoring ability of its players) grew. Women's colleges, including Mount Holyoke, Smith, Vassar, and Wellesley, all fielded basketball teams, and most offered intercollegiate archery, baseball, basketball, rowing, tennis, and track. Sport promised more than recreation; women used it to break free of restrictive codes of femininity. A writer in Wellesley's 1898 yearbook said of her basketball team, "The grimy and generally disheveled appearance of the players, as they emerge from the fray, fills our athletic souls with pride."[5]

In an 1898 *Scribners* magazine article, writer Abbie Carter Goodloe described a growing seriousness among female college rowers who had been training indoors on rowing machines: "In their dark blouses and bloomers, the muscular young rowers of today present a very different appearance from those of other years, when the formation of a crew was almost a social affair, and those who composed it were elevated chiefly for their good looks."[6]

In a letter to a female friend in 1884, the woman who would become Bryn Mawr president wrote of her visit to the Wellesley gym: "The girls in trowsers [*sic*] swinging on rings, twirling on bars, a newer race of athletes—ushers in of a new day."[7]

Some late nineteenth-century women even boxed, shot guns recreationally, and lifted weights in order to build big muscles. In 1876 Nell Saunders defeated Rose Harland in the first U.S. women's boxing match.[8] In 1885 Buffalo Bill's Wild West Show featured sharpshooter Annie Oakley.[9] And 1898 cigar box labels displayed front and back views of a bare-armed woman flexing her biceps.[10]

The All-England Croquet and Lawn Tennis Club held its first national women's championship at Wimbledon in 1884. British women created the Ladies Golf Union in 1893, the All-England Women's Field Hockey Association in 1895, and the Southern Ladies Lacrosse Club in 1905. In 1899 a popular British novel called *Miss Cayley's Adventures* featured a woman who rowed while at college and won a trans-Alpine bicycle race against male competitors.[11] The first women's sports magazine, *Hockey Field,* emerged in England in 1901.

Some outspoken feminists became avid athletes, creating an early association between women's liberation and sports. Senda Berenson, the Smith College professor who introduced basketball to American women in 1892, justified the strenuous game by pointing out that "all fields of labor and all professions are opening their doors" to women, and that therefore women would need "more than ever the physical strength to meet these ever increasing demands."[12]

Frances Willard, head of the Women's Christian Temperance Union, wrote an entire book about the liberating effects of cycling, *A Wheel Within a Wheel: How I Learned to Ride the Bicycle,* published in 1895. Alice Paul, founder of the National Women's Party and author of the Equal Rights Amendment, excelled at basketball while at Swarthmore College (class of '02). Charlotte Perkins Gilman (author of *Herland,* a feminist utopia; *The Yellow Wallpaper,* a novel about the devastating effects of the Victorian "rest cure"; and *Women and Economics*) played basketball with her teenage daughter. She also ran a mile a day and bragged of her ability to "vault and jump, go up a knotted rope, walk on my hands under a ladder, kick as high as my head, and revel in the flying rings."[13]

In a 1901 issue of *Munsey's Magazine,* Anne O'Hagen wrote, "With the single exception of the improvement of legal status of women, their entrance into the realm of sports is the most cheering thing that has happened to them in the century just past. . . . The revolution means as much psychologically as it did physically."[14]

Elizabeth Cady Stanton wrote in 1895, "Many a woman is riding to the suffrage on a bicycle."[15]

In 1890 the most famous female athlete in the United States was the "Gibson Girl," a slim, long-legged, fictional creation who graced many of Charles Dana Gibson's drawings. A cyclist, tennis player, and golfer, the nameless icon was "braver, stronger, more healthful and skillful and able and free, more human in all ways" than other prototypical Victorian women, Gilman declared enthusiastically.[16]

A Gibson cartoon that appeared in *Life* in 1902 showed a startled man standing on one side of a huge crevasse. Leaping across the divide, about to land on the other side, was a long-skirted woman. Title: "One of the Disadvantages of Being in Love with a Athletic Girl."

• • •

Men tried desperately to limit women's involvement, refusing women admission to most sports clubs,[17] mocking women who competed, and inventing numerous hazards, most gynecological, that might befall athletic women. Cyclists' saddles, for instance, were said to induce menstruation and cause contracted vaginas and collapsed uteri. While appearing to enjoy an innocent, healthful ride, female cyclists might use the upward tilt of the saddle to engage in the "solitary vice" of masturbation. And, skirts hiked provocatively above the ankle, female cyclists might contribute to immorality by inciting lewd comments from male pedestrians.

One writer insisted that when women overdo exercise, it "runs their flesh off."[18] In actuality, women's flesh was more endangered by rowdy male cyclists who would force female cyclists off the road. *Vogue* magazine reported in 1889 that the women of New York City protected themselves from such ruffians by riding with male companions.[19]

Physicians generally applauded women's cycling. By developing uterine muscles, they claimed, cycling eased childbirth; it also cured exhaustion and depression. Concurrently, doctors treated many male cyclists for testicular tenderness, constipation, bladder troubles, difficulty discharging urine, and "shrivelling of the penis."[20]

But in popular magazines, female "overexertion" was the overriding concern, a holdover from the midcentury cult of female invalidism. In 1902, women's tennis matches were reduced from best-of-five to best-of-three sets.[21] Meanwhile, female farmers and factory workers toiled for long hours without male complaint. This paradox—"how to convince women that heavy work was safe, while heavy play was dangerous," Canadian sociologist Helen Lenskyj writes in *Out of Bounds*[22]—proved challenging for opponents of women's sports.

In England, the *Birmingham Daily Mail* took an editorial stance against women's sports in 1881, calling cricket "essentially a masculine game" that "can never be played properly in petticoats." While the writer was right about the petticoats, he was less justified in his prediction that if women began to box they might become "horney-handed, wide-shouldered, deep-voiced . . . and with biceps like a blacksmith's." He attempted to dissuade women by implying that competition—especially with men—is unnatural: "Let our women remain women instead of entering their insane physical rivalry with men," he pleaded.[23] Perhaps in part to prevent such rivalries, through much of the 1890s female rowers were, against their desires, judged not on speed but on form and grace.[24]

Women who took sports (and especially sports feminism) seriously faced scorn. When Rhoda Anstey, founder of the Gymnastics Teachers' Suffrage Society, led a suffrage rally, hecklers yelled at the marching women, "Here come the elastic teachers. Let's see their biceps."[25] At Cambridge in 1896, male undergraduates celebrated their school's refusal to grant women degrees by publicly hanging in effigy a female cyclist in bloomers.[26] French poet René François Armand Sully-Prudhomme denounced the sportswoman's tendency to "borrow from the men the virile qualities that denature her and negate her charm."[27]

Gradually, men gave up trying to dissuade women from sports altogether. Instead they scurried to redefine female athleticism as sexy or romantic, intended not for women's health, enjoyment, or empowerment, but for men's pleasure. The popular image of the female cyclist was transformed from an adventurous, independent, bloomer-wearing feminist to someone who would "look sweet upon the seat"—the back seat—"of a bicycle built for two."[28] The cover of most issues of *Physical Culture* magazine featured a young, smiling woman in a semi-athletic, semi-cheesecake pose, the wind typically blowing her short skirt upward.[29]

The publisher of *Physical Culture* was a self-appointed professor of "kinesitherapy" named Bernard Mcfadden (in the 1890s he changed his name to Bernarr Macfadden). A staunch advocate of exercise, Macfadden was also an aggressive marketer, particularly of women's bodies. In 1901 he published *The Power and Beauty of Superb Womanhood,* a book that led to obscenity charges being brought against him because it included photographs of bare-breasted women exercising to improve their bust size.[30]

Women sometimes colluded in this strategy, peddling their own attractiveness as a way to justify sports participation. Lucille Hill, director of physical education at Wellesley, linked "the delights of athletics" with the "desirability of possessing a strong and beautiful body for both use and ornament."[31] Annette Kellerman, the competitive swimmer whose name became synonymous with tight-fitting, one-piece bathing suits shaped like today's triathlon suits, had her picture taken in poses that set the stage for today's *Sports Illustrated* swimsuit issue. Her autobiography, which included both her life story and the exercise regimen system she designed for women, was entitled *The Body Beautiful.*[32]

Advocating strenuous rowing in a series of 1880s and 1890s articles in the sports magazine *Outing,* Margaret Bisland wrote, "By some happy provision of kind Nature, no matter if the woman's biceps grow as hard as iron and her wrists as firm as steel, the member remains as softly rounded, as tenderly curved, as though no greater strain than the weight of jeweled ornaments had been placed on them."[33] A 1902 *Outing* article by Christine Terhune Herrick was entitled, "The Athletic Girl Not Unfeminine."[34] In an 1895 magazine, a writer named Winifred Ayers complained about Smith College's athletic program, describing a woman whose "arms were bare also, and the muscles were so developed that they appeared in lumpy protuberances, just as those of the professional athletes are wont to do."[35]

· · ·

Despite women's ambivalence, men got the message: women were changing. Men, too, were changing. Industrialization had destabilized American and European men's sense of themselves and their role in the social order. Moving from farms to factories, men's work became less physical, which led to self-doubts about virility. Men who had previously worked outside, and for themselves, began working inside, and for others, losing their independence and sense of control as the agricultural and small-business economy became urban, bureaucratic, and technological.[36]

In the United States, the gates to the new frontier gradually closed, stymieing European-American men who had been eager to demonstrate their courage, resourcefulness, or adventurousness. New immigrants flooded into the quickly expanding industrial cities, challenging American men's dominion over U.S. jobs. Women, too, were challenging men's jobs as they began to enter industrial and professional occupations previously closed to them.[37]

These changes brought about a "crisis of masculinity"[38]—at least for white, heterosexual men. Adding to the crisis was that women increasingly filled school teaching positions and raised their children virtually alone, since men spent more and more time working away from home. Rather than worry about the possible harm of male absence from family life, men worried about female presence. Might women teach boys to be more like women?

Male journalists began to warn against the "feminizing of culture" or its "effeminization." The Boy Scouts of America, founded in 1910, offered an all-male refuge designed in part to thwart this dangerous trend.[39] The YMCA, founded in 1852, became increasingly popular since it offered another all-male sanctuary where boys could escape "the feminizing clutches of mothers and teachers."[40]

Organized sports represented men's most enduring "weapon" in the struggle to redefine power, strength, and privilege as incontrovertibly male.[41] The ancient Greeks, Romans, Asians, and Egyptians had set the stage, using nude boxing and wrestling to prepare men for the constant threat of war, establishing sport as an almost exclusively male domain, and emphasizing in their legends male toughness and bravery, as well as the impressive size of male bodies. Greek games were particularly brutal: *Pankration,* a combination of boxing, wrestling, and kicking, even permitted genital kicks, pulls, and punches. Only biting and eye-gouging were forbidden.[42]

Drawing on this tradition of manly combat in a sporting context, late-nineteenth-century men promoted numerous sports from bare-knuckled prizefighting to wrestling to rugby. British and American proponents of a "muscular Christianity" movement equated stoicism, courage, tolerance for pain, and quick thinking under pressure with manhood. Men began to lift weights in earnest, attempting to accentuate a musculature they could call their own. Bigger became better: In the last decade of the 1800s, the ideal male body as portrayed in advertisements put on about two dozen pounds.

Men soon gave birth to the "he-man." The he-man was a redundant man, a man dedicated to the celebration of maleness. If women were determined to act like men, the ante would be upped: a woman could never be a he-man. A man could always develop more muscle. And this muscle would serve as a veiled threat: a reminder, to any who dared question male supremacy, that might makes right, and men have more might.

In contrast to the tennis-playing, golf-playing "Gibson girl," and in contrast to the thin, muscular "greyhound look" that represented the ideal male body in the 1860s, the most famous male athletes at the turn of the century were two wrestlers, a boxer, and a bodybuilder.[43] Historian Harvey Green wrote in *Fit for America,* "Perhaps men thought that by possessing great strength they would be forever superior—at least in one respect—to women."[44]

The modern Olympics, founded by France's Pierre de Coubertin, represented one of many attempts to accomplish masculine miracles through sports. De Coubertin insisted women be excluded from the games, as they had been in ancient Greece, and argued that sports could offer French men a "manliness" that would "reverse the decline of a French upper class grown weak and effete."[45]

Rugby, football's predecessor, became popular among middle- and upper-class men in late-nineteenth-century England. British sociologists Kenneth Sheard and Eric Dunning attribute its popularity to its rough, competitive nature and to its exclusion of women. It was a "mock battle" that enabled men whose work was increasingly sedentary "to measure up . . . to traditional ideals of masculinity."[46] Women, "particularly at these levels in the social hierarchy, were increasingly becoming a threat to men, and men, we should like to suggest, responded, among other ways, by developing rugby football as a male preserve in which they could bolster up their threatened masculinity and, at the same time, mock, objectify, and vilify women, the principle source of the threat."[47]

Theodore Roosevelt, who used boxing, wrestling, and tennis to overcome his own childhood frailty, advocated sports as a form of "controlled and channeled barbarism."[48] In speeches to male college students, he frequently used the words manly, manfully, manliness, and unmanly in reference to athletic courage and risk-taking. "The greatest danger that a long period of profound peace offers to a nation is that of [creating] effeminate tendencies in young men," he wrote. He designated "true sports for a manly race": baseball, running, rowing, football, boxing, wrestling, shooting, riding, and mountain climbing.[49]

Actually, Roosevelt's vision of manliness included traditional feminine qualities. "I want to see you game, boys," he said in one address; "I want to see you brave and manly, and I also want to see you gentle and tender."[50] He criticized college football for its early association with brutality and gambling, preferred mass-participation intramural sports to elite intercollegiate sports, and warned his own son not to let the desire for athletic excellence rule his life. So his message was not purely macho. After his presidency ended in 1909, he supported voting rights for women. But his manly stance had a more enduring legacy.

• • •

Everything that happened a hundred years ago is happening today. Women are reiterating the demands of their foremothers: abortion, birth control, dress reform, entry into the military and government, child-care, job training, equal wages. They have added new demands: an end to discrimination against lesbians and an end to sexual harassment, domestic violence, pornography, rape, incest, forced sterilization, and unnecessary Caesarean sections and hysterectomies. They have become lawyers and are using the law to help women gain justice. They are asking men to change diapers and become better lovers. They are demanding access not only to women's sports, but to men's.

Unprecedented numbers of women and girls are participating in everything from basketball, cycling, and golf to wrestling, horse racing, and rugby. No women have played college football yet, but they have played college baseball and men's basketball, and high school boys' wrestling, soccer, and football.

In 1993, two female place-kickers were crowned homecoming queen. Cheryl Zimmerman, cocaptain of her West Potomac High (Alexandria, Virginia) football team, successfully kicked six out of six extra points the night of her crowning. Sally Phipps, kicker for the Spanish River High football team in Boca Raton, Florida, missed her one attempted kick. Of receiving the crown she said, "I'd have rather made my extra point."[51]

As individual women discover their physical power, women's organizations are gaining political power. The National Organization for Women (NOW) led successful crusades to integrate both Little League and the Soap Box Derby in the early seventies. It was the Collegiate Council of Women Athletic Administrators that persuaded the National Collegiate Athletic Association (NCAA) to conduct the Gender Equity Survey that provided damning statistics pointing to widespread and illegal sexism among the nation's colleges. The Women's Sports Foundation, founded in 1974 by Billie Jean King and other athlete-activists, provides congressional testimony on sexism in college sports and serves as a clearinghouse for information about Title IX, the 1972 law that forbids gender discrimination in federally funded educational institutions. The Feminist Majority Foundation, cofounded by former NOW president Eleanor Smeal, established a Task Force on Women and Girls in Sports in 1993.

After a lull in the 1960s, 1970s, and 1980s, when many feminists didn't understand the importance of sports and most physical educators shied away from feminism, the alliances are once again becoming clear. Columnists such as Anna Quindlen, Ellen Goodman, and Judy Mann have begun to address sports as a feminist issue. Frances Willard's *A Wheel Within a Wheel* was republished in 1991. Women's sports conferences, once attended only by conservative coaches and professors, now feature openly feminist speakers and offer cultural events that include feminist singers, actors, and artists. At the University of Illinois, the Campus Task Force on Sexual Assault, Abuse, and Violence criticized the school's twenty-eight cheerleaders (the "Illinettes") for creating an image of "women as sexual objects."[52]

Male backlash has returned in full force. American rugby and football, the two most overtly misogynist sports, have become increasingly popular, as have men's basketball, baseball, and hockey. In the early sixties there were only about forty or fifty men's rugby clubs in the country; by the late 1980s there were about 1,200 clubs with 150,000 active players, with more predicted.[53]

Football, baseball, basketball, and hockey spectatorship have risen steadily in the past two decades. In 1973, 10.7 million people attended pro football games; by 1993, 13.8 million attended. In 1972, an estimated 80 million people watched the Super Bowl; by 1993, 133.4 million watched the game, the largest audience of any single sports spectacle.[54]

Attendance at pro baseball games has more than doubled from 30 million in 1973 to 70 million in 1993. Attendance at pro basketball games has almost tripled from 5.8 million in 1972 to 17.3 million in 1992. Pro hockey has set attendance records each year from 1972 (7.6 million) through 1992 (12.7 million).

All four major pro men's sports, according to Media Mark Research Incorporated, have primarily male audiences.

Men continue to bulk up, increasing the ideal masculine body size while the ideal feminine body size shrinks. Magazine advertisements feature bare-chested men with prominent muscles, adorned by sultry-looking skinny women. The average model, Naomi Wolf reports in *The Beauty Myth,* weighs 23 percent less than the average woman. In the 1970s, she weighed only 8 percent less.[55]

Football uniforms, propped up by huge protective pads, "have become the embodiment of manhood and have become the ideal form for today's unadorned male body," says Charlotte Jirousek, a costume historian at Cornell University. Richard Ryckman, psychology professor at the University of Maine, confirms from his own research that a supermuscular male physique such as Fabio's or Arnold Schwarzenegger's is seen by boys and men as significantly more desirable today than it was twenty or thirty years ago.

Most private golf courses allow women to play only during restricted hours, forbid women full voting privileges, forbid single women to join, and revert membership to the husband in the case of divorce. Most women's pro tennis matches remain best-of-three sets, despite the preference of some players for a best-of-five format.

Women's physical rivalry with men is again being portrayed as insane. Female football players and wrestlers at the high school level are often characterized as too weak to compete with young men, and denied opportunities even to try out for teams. Women who defeat men or simply break women's world records often must respond to accusations of steroid use; they must also pass official "sex tests" to prove that they are not male impostors. Real women, current reasoning goes, can "naturally" only achieve a certain level of athletic success.

Forced to accept female "superiors" in a work situation, some men desperately attempt to assert their own superiority through sports. A former football player told University of Southern California sociologist Michael Messner, a leading scholar in the field of sport and gender, "A woman can do the same job as I can do—maybe even be my boss. But I'll be damned if she can go out there on the [football] field and take a hit from Ronnie Lott."[56] Never mind that most men would not fare well if "hit" by Ronnie Lott—or any other pro football player—either.

The media often interpret female athletes not as powerful or strong, but as charming and seductive and vulnerable and sexy. *Playboy* poses models in "athletic" stances and sends "bunnies" to mingle with executives on ski slopes. Even sports magazines frequently feature models rather than athletes on their covers. Thin, nearly naked women pose passively, smiling, exuding neither strength nor exhilaration. One could get the impression that female athletes, who spend hours each day developing stamina and skill, aren't doing it for themselves. They don't train because they love basketball or soccer or swimming or each other. They do it in order to be sexy for men. *Washington Post* columnist Richard Cohen recently observed that many female runners do not become slimmer after "a million miles" of running. Assuming that weight loss "is probably why they started running in the first place," he seems mystified by their persistence.[57] Why would these women keep running, mile after mile, if they never lose weight? Why indeed? Could it be that, like men, they enjoy running? No. What could threaten the status quo—the growing strength and endurance of millions of women—becomes instead just another beauty technique, another way to win the real prize: a man.

Women still buy in. "Athletic girls" still try to prove that they're not unfeminine, meaning not lesbian and not threatening to men. Magazine ads often pair an action photo of a woman athlete with a shot of her lounging in glamorous evening wear, her face hidden under heavy makeup. Team sports seem to have become particularly threatening: female skaters, swimmers, tennis players, and golfers receive more coverage than do women who play basketball or even doubles tennis.

In the media, at women's bodybuilding championships, and in gyms, the "How much is too much muscle?" debate again rages for women—but not for men. Even in sports magazines, female muscles are often hidden through "soft" poses and occasionally even airbrushed away. A classic 1981 bodybuilding book by Joe Weider, the most influential man in the sport, offers this disclaimer: ". . . any muscle tissue a woman . . . might develop will show up on her body as feminine curves."[58]

"Virile qualities" are still said to negate woman's charm. To retain such indispensable charm, "media consultants" teach female basketball players how to dress and behave in a traditionally feminine fashion, as if to counterbalance their unfeminine behavior on the court. On college campuses, feminism has become a dirty word—a word male athletic directors use to designate female coaches as troublemakers, and a word many young women associate with man-hating or lesbianism.

Political satirists still aptly use sports as a metaphor for political power. In 1992, a few months before the national elections in which the number of female senators tripled (from two to six) and the number of women in the House of Representatives surged from 28 to 47, *Cincinnati Enquirer* cartoonist Jim Borgman drew a comic that showed two old, fat, disgruntled congressmen smoking cigars and looking nervously over their shoulders. Behind them, five women were hooping it up on a congressional basketball court, one spinning a ball on her finger, another launching a hook shot, another soaring through the air toward a dunk. The caption: "White men getting jumpy."

A year later, women played for the first time in the 32nd annual Congressional Baseball Game. The Democrats, who had two female players, defeated the Republicans, who had one female player, 13 – 1.

Charles Dana Gibson's image of the fisted female football players has also been reborn. Hysterical college football coaches accuse women who demand their fair share of the athletic dollar of trying to castrate football. At the 1993 NCAA convention, 26 percent of football coaches named gender equity (the elimination of sex discrimination) as the number one problem facing football today. There seems to be a growing male perception that active, athletic, angry women threaten football, threaten men, threaten manliness itself.

And perhaps they do. American manliness is defined, symbolically, by and through football and other combat sports. Women who refuse to stay in the bleachers or on the sidelines are refusing to be the kind of "sissy" that male coaches refer to when they tell their players, "Don't be a sissy!" If women aren't sissy (or wimpy or wussy or pussy), how will men motivate each other? How can you exhort a man, "Don't throw like my grandmother," if your grandmother plays shortstop on her company's softball team? How can you convince a man to injure himself and to deny his own physical pain in order to "prove" his masculinity if women resent— or worse, laugh at—that macho display? Masculinity has primarily been defined as not feminine. If women, too, reject stereotypical femininity, how will men define themselves? If women race onto the playing fields, "invading" even the few remaining exclusively male sports, men are going to have to stop clinging not only to outmoded and restrictive definitions of masculinity and femininity but also to power and privilege based on gender.

No wonder that football player in *The Coming Game* looks so frightened.

3

Stronger Women

Boy, don't you men wish you could hit a ball like that!

—*Babe Didrikson*

LAUGHING, PATRICK Thevenard would scoop his wife, Gail Savage, off the floor and carry her around the house like a squirming child. This was early in the marriage, and Patrick, an ecologist from Hyattsville, Maryland, thought it was funny, a joke. Gail, a history professor, didn't like it. Feeling helpless and angry, she would ask to be put down. He would refuse.

Later, Gail became a dedicated runner. Patrick argued that she was running too much, or in the wrong way, or at the wrong times. They would quarrel, and he would yell. Patrick didn't literally lift her off the ground then, but to Gail the sensation was similar: Patrick's criticisms felt like physical restraints, as if he were trying to prevent her from going where she wanted to go.

Patrick says Gail used running as a "weapon" against him, a way "to escape out of our relationship—to literally put physical distance between us."

Gail says running became "the focus of a power struggle over who would control me."

26

• • •

The way Gail gained strength, and keeps gaining strength, is through sports. Women can become strong in other ways, without being athletes, but athletic strength holds particular meaning in this culture. It's tangible, visible, measurable. It has a history of symbolic importance. Joe Louis, Jackie Robinson, Jesse Owens, Billie Jean King: their athletic feats have represented to many Americans key victories over racism and sexism, key "wins" in a game that has historically been dominated by white men.

Sports have particular salience for men, who share childhood memories of having their masculinity confirmed or questioned because of their athletic ability or inability. Along with money or sex, sports in this culture define men for men. They embody a language men understand.

Women also understand sports—their power, their allure—but often from a spectator's perspective. When a woman steps out of the bleachers or slips off her cheerleader's costume and becomes an athlete herself, she implicitly challenges the association between masculinity and sports. She refutes the traditional feminine role (primarily for white women) of passivity, frailty, and subservience. If a woman can play a sport—especially if she can play it better than many men—then that sport can no longer be used as a yardstick of masculinity. The more women play a variety of sports, the more the entire notion of masculine and feminine roles—or any roles at all assigned by gender—becomes as ludicrous as the notion of roles assigned by race.

Female athletes provide obvious, confrontational evidence—"in your face" evidence, some might say—of women's physical prowess, tangible examples of just what women can achieve.

• • •

An avid equestrian as a child, Gail thought of herself as "just one of those girls who loved horses." No one suggested that a girl who trains and competes in equestrian events is every bit as athletic as the boys her age who earn letters in baseball or track. Lately, thinking about her lifelong love affair with sports, she realized that she "was really being an athlete the whole time."

She rode during her first marriage, which lasted thirteen years. She taught riding and spent an inordinate amount of time at the barn, as equestrians do. Her husband did not object, but nor did he ask questions about her teaching, or speak proudly of her to his friends, or take an interest in her career. "What I did was OK because it was not considered important," says Gail. "He never took it seriously."

During her second marriage, Gail's horse grew lame and had to be put out to pasture. She discovered she "couldn't just sit around" so she began running. For three months she was "in agony," then she fell in love with the hypnotic process of landing, step by step, on the earth, as well as the fleeting moments of flight in between. She was forty-two.

At first, Patrick did not object. When her training was occasional, her schedule flexible, he didn't mind. "I was supportive when she started out because she had gotten a little overweight," Patrick recalls. "I was surprised she stuck with it as long as she did."

Gail increased her mileage. She joined a running club, where she learned about interval training, track workouts, and the value of taking one's pulse. She memorized *Runner's World* magazine. She went running for two, three hours at a time. Patrick started to get upset.

He didn't say he was upset, exactly. He said he was concerned. "A woman of your age shouldn't be doing this to her body," he would say.

Rapists also concerned him. "He would try to frighten me into not going out," Gail says. "I couldn't go out late in the afternoon because it would get dark. I couldn't go out at sunrise; he didn't like that either. It made it more difficult for me to exercise my judgment. It seemed like his conclusion was I should never go out."

Patrick's assessment: "It was a conflict between moral imperative and reality. Gail would say, 'A woman should be able to run freely.' I'd say, 'Of course, but in the real world, you can't.'"

He criticized her tactics, too, charging her with working too hard, risking damage to her joints. "I had been a runner myself," he explains. "I thought she should spend as much time stretching and doing yoga as running. I thought she should take some time off. She didn't."

"When you train hard, you run some risk of injury," Gail concedes. "But it was a double bind. No matter what I did, it wasn't right."

The more she ran the better she felt about herself, and the more she ran the more she believed that she had a right to this time, this pursuit of excellence. "I've always wanted to do everything as best I could, but women of my generation weren't supposed to try hard. That would mean you would sweat, you might make noises, you might fail." Running offered Gail an opportunity to test herself, to find out how good she might be.

The more she ran, the more running became "a lightning rod for the larger issues of who was in charge" in her marriage, Gail says. "Talking about it makes it sound like we sat down and had rational discussions about it. We didn't. Mainly I'd stomp out of the house and run, and he'd give me lectures about how I was hurting my knees and ankles."

As she was lacing her shoes, he would ask, "Where are you going?"

"Out," she'd say.

"When will you be back?" he'd ask.

"Later," she'd answer.

"I was very determined to go out on my own and not tell him where I was going," she admits. "That did exacerbate the conflict between us."

Eventually, after an eleven-year relationship, they divorced.

Now in her late forties, Gail's still running—farther, up to forty-five miles per week, at about an eight-minute-per-mile pace. She competes in 10Ks, recently placing second in her age group. She lifts weights and swims. She has tried orienteering, and is intrigued by the idea of competing in triathlons and marathons. "I seem to enjoy everything I try," she marvels. "I tend to acquire strength fairly easily."

· · ·

For a woman, especially for a married woman with a controlling husband, running is a feminist act. The athlete's feminism begins with the fact that her sports participation is, in Gail's words, "a declaration of independence." The runner runs on her own two feet, on her own time, in her own way, without male assistance. If a man wants to join her club, trot along next to her, watch her race, and leave a light on for her when she arrives home late, fine. If not, if she encounters male interference, she may not tolerate it. She may prioritize, instead, her own athletic joy. Running raises the possibility that the woman with the aggrieved husband will become the woman with no husband—that, in the process of running, women will run away from men.

Running also raises the possibility that mothers will leave fathers at home to wash dishes and put kids to bed. According to a 1993 Women's Sports Foundation survey of almost 1,600 working women, the more hours women devote to housework, the fewer they devote to sports or fitness. Twenty-nine percent of working women report that their husbands do no housework at all. Married women with children are the most likely to report a decrease in sports or fitness participation in the past five years.[1]

So if a woman runs in the morning while her husband dresses the children, feeds them, and gets them off to school, she tips the balance of power not only within the marriage but within the family. The runner who has no children, no husband, and no boyfriend—who instead carves out a life for herself with other athletes and other women—is likewise committing feminist acts. Her running represents a world in which women are neither running toward nor alongside nor away from men; where men and their ideas about what's too strenuous for women, what's acceptable for women, and what's attractive in women become irrelevant.

Female athletes don't necessarily see it this way. They don't necessarily call themselves feminists. They cycle or swim or surf because it's fun and challenging, because it feels good, because they like the way it makes them look, because it allows them to eat more without gaining weight, because it gives them energy and confidence and time spent with friends, female or male. Many are ignorant about the women's rights movement. I've heard college students confuse feminism with feminine hygiene.

Female athletes have a long tradition of dissociating themselves from feminism. Their desire to be accepted or to acquire or keep a boyfriend or a job has often equaled their passion for sports. Thus athletes have taken great pains—and it can hurt—to send reassuring signals to those who would oppose their play: "Don't worry, we're not feminists. We're not dykes, we're not aggressive, we're not muscular, we're not a threat to you. We just want to play ball." It has been a survival strategy.

It's time to tell the truth. We are feminists.[2] Some of us are dykes. Some of us are aggressive, some of us are muscular. All of us, collectively, are a threat—not to men exactly, but to male privilege and to masculinity as defined through manly sports. By reserving time each day for basketball dribbling, or for runs or rides or rows, women are changing themselves and society. Feminism is rarely an individual's motivating force but always the result: a woman's athletic training, regardless of the factors that lead to her involvement, implicitly challenges patriarchal constraints on her behavior. Sport for women changes the woman's experience of herself and others' experience of her. It alters the balance of power between the sexes. It is daring. It is life changing. It is happening every day.

• • •

Feminism is about freedom: women's individual and collective liberty to make their own decisions. For women, sports embody freedom: unrestricted physical expression, travel across great distances, liberated movement. Sports give meaning to the phrase "free time." Women find it, use it, and insist on retaining it. Their time for sports becomes a time when they free themselves of all the other people and projects they usually tend to. They become the person, the project, who needs care. They take care of themselves. For a group of people who have historically been defined by their ability to nurture others, the commitment to nurture themselves is radical.

Sports give a woman the confidence to try new things, including things previously defined as dangerous or unfeminine. "Boys grow up trying lots of new physical activities," notes University of Virginia sports psychologist Linda Bunker. "They develop an overall sense of their ability to handle unknown situations. Ask a male tennis player if he wants to play racquetball; he'll say 'sure,' even if he's never seen a racquetball court. But ask a nonathletic woman to play racquetball, and she'll say, 'Gee, I don't know if I can do it.' "

Several writers have used sports as metaphor, depicting women emancipated by the process of building muscle and endurance. In Fannie Flagg's film, *Fried Green Tomatoes,* a meek and depressed Evelyn Couch (played by Kathy Bates) takes aerobics classes, meets with a women's support group, and develops a deep friendship with an old woman. Soon she has acquired a new persona, Tawanda, who skips up steps, knocks down walls, and asserts herself with her husband. "I'm trying to save our marriage," she tells him. "What's the point of my trying if you're gonna sit on your butt drinking beer and watching baseball, basketball, football, hockey, bowling, golf, and challenge of the gladiators?"

In *Daughters of Copperwoman,* Anne Cameron creates a fictional world (based on the lives of the native people of Vancouver Island) in which prepubescent girls practice sprinting in the sand, running backwards, and swimming while tied to a log "until we were so tired we ached, but our muscles got strong and our bodies grew straight." Finally, after a girl's first menses, she is paddled by canoe out to sea, where she disrobes, dives overboard, and swims back to the village. As she approaches the shore, the villagers "sing a victory song about how a girl went for a swim and a woman came home."[3]

In Alice Adams' short story, "A Public Pool,"[4] a shy, anxious, unemployed woman who feels too tall and too fat and who lives with her depressed mother is slowly and subtly transformed by the process of swimming laps. At first she feels embarrassed to appear, even in the locker room, in her bathing suit. Swimming twenty-six laps, a half-mile, seems a struggle. She feels flattered by attention from a blond, bearded swimmer not because he is kind or interesting—in fact he cuts rudely through the water with a "violent crawl"—but because he is male.

By the end of the story she becomes "aware of a long strong body (mine) pulling through the water, of marvelous muscles, a strong back, and long, long legs." She applies for a job she'll probably get and looks forward to moving out of her mother's house. When she happens upon "Blond Beard" outside a cafe, she realizes that he is a gum-chewing, spiffily dressed jerk. The story ends with his inviting her to join him for coffee, and her declining. "I leave him standing there. I swim away."

No national statistics exist on the association between divorce and female athleticism, but stories are prevalent. The more she goes to the gym, the more he mopes. And the more she goes to the gym, the less willing she becomes to stop going, or to stop growing, to please him. She swims away.

Nancy Murray, an equestrian and public health doctoral student from Houston, Texas, quit riding the day she got married because she thought her husband wanted her to. She also quit graduate school and stopped talking to her friends in the evenings. "I was not a sane person," she recalls. She became ill with a severe thyroid disease that mysteriously cleared up when she started riding again, after eleven years. "It amazed the doctors," she says. Now she competes at fourth level, just below international level, in dressage.

"When I started riding again, I found my power," says Murray. That power transfers outside the ring. She is no longer able, she says, to play the subservient role her graduate school professors expect. Pursuing her dreams takes a toll, though. Murray says her husband now "supports my riding conceptually, but it's hard for him to have my attentions else-where." Like many of her married friends, Murray arrives at weekend competitions "blasted" with exhaustion, she says, "because it took so much energy just to leave—to leave our husbands, to get them to take care of the kids."

Traveling around the south to equestrian events, Murray drives a truck with horse-trailer attached. When she pulls off the road, she enjoys men's reactions. "My horse stands 17 hands high and weighs 1,500 pounds. I put a chain around his nose and hold a whip in my hand. He behaves. Men see me coming, controlling this huge beast, and they say, uh-oh." She laughs. She's in control. She's an athlete. She's free.

• • •

Feminism is about bodies: birth control, sexual harassment, child sexual abuse, pornography, rape, date rape, battering, breast cancer, breast en-largement, dieting, liposuction, abortion, anorexia, bulimia, sexuality.

Sports.

"The repossession by women of our bodies," wrote the poet and au-thor Adrienne Rich in *Of Woman Born,* "will bring far more essential change to human society than the seizing of the means of production by workers."

As athletes, we repossess our bodies. Told that we're weak, we de-velop our strengths. Told that certain sports are wrong for women, we decide what feels right. Told that our bodies are too dark, big, old, flabby, or wrinkly to be attractive to men, we look at naked women in locker rooms and discover for ourselves the beauty of actual women's bodies in all their colors, shapes, and sizes. Told that certain sports make women look "like men," we notice the truth: working out doesn't make us look like men, it makes us look happy. It makes us smile. More important, it makes us healthy and powerful. It makes us feel good.

According to the Women's Sports Foundation's 1993 survey, 71 per-cent of women who exercise said they work out primarily for the physical benefits.[5] The National Center for Health Statistics reports that physical fitness is linked to a general sense of well being, a positive mood, and lower levels of anxiety and depression, especially among women. The ath-lete is more likely than her nonathletic sisters to have a good body image, studies have consistently shown. Female athletes also report that sports reduce stress and enhance self-esteem. And University of Maine psychology professor Richard Ryckman has found that girls in the seventies derived their self-esteem primarily from their physical attractiveness, whereas for girls in the early nineties, physical competence is as essential to self-esteem as beauty.

As little as two hours of weekly exercise can lower a teenage girl's lifelong risk of breast cancer. According to the Women's Sports Foundation, female high school athletes are more likely than nonathletes to do well in high school and college, to feel popular, to be involved in extracurricular activities, to stay involved in sport as adults, and to aspire to community leadership. Female high school athletes are 92 percent less likely to get involved with drugs, 80 percent less likely to get pregnant, and three times more likely than their nonathletic peers to graduate from high school.[6]

Exercise reduces an older woman's chances of developing osteoporosis. Pregnant athletes report a lower incidence of back pain, easier labor and delivery, fewer stress-related complaints, and less postpartum depression than women who don't exercise.[7] And the effects of exercise seem to persist throughout a lifetime. Women who were athletic as children report greater confidence, self-esteem, and pride in their physical and social selves than those who were sedentary as children.[8] If, as a society, we were interested in the health and welfare of women, we would encourage and enable them to play sports.

In a country where male politicians and judges make key decisions about our bodies and all of us are vulnerable to random attacks of male violence, the simple act of women taking control of their own bodies— including their health, their pleasure, and their power—is radical. In a society in which real female bodies (as opposed to media images of female bodies) are unappreciated at best, the act of enjoying one's own female body is radical. It contradicts all feminine training to move, to extend our arms, to claim public space as our own, to use our bodies aggressively and instrumentally, and to make rough contact with other bodies. Temple University doctoral student Frances Johnston interviewed dozens of female ice hockey and rugby players and found that "physicality" was one of the most appealing aspects of the games. "They enjoyed the tackling, the checking, the falling down and getting up, the discovery that they had 'survived' another hard hit or rough game." Besides body contact, they enjoyed "kicking the ball, getting rid of the ball right before a tackle, the power of a well hit slapshot."[9]

Lunging for a soccer ball, we do not worry if our hair looks attractive. Leaping over a high bar, we do not wish we had bigger breasts. Strapped snugly into a race car, roaring around a track at 220 miles per hour, we do not smile or wave.

While playing sports our bodies are ours to do with as we please. If in that process our bodies look unfeminine—if they become bruised or bloody or simply unattractive—that seems irrelevant. Our bodies are ours. We own them. While running to catch a ball, we remember that.

• • •

I coach basketball. My players are girls (nine through twelve), teenagers (fifteen through eighteen), and grown women (twenty through forty). They all have trouble with the defensive stance, and with "being big."

The defensive stance requires a player to squat, low to the ground, her legs wide. Her knees should gape open, farther apart than her shoulders, her hands ready to deflect passes or shots. From this position she can react quickly to any moves an offensive player makes.

Why is this difficult for girls and women to learn? It's the leg spread. It's unladylike to yawn one's legs wide open. Even little girls growing up today are getting this message. I can tell because I tease them, imitating the way they try to squat without separating their legs. "It's OK," I say. "No one's going to look up your skirt." They laugh and I know I've hit the mark. Most little girls don't even wear skirts to school anymore. But their foremothers' skirts still haunt them, even on the basketball court.

My players are haunted, too, by size taboos. They don't like to feel tall, to seem wide, to make loud noises. They don't feel comfortable inhabiting a big space. Even many young ones talk quietly and act timid. In basketball, you need to snatch a rebound as if you own the ball, as if you're starving and it's the last coconut on the tree. You have to protect the ball, elbows pointed outward like daggers, lest others try to grab it. You have to decide where you want to be, then get there, refusing to let anyone push you out of the way. You have to shout, loudly, to let your teammates know who's cutting through the lane or who's open for a shot. Basketball teaches women and girls to renounce the suffocating vestiges of ladylike behavior and act instead like assertive, honest, forthright human beings. It's about unlearning femininity.

. . .

When Sarah Burton Nelson swims, she never follows a linear path for long. My mother will log her twenty laps "crawling" smoothly and efficiently from one end to the other; if anyone joins her, she'll eagerly offer to race. But she never enters a pool without also spending some time flat on her back, face to the sky. She has one of those rare buoyant bodies that, though thin, can float with hands and feet exposed; she wiggles all her fingers and toes, grinning. She likes, from that floating position, to point one leg then the other skyward, pretending she's Esther Williams. She likes to swim freestyle with one arm, then backstroke with the next, so that her body rolls like a spinning river log. She plays in the water the way children play, bobbing, twirling, languishing. Like children, she unabashedly savors the weightlessness, the wetness, the automatic grace granted to swimmers who dare to sink as well as to swim.

Sports offer women a chance to enjoy their own physical natures: graceful, expansive, experimental, joyful, sensuous. The athlete breathes not with the shallow breaths of a woman trying to hold her abdomen flat but with a deep, full sort of breathing that expands the lungs with air, the mind with possibility. The athlete knows movement, sweat, stretching. She knows how to use her body to get what she wants.

This can be scary. "We have been raised to fear the *yes* within ourselves, our deepest cravings," wrote the author Audre Lorde in an essay entitled "Uses of the Erotic: The Erotic as Power."[10] Many women feel vaguely embarrassed by their bodies: their muscles, their fat, their breasts, their hair, their desires. Many women feel uncomfortable about their own perspiration. Their first reaction, upon noticing sweat, may be to get rid of it. They may feel too self-conscious to fully appreciate other sensations—racing pulses, stretching muscles—that arise in the course of jumping, throwing, lifting weights, skating. They may feel embarrassed by public displays of sensuality, too inhibited to turn slow somersaults in a pool.

But the popular sports maxim could aptly be inverted: no pleasure, no gain. Sports require athletes to pay attention to their bodies. It is through this careful attention that athletes improve. Surely it is not gold medals but pleasurable perceptions—two skis caressing a mountain; a hand rolling a heavy ball toward ten pins; the welcome ache of powerful thighs kicking through ocean waves—that keep the athlete returning to her sport again and again despite fatigue, frustration, or grumpy husbands.

Nancy Nerenberg compares the onset of perspiration to orgasm. Nerenberg played basketball for the University of California, Berkeley, in the late seventies. Now a freelance writer and mother of two, she still plays pick-up games with men.

She enjoys sweating. After several trips up and down the court, when her pores open and her skin begins to glisten with moisture, Nancy notices. She's paying attention not only to the ball, to her teammates, and to the opposing team but also to her own physical sensations. "It's like a climax," she says. "It's like a faucet turning on. It's a rush."

Maybe you haven't noticed this. Maybe sweating doesn't feel like orgasm to you. Maybe Nancy Nerenberg is eccentric.

But maybe she's right. Maybe, if we pay attention, we'll notice that sweating feels, for starters, good. Maybe, if we open our minds to new possibilities, sweating could feel, if not like orgasm, at least interesting. Relaxing. Luxurious. After all, doesn't all personal, physical experience have sensuous, even erotic potential?

Ever since they stopped riding sidesaddle, horsewomen have shared an erotic secret alluded to with smiles, nods, and the phrase "girls love horses." One woman I know had "sensations very similar to the sensations that precede orgasms" while squeezing her legs closed on the adductor machine at the gym. It actually became a problem for her. Afraid of "going all the way" in front of dozens of other gym members, she eventually stopped using the machine altogether.

But sports don't have to feel sexual to feel sensual. They don't have to feel sensual to feel pleasurable. One definition of Eros is "love directed toward self-realization." There's something about physical joy that teaches an athlete who she is. "Sport holds a mirror to a woman's life," LaFerne Ellis Price wrote in *The Wonder of Motion*.[11] The athlete learns to love herself the way we all want to be loved: with eyes open, with forgiveness and enthusiasm. She becomes her own cheerleader. Moving alone, she discovers that physical joy resides in her body, regardless of how pleasing or attractive that body might be to others. Moving in concert with other women, she discovers the beauty of those women, and of women in general. Surely these twin pleasures: personal pleasure and communal female pleasure—go a long way toward explaining the powerful potential of women's sport.

• • •

Almost two million girls play soccer. Sixteen million women play softball. College volleyball is second only to football in autumn participation rates. Basketball is the most popular high school and college sport for women. Not gymnastics. Not tennis or golf. Basketball: Big, sweaty, strong, and requiring complex, intricate, intimate teamwork. This is the essence of much of women's athletic joy and much of women's athletic power. Feminism is about female bonding.

Adrienne Rich wrote a poem about a team of women who died during an ascent of Lenin's Peak in 1974. Imagining the leader's thoughts before she froze to death on the mountain, Rich wrote:

> *I have never loved*
> *like this   I have never seen*
> *my own forces so taken up and shared*
> *and given back*
> *After the long training   the early sieges*
> *we are moving almost effortlessly in our love . . .*
> *We know now we have always been in danger*
> *down in our separateness*
> *and now up here together   but till now*
> *we had not touched our strength.*[12]

We're not used to hearing such passionate depictions of love by women, for women—neither by lesbians, who still remain largely invisible in this culture, nor by heterosexual women. When Magic Johnson retired from basketball in 1992, he said he would most miss his "buddies"—his teammates and opponents. Sportscaster Dick Vitale, introducing the cancer-stricken former coach Jim Valvano at the publicly televised "Espy's," the first American sports awards, said of his friend, "I love him." When was the last time we heard a woman publicly declare her love for another woman or team of women? When Chris Evert retired after playing almost two decades of phenomenal tennis, did Billie Jean King or Martina Navratilova or any other woman publicly say, "I love her?" I don't think so. Women finishing college basketball careers or returning from overseas professional careers surely feel the same way Magic Johnson did—affectionate toward and dedicated to their teammates. But these women—Heidi Wayment, Kamie Ethridge, Lynette Woodard—are not household names. No one even asks them whom or what they'll miss most.

Teams can offer women a welcome all-female world devoid of male commentary or competition. This sanctuary is one of sport's delights. "We want to be away from men, playing our sport for ourselves, with ourselves," one softball player told University of Iowa sociologist Susan Birrell. "We have a good time, stay in shape, and share being women— but mostly without men. It's refreshing." [13]

All-female sports participation places women somewhere along what Adrienne Rich calls the lesbian continuum.[14] Which is not to say that women who join sports teams become lesbians. Most don't; most female athletes, like most male athletes, are heterosexual. But Rich expands the usual definition of lesbian in this continuum to mean "not simply the fact that a woman has had or has consciously desired genital sexual experience with another woman," but also "many more forms of primary intensity between and among women, including the sharing of a rich inner life, the bonding against male tyranny, the giving and receiving of practical and political support." Even heterosexual athletes, especially team sport athletes, could be classified as falling somewhere on this continuum, which is based on love and commitment to women rather than sex. In a society in which "lesbian" is a pejorative used against women who become strong and assertive, the athletic act of enjoying one's female body as it moves with and against other female bodies becomes a feminist act.

Much of male pornographic lore depicts women as having intimidating, insatiable sexual appetites, but Rich says "it seems more probable that men really fear, not that they will have women's sexual appetites forced on them, or that women want to smother and devour them, but that women could be indifferent to them altogether, that men could be allowed sexual and emotional—therefore economic—access to women *only* on women's terms, otherwise being left on the periphery of the matrix." [15]

The lesbian label used against female athletes (and against politicians, pilots, and other women who enter traditionally male domains) becomes clearer in this context: it names male fears of female empowerment. In the case of athletes, there's some truth to the rumors. Some of the best athletes in this nation's history were lesbians, largely because straight women were constrained by husbands or by restrictive definitions of appropriate female behavior. Nowadays, fewer women tolerate male interference in their athletic pursuits. But female athletes still symbolize this threat: women will devote their passions to women. In a significant power shift, millions of women are now becoming "team players"—not with men in corporations, but with women on softball, volleyball, and soccer fields.

Sports are more than games. When they work together toward communal goals, regardless of differences in race, class, physical ability, and sexual preference, women create unity through diversity, laying the groundwork for empowering political change. What if women really bonded against male tyranny? How bonded could we get? What if women truly trusted other women? What if we became comfortable in female worlds, with female leaders? Women are, after all, the majority. The majority rules, usually.

Simone de Beauvoir wrote in *The Second Sex* that the athlete receives from sports a sense of authority and an ability to influence others. "To climb higher than a playmate, to force an arm to yield and bend, is to assert one's sovereignty over the world in general." By contrast, the woman deprived of sports "has no faith in a force she has not experienced in her body; she does not dare to be enterprising, to revolt, to invent; doomed to docility, to resignation . . . she regards the existing state of affairs as something fixed." [16]

Thus the very desire to change the conditions of our lives—to demand the equal rights that are a cornerstone of feminism—may be traceable to our own sense of our physical power. This is supported by anecdotal evidence that many female politicians, business leaders, and other successful women were athletic as children.

This may also explain, in part, how dozens of female athletes have of late developed the chutzpah to sue their universities. Historically, boys and men have been granted more and better of everything athletic: facilities, coaches, travel, training, scholarships. In 1991, women made up more than half (50.3 percent) of the overall college student population but less than a third (30.9 percent) of all athletes. Men received 83 percent of recruiting funds, 77 percent of the athletic budget, and 70 percent of the scholarship money: approximately $179 million more per year in scholarships than their female counterparts.[17] Men now coach 52 percent of the women's teams and 99 percent of the men's teams.[18] Even when women and men coach identical sports, men receive bigger paychecks;[19] female basketball coaches typically receive $23,000 less than male basketball coaches.[20] At the Division I level, 289 out of 298 athletic directors are men.

Lately, to save money, athletic directors have been cutting programs. Usually they eliminate one men's sport and one women's—or two men's and two women's—despite the fact that men begin with more opportunities, so the cuts detract disproportionately from women. "It's the only time we experience equity—when they're dropping sports," University of Iowa women's athletic director Christine Grant notes wryly.

But the law is on women's side, and they're beginning to use it effectively. Title IX, a 1972 amendment to the Civil Rights Act, forbids gender discrimination in educational institutions that receive federal funds. Most schools and colleges receive federal funds. The Supreme Court's 1992 *Franklin v. Gwinnett County* decision further strengthens the law, enabling plaintiffs to receive monetary damages.

From 1991 through the first half of 1993, at least thirty-four colleges and universities were sued by their female athletes or coaches, threatened with lawsuits, or had complaints filed against them.[21] Judges, juries, and the Office of Civil Rights virtually always ruled in favor of the women. When schools appealed the decisions, they virtually always lost.

Five colleges—William and Mary, the University of Oklahoma, the University of New Hampshire, the University of Massachusetts at Amherst, and UCLA—canceled women's teams only to reinstate them a few months later after women's groups, legal advisors, or judges reminded them that they were violating the law.

The University of South Carolina in 1991 announced a plan to eliminate women's softball but add women's track—a net reduction of the women's athletic budget (then $1.5 million, compared to $18.5 million for the men). Public pressure, galvanized by women's sports organizations, persuaded South Carolina to add track *and* keep softball.

Indiana University in Pennsylvania dropped women's gymnastics and field hockey, along with men's soccer and tennis, in the 1992 season to save $350,000. The football team took over the hockey field for their practices. But U.S. District Judge Maurice Cohill ordered the University to restore funding of the two women's teams, ruling that financial problems were no excuse for sex discrimination.

At Brown University, athletes filed a class action suit after the school cut its women's gymnastics and volleyball programs. A U.S. District Court judge ordered the school to reinstate both sports. University of Texas students also filed a class action suit. In an out-of-court settlement, the university agreed to increase the number of female athletes from 23 percent to 44 percent by 1996.

All of this was mere warm-up for the landmark decision in 1993, when Howard University women's basketball coach Sanya Tyler was awarded $1.11 million by a U.S. Superior Court in Washington, D.C. The 1991 sex discrimination suit claimed that Tyler and the men's basketball coach had identical job descriptions but he was paid almost twice as much and was given more office space and more assistants.[22]

As if to stave off such lawsuits, college administrators have recently given five top women's basketball coaches (Tara VanDerveer of Stanford, Vivian Stringer of the University of Iowa, Pat Summitt of the University of Tennessee, Ceal Barry of the University of Colorado, and Debbie Ryan of the University of Virginia) phenomenal raises—between $20,000 and $60,000 annual increases—to bring their salaries in line with or closer to the men's.

Dozens of girls, too, are suing. A 16-year-old named Jennifer McLeery successfully sued the U.S. Amateur Boxing Association in 1993, overturning their rule barring women from competition. Her goal: to box in the Olympics.

Sometimes athletes flex their political muscles beyond the sporting arena. Run, Jane, Run, which bills itself as the largest U.S. amateur sports competition for women, each year donates more than $655,000 to battered women's shelters, rape crisis hotlines, job training programs, YWCAs, and other women's groups. Women have also organized benefit runs and walks for breast cancer research and against rape.

A few pro athletes in the post–Billie Jean King generation have become outspoken advocates for women. Golfer Carol Mann, race car driver Lyn St. James, and Olympic swimmers Nancy Hogshead and Donna de Varona have served as Women's Sports Foundation presidents.

Zina Garrison has talked openly about a troubling feminist issue: the body/self hatred that in her case led to bulimia. Martina Navratilova has become an outspoken advocate of lesbian rights, supporting the Gay Games and joining a successful 1992 suit against the Colorado antigay amendment.

Many women, particularly women of color, believe that sports participation is an asset in gaining access to the business world. The energy, confidence, and connections that accrue from sports seem to spill over into job success. According to the 1993 survey of working women, about 50 percent of women of color believe their sports participation—not talking about the Dallas Cowboys but actually playing sports—helps them to access decision-making channels outside the office, gain acceptance by coworkers, advance their careers, and tap into business networks. About 36 percent of white women agree.[23]

Women who have played college sports rate themselves higher in their abilities to set objectives, lead a group, motivate others, share credit, and feel comfortable in a competitive environment. Former high school athletes also rated themselves fairly high in these abilities, followed by former youth sport athletes. Women with no childhood competitive experience felt least adept.[24]

Surely sports experience helps women obtain coaching jobs; female coaches are even more likely than male coaches to have played college sports.[25] Men have taken over most women's teams, but a handful of former female athletes are breaking through a cement ceiling to gain men's leadership positions. Meg Ritchie, for example, the first female strength and conditioning coach at a major university with a football program, was a former 1984 Olympic discus thrower. When she arrived for work at University of Arizona in 1985, she could power clean (a type of lift) 350 pounds, more than any of the football players.

Wanda Oates has coached boys basketball at Ballou High School in Washington, D.C., since 1986. Since 1990, Bernadette Locke-Maddox has served as assistant men's basketball coach at the University of Kentucky. Carol White, a former assistant football coach at Georgia Tech, now works with Tech as a freelance kicking instructor. It's only a matter of time before a woman coaches an NFL team. Only sexism now keeps women from those positions. They needn't have playing experience. Some of the best male coaches have never played the game.

In 1991 Sandra Ortiz-Del Valle became the first female official to call a men's pro game, in the United States Basketball League. In 1992, Constance Hurlburt was named executive director of the Patriot League, the first woman to head a Division I all-sports conference for men and women. Sally John, a Little League coach since 1986, became in 1992 the first woman appointed to the sixteen-member international Little League board of directors. The following year, Kathy Barnard became the first woman to coach in a Little League World Series.

Susan O'Malley serves as President of the Washington Bullets. Joan Kroc inherited the San Diego Padres from her husband. Georgia Frontiere owns the L.A. Rams. Marge Schott owns the Cincinnati Reds (a dubious victory, considering her racist remarks and hiring practices). Marian Illitch of the Detroit Red Wings co-owns the hockey team with her husband, Mike. Ellen Harrigan-Charles serves as general manager of the St. Catharine's (Ontario) Blue Jays, a minor-league baseball team. She has assembled the only all-female front office in professional sports.

In 1993, *The Sporting News* named Anita DeFrantz, director of the Amateur Athletic Foundation and a member of the International Olympic Committee, one of the 100 most powerful people in sports. Women's Sports Foundation executive director Donna Lopiano, U.S. Figure Skating president Claire Ferguson, and NCAA President's Commission chair Judith Albino were also on the list.

Judith Sweet became the first female NCAA president in 1992. Barbara Hedges of the University of Washington and Merrily Dean Baker of Michigan State are the first two female athletic directors at major college programs (Division I-A) that include football. Two African-American women, Vivian Fuller of Northeastern Illinois University in Chicago, and Barbara Jacket of Prairie View A&M, are among the nine female athletic directors at Division I schools. Fuller says of working with sexist men, "The good old boys can ride my train or get off. It's up to them." Where did she obtain such self-assuredness? "I ran track in college."

• • •

Athletes are some of the strongest women in America. Perhaps our greatest potential for changing the gender balance of power lies in our strength. Physical power is not the only kind of power there is, but it's an important power: measurable, salient, symbolic, and understood by men. "Violence is the authentic proof of each one's loyalty to himself, to his passions, to his own will," wrote de Beauvoir. "For a man to feel in his fists his will to self-affirmation is enough to reassure him of his sovereignty. Against any insult, any attempt to reduce him to the status of object, the male has recourse to his fists."[26]

Many women don't even know how to make a fist. We weren't raised to fight. As girls, we weren't taught how to scream, run, hit, or kick—in short, how to take care of ourselves. Girls who live near the water are taught to swim, and girls who drive cars are taught to steer and brake. But while verbal, physical, and sexual assaults are common, most girls are not taught to develop the strength and technique necessary to resist attacks. "Don't take candy from strangers," they warned us in school. Big help. Almost 90 percent of rapists are acquaintances.[27]

Denied sports training as well as fighting skills, many women have become physically retarded, literally: slowed or delayed in their physical development. "I've taught black women, Hispanic women, and white women," says karate black belt Susan Erickson of Arlington, Virginia. "What they have in common is they have no sense of their physical prowess."

Women's physical inferiority, and our concomitant fear, is not incidental. It's not natural. If we are the weaker sex, it's because men have denied us the opportunity to build strength. "All patriarchal cultures idealize, sexualize, and generally prefer weak women," writes Gloria Steinem in *Revolution from Within*.[28]

Girls learn that female strength is unattractive to men, and that being attractive to men is paramount. "There are young girls who could be a lot better at taekwondo than they are, but they're afraid of what the boys will think," laments Olympic gold medalist and four-time taekwondo world champion Lynnette Love. "For so long they've been taught that if there's a boy and a girl the same age, the boy must be naturally better. If they do something to assert that they are stronger, then they have to apologize for it. It's frustrating because it takes such a long time to remold that."

Women learned from Billie Jean King's 1973 victory over Bobby Riggs that we can exceed male expectations—and often our own. That we can, brick by brick, dismantle the Gender Wall the men have constructed to keep women out. Relatively, men's upper bodies are usually stronger than ours, even if we are equally well trained. But their legs aren't. We could learn to kick, as Lynnette Love does. She can kick to the chest, the neck, the knee, the groin—anywhere she wants. With a kick to the head, she can kill.

In the film *Necessary Roughness* a college football team, short on players, invites a soccer player named Lucy to be their place-kicker. Team members fear that they'll be the laughingstock of the conference, and they make sexual comments about her body.

But Lucy scores the tying kick in the final game. A player from the opposing team, his sense of masculine dominance clearly threatened, gratuitously and angrily knocks her to the ground, saying, "Welcome to football." Her teammates, by then appreciative of her ability but still ensconced in their mythic man-as-protector role, run toward the guy who had tackled her as if to retaliate.

No need. Lucy can take care of herself. She kicks him in the groin, saying, "Welcome to football."

What interests me about this scene is the kick, this refreshing double-entendre on the word football. When a strong female foot connects with and injures delicate male "balls," it breaks all the rules, not only in the game of football (surely this would be ruled unnecessary roughness) but also in the game of life. Yet the title of the film is *Necessary Roughness*.

Six months pregnant, Amelia Brown[29] was walking along a street in the financial district of a major city, lost in maternal daydreams. It was Saturday; the street was quiet. Suddenly a man grabbed her by the arm, said, "Fuck me, bitch," and pulled her toward an alley.

Brown struck him in the face. It sent him backward. She stepped into him and jabbed his stomach with her elbow. He doubled over. She grabbed him by the hair, yanked his head down, and brought her knee up as if to smash him in the jaw, but stopped short, as if to say, "See what I could do?"

He fell on the sidewalk. Waving her finger in his face, she yelled, "You asshole. Don't you ever, ever do that again."

She felt a little better at that point. "My next thought was, I can't miss my train," she recalls. "I was going to see my obstetrician, and it was difficult to get appointments. So I just left him there."

A legal secretary, Amelia Brown had been raped by her husband's brother one morning in 1987, when she was alone at her house. She had let him in; she had trusted him. For weeks afterward she had been debilitated by fear, unable to stay home alone, to answer the door, or even to answer the phone. At the suggestion of a friend, she began to study and eventually to teach a women's self-defense program called Chimera. That prepared her for the attack, four years later, by the man on the street.

It also prepared her for life at work. Since studying self-defense, Brown deals with co-workers and superiors "from a position of strength. I'm the only legal secretary who'll march into the partners' corner offices and tell them what I really think."

Her physical training transformed Brown's marriage. "Before, when my husband would raise his voice, I'd run and hide. He never intended to threaten me, but occasionally he would get angry, and we couldn't continue the argument because I was frightened. He'd have to reassure me: 'I'm not going to hurt you.' One day we realized that my old fear was completely gone."

Amelia Brown is not alone. Women who study self-defense or otherwise build strength often have previously been assaulted. Their interest in physical power emerges as a direct result of their awareness of their vulnerability and their desire to become less vulnerable.

Psychologists say that the best antidote to depression and helplessness is action. Athletes, with their proud muscles and trained minds, are poised to take those actions, and to provide leadership for women who are sick of living in fear. When asked what she'd do if a man tried to rape her, Donna Lopiano, executive director of the Women's Sports Foundation, replied, "I'd kill him." She did not hesitate. She did not seem to worry that killing him might be unkind or unladylike. She'd kill him. Lopiano played in twenty-six national championships in four sports and was inducted into the National Softball Hall of Fame. Now in her late forties, she's still, she says proudly, "strong as a horse." If a man were foolish enough to attack her, she'd have the means to resist.

Ailene Voisin, a sportswriter for the *Atlanta Journal-Constitution,* was attacked in her own house by an employee of a professional moving company, whom she had recently hired. He returned to her new home the following week, knocked on her door, and asked to use her phone. When she let him in, he grabbed her from behind in a choke hold, lifted her off the ground, and tried to drag her toward the bedroom. Though she was much smaller, she wrestled him across the kitchen, where she was able to activate an alarm. Her sports training, she believes, helped save her life.

From years of playing basketball, volleyball, softball, and other sports, Voisin acquired "strength, quick thinking, and also aggression," she says. "In sports, aggression is not only necessary, it's rewarded. It becomes automatic."

Tennis player Chris Thayer, furious about daily harassment from a construction crew near her home, decided to take matters into her own hands one day when walking to her car in a tennis dress. "The more I thought about it, the madder I got," she wrote in a letter to the *San Diego Union*. "Why should I be intimidated every time I enter or leave the place I live? I grabbed my tennis racket as though it were a weapon. I marched from my apartment straight past the construction workers, staring at them with sheer hate in my eyes. Guess what? I got in my car, slammed the door, and drove off without getting so much as a peep!"

Are female athletes, with their quick minds and swift feet, less prone to rape than nonathletes? Researchers have not yet answered—or even really asked—this question. But in one study, University of Arkansas psychologist Thomas L. Jackson found that female athletes reported significantly less rape victimization than has been reported by other researchers studying general female populations.[30]

Our problem is not so much superior male strength, but superior male training, combined with a culture that encourages male violence. Men have culturally sanctioned *rights* to violence. Sports—particularly football, boxing, and ice hockey—train men to use their bodies to injure others. Not only do women miss out on military-style sports training; many of us are actively discouraged from fighting. Amelia Brown says she was "socialized not to be angry. I was always told I was a hothead, I flew off the handle, and that was bad."

What if women became hotheads; what if we flew off the handle?

The Reverend Jesse Jackson, noting the social influence of sports heroes, said of the late great boxer, "Joe Louis taught us we can fight back with dignity and conquer." By "we" he meant African-American people and he seemed to mean primarily men, for whom boxing tends to be a more meaningful metaphor than for black women.

Do African-American women—and other women—know that we, too, can fight back with dignity and conquer? What if we learned that lesson from the story of Amelia Brown? Or from Lynnette Love, who now co-owns the National Institute of Taekwondo and Fitness in Temple Hills, Maryland? Or from our own sports training?

Surely we have discarded that bad, old advice: "If you don't resist rape, you won't get hurt." Since when can a woman be raped without being hurt? Surely it must be appropriate, sometimes, to "act like men." Otherwise we're defenseless against their attacks.

What if we did act as men act? What if women became not merely assertive, but aggressive—or, more precisely, counteraggressive? What if, when attacked, we retaliated? What if, before being attacked, we knew that we could fight back? What if, walking down the street or sleeping in our own beds, we didn't feel so damn vulnerable? Historically, men have used sports training to prepare for war. What if we used sports training to prepare for what Marilyn French calls men's "war against women"?[31] What if female coaches openly encouraged their athletes to transfer their strength, power, and presence of mind into self-defense off the playing fields?

· · ·

Daily, I walk with Kabir, a big friend of German shepherd ancestry. Men never hassle me. I'm big, too, and that may be part of it. But I think it's mostly the dog. Many men are afraid of dogs, in particular German shepherds, in part because the police commanded the dogs to attack demonstrators during the Civil Rights marches of the sixties. I abhor any police or dog brutality, but what interests me is that many men are wary of dogs the way they're wary of each other. I'd like them to be wary of women, too.

Any athlete knows that smaller is not necessarily weaker. Women are getting strong, and we could get stronger. We could make men wary of us, make them walk a wide circle around us, even if we weren't accompanied by dogs. It won't work, my friend Susan says. Men will only start using more weapons. Or they'll gang-rape more. That may already be happening. Still, I'd like men to know that they can't trust women to be passive, to be victims, to be nonviolent, the same way they can't trust dogs.

We could also team up. Remember: sports teach women how to rely on each other, help each other, trust each other. One-on-one, the average man may win a fight with the average woman. His greater size, upper-body strength, athletic and aggression training, and culturally granted rights to violence give him the advantage. With training, she could fare better. With the help of her sisters, she could win.

Rarely do we hear of women banding together to protect each other or children from male violence. But it could happen, and athletes could lead the way. Wasn't this the appeal (for women) and horror (for rapists) of *Thelma and Louise?* It represented what editor Merle Hoffman called "two women giving the ultimate 'fuck you' to the patriarchy." Male reviewers expressed disgust that women would "act like men," proclaimed the film "toxic feminism" and worried about, in Hoffman's words, "the film's catalytic possibilities for general female revolt."[32]

If athletes lead the way in resisting male violence, those athletes may be girls. A 14-year-old named Hannah Alejandro recently wrote to *Ms.* magazine: "At school today I walked in on a group of my friends, two 15-year-old girls and a 15-year-old boy. The boy was playfully threatening to slap one of the girls. I leaned over to her and said loudly, 'Let me know if he bothers you, and I'll take care of him. I can body slam him, you know.' I made this comment partly to be funny, partly to warn. The boy immediately yelled that 'guys don't like to go out with big strong manly girls.' This is a boy who weeks ago asked me if I took pride in being manly, because I was discussing weightlifting with other boys. (I was forced to break it to him that it is possible to be a woman and strong.)

"I reacted to today's incident with indignation, and I think I've lost him as a friend. (I wonder if it was a loss?)"[33]

• • •

We have been ridiculed for throwing "like girls." What does it mean to throw like a woman? Maybe it means to throw hard, imagining oneself playing in the All-American Girls Pro Baseball League of the 1940s and 1950s. Maybe it means to throw with pride, having trained oneself, at age fifty. Maybe it means to throw often and publicly, hoping to inspire young girls. Maybe it means never throwing anything *at* anyone—unless in self-defense.

Sport, by definition, strengthens. Like Gail Savage, we all tend to acquire strength fairly easily. At 5'5", Gail can now bench-press eighty-five pounds and leg-press 325. She knows she's not "a total weakling." No female athletes are. The athlete dedicates herself to women's rights, beginning with her own. The team athlete becomes appreciative of women's bodies, beginning with her own. She cares for women, respects women, and becomes willing to take physical risks for and with women. Sport for women represents autonomy, strength, pleasure, community, control, justice, and power. It disrupts men's attempts to elevate themselves above women. It changes everything.

Patrick Thevenard, for example, has been changed. Thinking back on the times when he would lift and carry his ex-wife despite her objections, Patrick says, "That was years ago. That was before I'd done enough reading and thinking to understand that it was another one of those nice reinforcements of physical masculine dominance. You can pick up someone and show them to be helpless, but it's all a good joke, ha-ha-ha, so the woman is not in a position to put up much of a struggle. It maintains an underlying physical domination."

He would not, he says, do it again.

Meanwhile, President Clinton moved to Gail Savage's town. I mentioned to her that they're the same age. "I can run faster than Bill," she responded immediately. News reports have described his jogging regimen—about two to three miles a day—as "real slow, not too strenuous." Gail noticed. She added generously, "That's OK for him."

As for herself, she has faster goals, including a 10K at a seven-and-a-half-minutes-per-mile pace. Meanwhile, it's nice to know that already she can outrun one of the most powerful men in the world. It makes her feel good about herself. It makes her feel like running.

4

Boys Will Be Boys and Girls Will Not

> *My aunts washed the dishes while the uncles*
>
> *squirted each other on the lawn with*
>
> *garden hoses. Why are we in here,*
>
> *I said, and they are out there?*
>
> *that's the way it is,*
>
> *said Aunt Hetty, the shriveled-up one.*
>
> —*Paulette Jiles, "Paper Matches"*

TWO SCIENTISTS recently made this forecast: The fastest woman may eventually outrun the fastest man. Their prediction appeared only as a letter to the editor in *Nature* magazine,[1] yet it generated a stampede of interest from the media. *Time,* the *Chicago Tribune, USA Today,* the *New York Times,* the *Washington Post,* and *Sports Illustrated* printed stories. All quoted experts who ridiculed the conjecture as "ludicrous," "sheer ignorance," "a good laugh," "absurd," "asinine," "completely fallacious," and/or "laughable."

In one Associated Press report, the word ridiculous was used five times. *Science News* ran the headline "Women on the verge of an athletic showdown." *Runner's World* entitled its article "Battle of the Sexes." Unlike questionable projections that are dismissed without fanfare, this one seems to have struck a nerve.

The researchers, Brian Whipp and Susan Ward of the University of California, Los Angeles, calculated runners' average speeds during record-breaking races over the past seventy years, then compared the rates of increase. Noting that women's average speeds are increasing at a faster rate than are men's, they projected that in the future, the best women may catch up to and even surpass the best men at various distances. For example: By 1998, the best woman and man would, if they continue to improve at current rates, complete the 26.2-mile marathon in two hours, two minutes. In subsequent years, the woman would sprint ahead.

Indisputably, neither women nor men will continue to improve at their current rates forever. Otherwise, humans would one day run the marathon in a matter of minutes. But the very idea that women might someday beat men elicited passionate responses. *Runner's World* writers Amby Burfoot and Marty Post, as if verbally to stop women in their tracks, pointed out that in the past five years, women have made few improvements in world-record times. This is a sure sign, they said, that women "have already stopped" improving.[2]

• • •

When I appear on radio and television shows to discuss women's sports or my first book, *Are We Winning Yet? How Women Are Changing Sports and Sports Are Changing Women,* I encounter a similar fury. Female callers are not the problem; they brag about their triceps or gripe about male egos or ask for advice about discrimination. Some male callers tell stories about female martial artists or mountain climbers who taught them, in a way they could understand, about female strength. But at least half of the male callers act as if my views were heretical. Angry and antagonistic, they belittle me, my ideas, my book, and female athletes in general.

What seems to make them angriest is my observation that men are not better athletes than women are. In no sport are all men better than all women, I point out, and in many sports, women routinely defeat men. Although single-sex competitions are often appropriate, and men do have physical advantages in some sports, women should see themselves as men's peers, I suggest, rather than exclusively competing against women.

These men don't want to hear any of that. In voices I can only describe as high-pitched and hysterical, they say, "Yeah, but you're never going to see a woman play pro football!"

It is a taunt and, I think, a genuine fear. I'm not talking about football. I've never met a woman who aspires to play pro football. I'm talking about auto racing, horse racing, dog sled racing, equestrian events, rifle shooting, and marathon swimming, where women and men compete together at the elite levels. I'm talking about tennis, golf, racquetball, bowling, skiing, and other recreational sports, where a wife and husband or a female and male pair of friends are likely to find themselves evenly matched. In sports, as in the rest of life, women do compete with men on a daily basis, and often win.

So it intrigues me that in response to my discussion of women's athletic excellence, men change the subject to football. They try to assert football as the sine qua non of athleticism. Because "women could never play football," they imply, men are physically, naturally, biologically superior.

Most men can't play pro football themselves—but they can take vicarious comfort in the display of male physical competence and aggression.

They take comfort in professional baseball ("Women could never play pro baseball") and in professional basketball ("Women could never play pro basketball") and in boxing ("Women could never box") and in footraces ("Women could never win the marathon").

Here are a few more quotes from men on radio shows, on airplanes, at restaurants:

"Women can't dunk."

"OK, women can play golf, but they can't drive the ball as far as men can."

"OK, female jockeys win, but there's a horse involved."

"Women win at marathon swimming? Who cares? You call that a major sport? I'd like to see a 320-pound female linebacker. That's a laugh."

Most men are not 320-pound linebackers. But, identified with these hulks, average men take great pleasure in the linebackers' exploits (a revealing term). Football, baseball, basketball, boxing, and hockey are important to men in part *because* they seem to be all-male pursuits, because they seem to be activities that *only men can do*. When women demonstrate excellence in sports like running, tennis, and golf, men take great pains to describe that excellence as less important, less worthy, less of an achievement than male excellence.

Psychiatrist Arnold R. Beisser explains the phenomenon this way: "It is small wonder that the American male has a strong affinity for sports. He has learned that this is one area where there is no doubt about sexual differences and where his biology is not obsolete. Athletics help assure his difference from women in a world where his functions have come to resemble theirs."[3]

．．．

Sports are about distinction. Who is better? One inch, one point, or one-hundredth of a second can differentiate winner from loser. One pound, one meal, one more set of two-hundred-meter sprints in practice can determine, or seem to determine, whether a person finishes first or last. Athletes may train for the sheer joy of moving their bodies through space, but eventually they grow curious to see how fast they can move, or how well they can perform, compared to others. They want to compare, to contrast, to differentiate. To know where they stand. To win.

It is in this comparative, competitive arena that we are repeatedly told that women and men are different. And men are better.[4] Women may no longer be weak, granted, but they are still weak*er*. Weaker than men. Still the weaker sex.

Still, as de Beauvoir said, the second sex.

Actually, in many ways, men are the weaker sex. Men die on average seven years earlier than women. Women have a better sense of smell, taste, hearing, and sight (colorblindness affects one woman for every sixteen men). Women are more susceptible to migraines, arthritis, and depression, but men commit suicide more and have higher rates of heart attack and stroke. "Women are sick, but men are dead," Edward Dolnick wrote in his *In Health* magazine article on the subject.[5]

Yet men keep pointing to one physical advantage—upper-body strength—to maintain their illusion of supremacy. Sports that depend on such strength—that, indeed, were designed to showcase that strength—bolster the myth.

Those who claim male sports superiority are not thinking of male gymnasts, who lack the flexibility to use some of the apparatus women use. Or male swimmers, who can't keep up with women over long distances. Or male equestrians, who gallop side by side with—or in the dust of—their female peers.

They are not considering how much women and men have in common: the human experience of sport. These same people would never think of comparing Sugar Ray Leonard to Muhammad Ali. One weighed sixty pounds more than the other. Clearly, they deserved to box in different classes. Yet the top female tennis player is often compared to the top male tennis player ("Yeah but, she could never beat *him*"), who usually outweighs her by sixty pounds.

Those who claim male superiority are not remembering jockstraps. Because men's genitals dangle precariously outside the pelvis, they are vulnerable to speeding baseballs and to angry fists or feet. In addition, "bikes with dropped handlebars bring the rider's legs close to the stomach, and the testicles can get squashed or twisted against the saddle," notes sportswriter Adrianne Blue in *Faster, Higher, Further*. "This can lead to gangrene and amputation." Such cases have been noted in medical journals.

Blue also suggests that men's bigger bodies make more "dangerous missiles" that are more likely than women's bodies to cause injury when they collide. For this reason a case could be made, she says, for banning men from contact sports.[6]

If women and men were to compete together in noncontact sports, a man would currently win at the elite levels of most existing events: running (as long as the race is under 100 miles); swimming (under about 22 miles); throwing shot, discus, or javelin. On average, men can carry and use more oxygen. They tend to be heavier—an advantage in football—and taller: handy in basketball and volleyball. Men have more lean muscle mass, convenient in sports requiring explosive power—which happens to include most of the sports men have invented.

Less muscle-bound, women generally have better flexibility, useful in gymnastics, diving, and skating. Our lower center of gravity can help in hockey, golf, tennis, baseball, and even basketball. We sweat better (less dripping, therefore better evaporation), which is critical since, like car engines, human bodies need to remain cool and well lubricated to function efficiently.

Physiologist Diane Wakat, associate professor of health education at the University of Virginia, tested athletes under various conditions of heat, humidity, exercise, and nutritional intake, and concluded that women are better able to adjust to the environmental changes. "In every case, females were better able to handle the stress," says Wakat.

The longer the race, the better women do. Women's superior insulation (fat) is, believe it or not, prized by some because it offers buoyancy, heat retention, and efficient use of fuel over long distances, whether by land or by sea.

Ann Trason, a California microbiology teacher, became in 1989 the first woman to win a coed national championship—the twenty-four-hour run—by completing 143 miles. The best male finisher completed four fewer miles. Of Ward and Whipp's prediction that women will one day hold the overall world record in the relatively short (26.2-mile) marathon, Trason says: "I'd be there and be really happy to see it, but it seems unlikely. I do think women will get closer."

Helen Klein's world-record distance in a twenty-four-hour race— 109.5 miles—exceeds the best distance for an American man in her age group (65–69). She says of the possibility that a woman will one day set the overall marathon record, "I would not say no. There is hope. If I were younger, I might try it myself."

In marathon and long-distance cold-water swims, "women usually out-swim the men," says Bob Duenkel, curator of the International Swimming Hall of Fame. Penny Dean still holds the English Channel record she set in 1978. Diana Nyad is the only athlete to complete the swim from Bimini to Florida. Lynne Cox holds the records for swimming the Bering Strait and the Strait of Magellan. The first person to swim all five Great Lakes, and the first ever to cross Lake Superior (in 1988), was Vicki Keith.

Susan Butcher has been the overall winner of the 1,100-mile Iditarod dog sled race four times. A woman named Seana Hogan recently cycled the four hundred miles from San Francisco to Los Angeles in nineteen hours, forty-nine minutes, breaking the previous men's record by almost an hour.

But women's successes are rarely attributable to gender. In ultra-distance running, swimming, and cycling, as well as in equestrian events, horse racing, auto racing, and dog sled racing, success is determined primarily by physical and mental preparation, competitive spirit, self-discipline, or other nongender-related factors. Because upper-body strength is not paramount in these sports, women and men become free to compete together as individuals, even at the highest levels of competition.

Men's strength advantage is actually marginal, meaning that there is more variation among individual men than between the average man and the average woman. It only becomes relevant when comparing trained, competitive athletes. On any recreational doubles tennis team, the female player might be stronger.

Age is also important. Men's strength advantage occurs primarily during the reproductive years. Before puberty, girls, who tend to mature faster, have a height and strength advantage which, if not nullified by institutional and cultural discrimination, would actually render the best of them superior to the best boys. In old age, there is little physical difference between female and male strength.

But we've so long been told that men are better athletes. I even catch myself thinking this way, despite daily evidence to the contrary. For instance, in my masters swimming program, the fastest athletes—including college competitors—swim in Lane 1, while the slowest—including fit, fast, white-haired folks in their seventies—swim in Lane 6. There are women and men in all the lanes.

I swim in Lane 3. In Lane 2 is Ken. Because he's about my age and height, I identify with him. We have the same stroke length, so we look at each other sometimes, his breathing to the left, my breathing to the right, as we windmill through the water. But eventually he pulls ahead. He's faster. At first, I attributed his greater speed to the fact that he is male. His shoulders are broader; his muscles are more prominent than mine.

But then I looked over at Lane 4. There swims Bruce. Also about my height and my age, Bruce is slower than I am. He's got those same broad shoulders and big muscles, but there he is anyway, poking along in Lane 4. I'm faster because I've trained longer, or I have better technique, or I'm in better shape, or I'm more competitive, or some combination of those factors—the same reasons Ken is faster than both Bruce and me, and the same reasons Susie, Karen, Diane, Denise, Lynn, and Martha are faster than Ken. It has nothing to do with gender.

Does it make any sense to ask whether women—even marathoners—will catch up to men? Most women don't think so.

"Let's just run as fast as we can and not compare ourselves to men," proposes Henley Gibble, executive director of the Road Runners Club of America. "It seems like a silly thing to do anyway. In the open distances, we're already winning."

"It's only relevant for me in terms of, Have women been given the same opportunities to explore what their own potential is?" says sports psychologist and University of Virginia professor Linda Bunker. "The bottom line—Will women ever be as good as men?—is not necessarily of interest."

Men are arrogant to think we want to catch up to them, says Susan Birrell, a trailblazing sports sociologist from the University of Iowa. "As if we don't have any ambition at all. As if all we want to do is catch up to men. Remember that quote: 'Women who want to be equal to men lack ambition.' "

In addition to being the overall winner of the twenty-four-hour race, Ann Trason has five times won the women's division and in 1992 and 1993 finished third overall in the Western States 100-Mile Endurance Run. I ask her: "The whole concept of women catching up to men is off the mark for you, because you're already beating men, right?"

"I guess you could look at it that way," she replies. "That's sort of nice."

"Is it nice?" I ask. "Does it matter?"

"Yeah, it is important to me," she says. "It shows what women can do. It's not like I go out there intentionally to outrun men, but I'm proud of that achievement."

Male competitors have told Trason they'd "rather die" than "let" her pass them. But for Trason, competitions are not "athletic showdowns" or "battles of the sexes." In fact, the races nearly transcend gender, which appeals to her. "The nice thing about ultras [one-hundred-mile or twenty-four-hour races] is, you're just competing against whoever's out there. The sex barrier comes down. It's not gone altogether, but it's a lot less than if you were doing a 10K."

Because "being masculine" has included access to diverse sporting opportunities and "being feminine" has not, it's shortsighted to postulate that current gaps between male and female athletic potential will not close, at least partially, in the future—or that, as Post and Burfoot asserted, women "have already stopped improving." Men prevented women from running marathons until 1967. The Olympics did not offer a women's marathon until 1984, and still doesn't offer a women's swimming event longer than eight hundred meters (the men swim fifteen hundred meters). For every college woman who gets a chance to play college sports, 2.24 men do. For every woman who receives a college scholarship, 2.26 men do. The more women run, the greater the likelihood that some of them will run fast. Increased numbers of female runners—along with female-focused training, coaching, scholarships, equipment, and even clothing—account for the historical improvements in women's times, and greater numbers in the future are likely to improve times further.

If marathon swimming were our national sport, as it is in Egypt—if there were a nationally televised Super Bowl of marathon swimming, and spectators packed college swim meets like sardines—we might think differently about women's and men's athletic capabilities. If men competed against women on the balance beam, or in synchronized swimming, or in rhythmic gymnastics, we might rephrase the question about who might catch up to whom.

Maybe, in a world where gender differences were no more relevant than hand sizes, we could innocently wonder if the best women will catch up to the best men in running while also pondering the possibility that the best men will catch up to the best women in gymnastic floor exercise. Neither would have emotional import.

But in this society, the question of women catching up to men has enormous emotional significance. Scientific inquiry is always influenced by the value system of the scientists: What questions are asked? Since most women runners express no desire to "catch up" to men, and indeed seem to want to avoid the comparison, more appropriate questions might be, Do women feel behind? If so, why? In what ways?

We might ask how many women will ultimately have opportunities to play sports. By what date will the percent of college women athletes—currently about one-third—reflect the percent of college women students—one-half? When will women "catch up" in terms of social support?

We might also ask why was the outcry about the letter to the editor of *Nature* far greater than the outcry about the National Collegiate Athletic Association's comprehensive study that described vast gender inequities in college sports.

· · ·

One reason male–female athletic comparisons are tempting to make, and hard to argue with, is that they seem natural.[7] What could be more natural than human bodies? Sports seem to offer measurable, inarguable proof of human physical potential. Especially when no machines or animals are involved, sports seem to represent a raw, quintessentially fair contest between individuals or teams. *Ready? Set? Go. May the best man win.*

In fact, few professional athletes have "natural" bodies; otherwise we'd bump into pro football–sized men in the supermarkets. The linebacker has been shaped by many behavioral (nutrition, weight lifting) and often chemical (steroids, growth hormones) factors. Women who play or do not play sports have also been shaped by various factors, including restricted access to training opportunities, restrictive shoes and clothing, ridicule by peers, and cultural pressure to limit food intake for the sake of creating a thin, rather than strong, body. There's nothing natural about any of that.

But because sports seem natural, and because in the sports media we so often see men who are bigger and stronger than the biggest, strongest women, these men make a convincing subliminal case: not only are men better athletes, men are superior physical specimens. And because the men engaged in sporting events are so often enacting some form of mock combat, we receive the message: Men are inherently, naturally aggressive and, as a gender, dominant.

By framing women as "catching up"—or "naturally" incapable of catching up—writers and researchers obscure the value of women's achievements in and of themselves, regardless of men's achievements. We say that women have an "extra" layer of fat, but not that men have "extra" testosterone. What if we used women's behavior as the standard? In sports, we would compare violent crimes committed by male athletes to violent crimes committed by female athletes. Or sexual abuses committed by male coaches compared to sexual abuses by female coaches. Instead, it's women's physical "inferiority" that captures the public attention.

In Carol Tavris's book, *The Mismeasure of Woman: Why Women Are Not the Better Sex, the Inferior Sex, or the Opposite Sex,* she notes that most gender differences are invented or exaggerated, and women are erroneously compared to a male "norm" for the purpose of maintaining male privilege. "Those who are dominant have an interest in maintaining their differences from others, attributing those differences to "the harsh dictates of nature" and obscuring the unequal arrangements that benefit them," she writes.[8]

Tavris recently told the audience of a Washington, D.C., radio station,

"We see differences as deficiencies and conclude men are better. It's not true that men are better or women are better."

Immediately a male caller protested. "What do you mean, neither men or women are better? It depends what you're talking about: bench-pressing 240 pounds or having labor pains."

Funny: Tavris had not been talking about sports at all. Yet suddenly, irrationally, the caller used a testosterone-aided strength sport (notice he didn't choose gymnastics) to assert not only difference but superiority. Since men do not have labor pains—a rather negative way to refer to women's unique capacity for giving birth—it makes no sense to say women have labor pains "better" than men do. Yet this man angrily contrasted women's particular reproductive capacity—something men can't do at all—with a sport that men can do "better."

A female caller, obviously unimpressed (and comically unfamiliar with weight lifting), responded, "I hope we get this discussion beyond bench pressing. Maybe someday women will be able to press benches. So what?"

So what? Who cares if men are stronger, heavier, taller? Who benefits when this comparison is repeatedly made, and women come out on the shorter, lighter, weaker end of the stick? Might it be *because* only women can "have labor pains" that men cling so tightly to their strength advantages? Why are some men so vociferously asserting these differences *now?* And what is sport's role in creating and sustaining gender differences?

As every first-grader knows, there are physical differences between women and men, but these differences would be largely irrelevant except in matters of sex, reproduction, urination, and toupee purchases if it weren't for our culture's insistence on categorizing people first and foremost as "male" or "female." It is from these cultural categories—not from biological realities—that most "masculine" and "feminine" behaviors emerge. Cynthia Fuchs Epstein, author of *Deceptive Distinctions,* writes, "The overwhelming evidence created by the past decade of research on gender supports the theory that gender differentiation—as distinct of course from sexual differentiation—is best explained as a social construction rooted in hierarchy."

Here's where the hierarchy part comes in: we don't just say, boys shouldn't play with dolls and girls shouldn't play with pistols. Through our economic structure and through the media, we say that taking care of children—"women's work"—is less important than war—"men's work." We don't just say that football is for boys and cheerleading is for girls. We say that playing football is more valuable than cheerleading or field hockey or volleyball or Double Dutch jump rope or anything girls do—more important, more interesting, more newsworthy: better.

Thus boys have an incentive to cling religiously to "boy behaviors," and they do. Boys are more likely than girls to insist on sex-typed activities and toys,[9] and with good reason—it cements their place in the dominant class. Boys also have an incentive to keep girls out of their tree forts and clubhouses and sports associations and military elite: like "undesirables" moving into a pricey neighborhood, females lower the property value. Women's participation challenges the entire concept of relevant differences between women and men. "To allow women into sport would be an ultimate threat to one of the last strongholds of male security and supremacy," write Mary A. Boutilier and Lucinda SanGiovanni in *The Sporting Woman*. To put it another way, if women can play sports then "men aren't really men."[10]

Of course, it's too late to keep women out of sports. But they can be kept out of the public eye and kept out of key, visible, highly paid positions like a football or men's basketball coach. Their accomplishments can be ignored or trivialized or sexualized. They can be barred from "masculine" activities—a term having nothing, really, to do with who men are, and everything to do with what men want to claim as their own.

Consider the case of skateboarding. You may have noticed: few girls careen around city streets or suburban malls on skateboards, leaping high over curbs. It's primarily a teenage boys' sport. But in contrast to other male-dominated sports, skateboarders tend not to compete with each other and tend not to establish hierarchies based on ability. Skateboarders value what are often considered feminine qualities: balance, grace, cooperation, and artistic style. One male skateboarder told Greeley, Colorado, researcher Becky Beal, "If you're the worst one on the baseball team, others give you shit and that makes you feel bad. In skating if you are bad, no one makes you feel bad about that." Skaters considered "cool" are those who are supportive, and who do not try to dominate by competing with others.[11]

Yet Beal found during her two-and-a-half-year study of a forty-one-member skateboarding community (37 boys, 4 girls) that teenage boys construe skateboarding as a "naturally" male activity. Despite its coopera-tive, nonhierarchical, grace-oriented value system, boys insisted that few girls skate because boys and girls are intrinsically different sorts of people suited for different domains. Girls were seen by the boys as lacking the "innate abilities" to skateboard. When Beal pointed out that women suc-ceed at plenty of sports that require balance and coordination such as gymnastics and figure skating, the boys were unshaken in their belief that girls lack what skateboarding requires.

The boys seemed unaware that their own behavior might be making the environment unattractive to young women. Girls who did skate were slighted by the boys as "trying to skate around" or "just trying to balance on the board." Female skaters were labeled "skate Betties" and presumed to be primarily interested in dating the boys. The male skaters did not want to date girls who were engaging in this "masculine" activity. "You don't want your girlfriend to skate," but it's OK for other girls, one boy explained.[12]

The four female skaters in the group reported that "skating is seen as unfeminine" and that their male friends were patronizing and overprotec-tive. The boys "feel threatened," one girl said.[13]

• • •

In sports, women do various activities men have claimed as masculine. They shove, sweat, strain, flex, groan, take large strides across open spaces, prioritize their own pleasure, and even, occasionally, receive ap-plause for their accomplishments, regardless of their physical beauty. They violate the fundamental principle of gender inequality as expressed by Holly Devor in her book, *Gender Blending:* "Boys will be boys and girls will not."[14]

In sports, girls "will be boys," too. When this happens—when girls trample on "male" territory, men use myriad institutional, cultural, social, and personal means to reinforce the myth of gender difference. These include restricting women's access to sports, ignoring women's participa-tion in sports, controlling women's sports involvement, trivializing women's interest in sports, and sexually harassing women who play sports.

Restricting women's access is becoming increasingly difficult since the law is on women's side, but college administrators plan to go down fight-ing. In 1993, both Brown and Colgate universities appealed legal decisions that granted their female students expanded sports opportunities. Both schools admitted offering inequitable sports programs, yet resisted, at considerable legal cost, the students' insistence on improved programs. Colgate won; the Second U.S. Circuit Court of Appeals ruled that the Title IX lawsuit was moot because none of the five students who sued would be attending Colgate the following season. Younger students have sued Colgate again. Brown lost the first stage of its appeal; the result is pending as this book goes to press.

Newspapers, magazines, radio, and television ignore women's participation every day. The coverage granted to female athletes—less than 5 percent of total sports coverage—gives the erroneous impression that very few women compete in sports.

Controlling women's sports participation is easy now that more than half of all coaches and administrators of women's sports are men. These men decide what sports will be offered for women, what those women will be taught, what dress and behavior codes will be established, and how the young women will be coached. National and international sports organizations are also overwhelmingly controlled by men. So men can decide, as the Barcelona Taekwondo Federation did in 1992 without consulting its female athletes, that women must wear breast protection and groin cups, must undergo pregnancy tests, and must not compete if pregnant.

They can decide, as they often have when female performance matches men's, that women should compete separately. In the case of bowling, this means separating tournaments (and offering men more money) on the pretext that men require different lane conditions. (All pro bowlers use the same size and weight balls, but men's lanes are conditioned with what's known as "longer" oil.) In the case of archery, it means offering slightly different distances for women and men (men shoot at 30, 50, 70, and 90 meters; women at 30, 50, 60, and 70 meters) so that total scores cannot be compared. Segregation begins with children. The National Marbles Tournament, held annually in Wildwood, New Jersey, offers separate competitions for girls and boys.

Rifle-shooting used to be coed. But in the three-position small-bore event, Margaret Murdoch tied teammate Lanny Bassham for first place in the 1976 Olympics. The gold was given to Bassham (a man) based on a tie-breaking rule, though at the awards ceremony, he graciously invited

Murdoch up onto the winner's platform with him. Immediately afterward, the international shooting federation segregated most events in the sport. There are now four events for women and seven for men—apparently a more "natural" order of things.

In a variation on the women-shouldn't-go-in-the locker-room rationale, bass fishermen exclude female participants on the grounds that women shouldn't watch men urinate over the side of the boat. When the Army Corps of Engineers recently refused to allow the men use of a lake for a scheduled tournament unless they integrated, the bass men reluctantly admitted one woman. Reporter Julie Vader wrote, "A whole generation of men may now have to learn two of life's most crushing lessons: one, sometimes a woman can catch a lot of fish, and two, she really isn't interested in looking at him with his zipper down." [15]

Go only as far as your nearest college and you'll see that while men's teams tend to have nicknames such as the Panthers, women tend to have nicknames such as the Pantherettes or the Pink Panthers. So men are the norm, women a cutesie deviation from the norm, often absurdly so: consider Lady Rams, Lady Redmen, and my favorite, Lady Gamecocks. To attend a women's sporting event is to have a bizarre zoological experience: fans see Tigerettes, Beaverettes, Eaglettes, Leopardettes, Bulldogettes, Thorobrettes, Yellow Jackettes, Rambelles, Rammettes, Lady Eagles, Lady Centaurs, Teddy Bears, and Wildkittens. More than half of all women's college teams have demeaning or sexist nicknames. [16]

Why can't a panther just be a panther? Because panthers will be panthers, and girl panthers will not.

Sexual harassment is a new term for an old strategy: humiliating women in order to undermine their power. I was sitting in the stands at a women's college basketball game in 1992 when I overheard a vivid illustration of how men employ sexual remarks when threatened by female strength. It was big game, between the two teams ranked best in the country: the University of Maryland and the University of Virginia. More than 14,500 fans packed Maryland's Cole Field House, screaming when Maryland scored and groaning when they missed. Cheerleaders cheered and band members played, offering the support and enthusiasm most people associate with men's games. For that evening at least, watching women play basketball had become cool.

Suddenly a group of male students sitting behind me began loudly harassing the Virginia players with sexual epithets. "You've got too much testosterone," they shouted at one muscular woman. They taunted Virginia's 6'5" Burge twins with, "Amazons!" And when Virginia players stepped to the free-throw line, they tried to rattle them with, "You're bleeding, bitch!"

Male fans are known to be rowdy. But these taunts were telling. All seemed designed to belittle the women *as women*—to punish them for stepping beyond the bounds of traditional femininity, for daring to act like men. The "too much testosterone" accusation implied that muscles and athletic skill are strictly male domain; that the athlete was somehow defective, freakish, or artificially bulked up, not authentically female. The amazon label ridiculed the women for being too tall and too strong; too masculine. With, "You're bleeding, bitch," the men continued their misogynistic tirade, perhaps hoping to remind the women of their inescapable femaleness, to shame and humiliate them about their bodies, and thus to distract them from shooting free throws. (It didn't work.)

Few if any of the male spectators could have won a one-on-one contest with either of the towering Burge twins, or, for that matter, with their 5'6" point guard. These women were more skilled than most if not all of the male fans. This is the reality young men face: female power—physical, political, social—is multiplying daily. By demeaning "amazons," by extolling the sexist traditions inherent in manly sports, and by scrambling to differentiate women from men in a significant, limiting way, men seem to be struggling to nullify the immediate evidence of female strength.

My dictionary defines "amazon" as "a tall strong masculine woman." [17] We don't have a word—or even a concept—for a "tall strong feminine woman." What would she look like, act like? We have instead the word amazon, a term equated with female power and in the same breath with masculinity, and therefore deviance or aberrance.

Amazon is also defined as "a member of a race of female warriors repeatedly warring with the Greeks of classical mythology." At very least, this reveals that the Greeks spent some time thinking about female power, which may explain why they excluded women from their Olympic Games.

But Amazons were also real women and men: goddess-worshiping tribes in North Africa, Bulgaria, Greece, Armenia, Anatolia, and the Black Sea area. Roman and Greek historians of the first century described Amazons as "the warlike women of Libya" (Libya was then all of North Africa west of Egypt); women who "fight like men and are nowise inferior to them in bravery," and women who dressed in black, waved swords, and cursed their enemy "like the Furies."[18] According to Barbara G. Walker, author of *The Woman's Encyclopedia of Myths and Secrets*, "In the Amazons' territory near the Black Sea, women retained certain Amazon customs up to the 18th century: dressing in men's clothes, riding horseback astride, and fighting beside the men in war."[19]

The word Amazon was once thought to derive from *a-mazos*, meaning "breastless," based on the impression that female Amazon warriors amputated a breast to facilitate drawing the bow, but Greek depictions feature no such maiming. The missing breast concept, Walker says, "may have arisen from Asiatic icons of the Primal Androgyne with a male right half and female left half, echoed by a coalescence of the Amazon Goddess Artemis with her brother-consort Apollo."

Nowadays, on basketball courts nationwide, we see women who dress in what used to be men's clothes and are "nowise inferior to them in bravery." At racetracks and equestrian competitions we see women who ride horseback astride. In martial arts dojos and on recreational soccer teams, rugby teams, and softball teams, we see women who "fight" alongside men. In bodybuilding contests, we see small-breasted, large-muscled women—appearing, to some, half male, half female. We see, in other words, amazons.

The "enemy" these amazons face is no longer a military one. It's a legal, cultural, political one, and as such is often less easy to identify and defeat. It ranges from the derision rained on the Virginia basketball players to more subtle behind-the-scenes efforts of college administrators to resist and control female athletic power.

Why are amazons so threatening? Why, when women refuse to "act ladylike," do men react with fear? Why does female strength somehow diminish male strength?

To assert that women are really not so different from men disturbs our dualistic, bipolar way of viewing the world. If women can participate fully in an activity, whether that activity is combat or coaching or computer programming, that activity can no longer be used to grant men superior status. So when women demonstrate strength, some men respond nervously to the impending power shift. "Amazons" with "too much testosterone" threaten the concept of men as meatier, mightier, and as warranting special privilege.

Thus men characterize women as "different." Opponents of Title IX keep turning to women's "difference" to justify cheating women out of sports opportunities. From "women can't play football" to "women's sports don't raise money" to "women don't really want to play sports," men scramble to preserve sport as a bastion of male power. After *USA Today* ran a two-day series of reports on the status of female college athletes, numerous angry male readers wrote to justify discrimination. The most telling letter came from an Alabama man who wrote, "Back off, you guys at *USA Today* . . . This equality kick long ago passed the absurdity redline mark. I suggest you get a recent issue of *Playboy, Penthouse,* or *Hustler.* Study it closely. If you can't detect some significant differences between the sexes, get in out of the sun."

This is what it comes down to: women deserve fewer sports opportunities not because women and men have physical differences that matter in sports, but because women are rightfully objects of sexual pleasure for men. The ancient Greek *porne,* from which the word pornography is derived, was the lowest class of prostitute, a sexual slave available to all male citizens. Pornography does not consist of depictions (*graphos*) of naked women; it consists of depictions of women *as prostitutes.*[20]

• • •

At the "Femininity Control" outposts of international competitions, the world's best female athletes are tested to determine if they are male impostors. Supposedly, the tests are designed to protect female athletes from men who would attempt to use their superior muscle and stature to unfairly sneak into and win women's competitions. In actuality, the tests reinforce the myth of female athletic inferiority.

The tests seem misguided at best, misogynist at worst. They are ineffective, detecting women with genetic anomalies who have no unfair advantage, and passing over steroid users, who do have an unfair advantage. They are insulting: simply being a man would not give one an advantage over the best women athletes. And they are philosophically unsound. In some sports, women have an advantage, yet men are never tested to see if they might be women in disguise.

"The problem with sex testing is it implies that women's capabilities are more limited than they really are," says Alison Carlson, a tennis coach and writer who has spent five years researching, writing, and speaking about gender verification. "If you've got capabilities beyond a certain point, you're not a woman. It's backwards. Instead we should say, by definition, if a woman does this, women can do it."

The first modern "sex check" was conducted in 1936 after Helen Stephens defeated Stella Walsh in the Olympic 100-meter dash, and Walsh's Polish coach complained, insinuating that Stephens might be a man. Stephens, now in her seventies, recalls feeling "hurt and embarrassed, of course," but went along with the United States Olympic Committee's request to have a male doctor "look her over" to make sure she was female. She passed.

Walsh, ironically, fared worse during the inadvertent sex check that occurred during an autopsy after her death in 1980. The coroner found that Walsh, who had lived her entire life as a woman, was not a man exactly, but had been born with ambiguous genitalia. "So it was a case of the pot calling the kettle black," says Stephens with a lighthearted laugh.

Dora Ratjen, a 1936 Olympic high jumper from Germany, was never tested but admitted in 1955 that he was in fact a man, and had been forced by the Hitler Youth Movement to compete as a woman "for the honor and glory of Germany." Three women had jumped higher than he did at those 1936 Games, but he had set a women's world record two years later. Of his disguise he said, "For three years I lived the life of a girl. It was most dull."[21]

In 1946, two French runners who had led a women's relay team to second place in a European championship were found to be living as men. "Whether they had pretended to be women or were later pretending to be men was not absolutely clear," writes Adrianne Blue in *Grace Under Pressure.*[22]

In 1967, organizers first officially instituted what have variously been called sex tests, femininity tests, and gender verification tests at international competitions. Not coincidentally, this new policy arose during a decade when women were beginning to shatter previous records and to narrow the gap between male and female performances. It was also a time when women (and men) were beginning to take steroids to build strength. Because the drugs can produce malelike secondary sex characteristics in women, female athletes with deep voices and beards were showing up at meets. Other women were eyeing these athletes suspiciously, unsure what was going on. They heard rumors that men were masquerading as women.

In the prefeminist era of the late 1960s, women were barred from marathon running and other "masculine" competitions, but they were beginning to resist those restrictions. Serious female athletes were more severely harrassed than they are today, often publicly ridiculed as "manly" or "dykes." Such gibes inspired some women to welcome testing as a way to quell rumors, to prove that they were female, and to weed out the "masculine" women, whether those women seemed masculine because they were on steroids, because they were actually men, or because they were lesbians.

Pat Connolly, a three-time Olympian from that era, explains: "At 17, I . . . knew that some of my competitors had deep voices, beards, and seemed to like women more than men. We felt a mix of emotions: resentment, anger, pity, and empathy . . . but . . . I was sick of being called a dyke. These things prompted us to say, Let's get the men out of our competitions. We had to overcome the stigma of overmasculinization, regardless of whether it was right or wrong."[23]

The justification for testing put forth by the International Olympic Committee (IOC), then and now, is that the tests are designed to "ensure femininity," to "establish physical equality," and "to prevent unfair, malelike physical advantage."[24]

It hasn't worked. During 1967, testing's first year, women at major competitions were obligated to lift their shirts and pull down their pants in front of a group of gynecologists. They then had to wait while the physicians (male) decided if they were "feminine enough." The press jocularly referred to these as "nude parades." Athletes protested that the test was humiliating.

The next year, beginning at the Winter Games in Grenoble, the IOC rejected the nude parade in favor of a chromosome test known as the Barr body test. With this method, a technician scrapes some cells from the lining of a woman's mouth (a buccal smear), examines the cells under the microscope, and looks for XX (female) or XY (male) chromosomes.

But biology is not as simple as culture would have us believe. Not all women have XX chromosomes, it turns out, and not all men have XY. The differences between men and women, so obvious to any gradeschooler, are actually less salient than they seem.

Ewa Klobukowska, for instance, was found to have an XXY genotype. Klobukowska, the first woman to fail the chromosome test, was a Polish sprinter who had won a gold medal with the 4×100 relay in the 1964 Olympics. In 1967, physicians had declared her female during a visual inspection. But the 1968 test revealed her to be one of the six women in a thousand who have XXY chromosomes. At the world championships before the 1968 Olympics, doctors reported that she had "one chromosome too many to be declared a woman for the purposes of athletic competition." She was stripped of her Olympic and other medals.

"It's a dirty and stupid thing to do to me," she said. "I know what I am and how I feel."[25]

This sort of thing keeps happening. The tests aren't turning up any male impostors—zero, in twenty-five years of testing—but, like people who fish for lobster but keep catching eel, test-takers keep uncovering people with genetic anomalies. The IOC does not release test results, but each year, about twelve women fail the test and are banned from competition for life, researcher Alison Carlson has found. There is no reason to believe, Carlson says, that any of these were male impostors. Shocked and humiliated, the women usually withdraw quietly, often faking an injury at the suggestion of tournament officials. Countless others withdraw after failing precompetition tests.

The only woman publicly to contest her disqualification so far is Spanish runner Maria Jose Martinez Patino. In 1985, at age twenty-four, Patino failed the sex test at the World University Games in Kobe, Japan. She had passed at the Helsinki World Championships in 1983, but had forgotten to bring her "femininity certificate" to Japan.

"I could barely comprehend what was happening," she told Carlson. "I was scared and ashamed, but at the same time angry, because I couldn't see how my body was different from the other girls." In shock, she did as told: feigned a foot injury.[26]

Patino's genetic anomaly is called androgen insensitivity. To understand it is to understand the mind-blowing concept that human beings do not fall exclusively into two categories, male and female.

People *generally* fall into two categories, but not all of us are so cleanly in one camp or the other. Says psychologist John Money, a leading sex researcher from Johns Hopkins University, "The difference between male and female is not black and white. It is a biological continuum."[27]

Gender is determined by five variables: chromosomes, hormones, gonads, external genitalia, and the most definitive one, the gender of assignment: what midwives, doctors, or parents say when they look at a newborn and proclaim, "it's a girl" or "it's a boy." Usually, all of the variables are consistent: a baby with XX chromosomes, for instance, will have more estrogen than testosterone,[28] will have ovaries, uterus, vulva, and vagina, and will be called a girl at birth.

During the first six weeks of embryonic development, internal and external genitalia are undifferentiated. This "bipotential" tissue could develop into either ovary or testes, labia or scrotal sac, clitoris or penis. Which way it goes depends on hormonal secretions: if androgens are secreted, the tissue usually develops along male lines. If no androgens are secreted, the embryo will become female. Female is what happens if no hormones intervene, regardless of genetic XX or XY designation.

But sometimes, XY embryos can't react to androgens, so the fetus develops along female lines. This is what happened to Maria Patino and the approximately one out of 5,000 to 10,000 people who are androgen-insensitive. Patino's body ignored the androgens and went ahead and developed as a girl. Thus the physicians declared her female and she always thought of herself as female until astonished by the XY test results.

The athletic relevance of androgen insensitivity is that these people are immune not only to the hormones their own bodies produce, but also to steroids. Rather than giving them an unfair advantage in competition against women, their condition ensures that they will have no unfair advantage. There is no reason to disqualify them from Olympic competition against women. But they are disqualified.

Patino was banned from competition; she was ridiculed as a freak in newspapers and on the streets of Madrid; she lost her athletic scholarship; she was expelled from her Spanish national athletic residence; her coach was told he could no longer train her; and her girlfriends and boyfriend left her. Her records were struck from the books.

Men, too, have anomalies: some appear male but are genetically XX; others have XXY chromosomes; others are XX or XY hermaphrodites (possessing some aspects of both male and female anatomy, both internally and externally) who were assigned the male gender at birth. Some boys and men have no testicles, or even a uterus. Some men have genetic conditions that lead to unusual height or weight or strength. But men are never banned from competitions for being "too malelike" or "too femalelike."

Ironically, the Barr body test and the updated (since 1992) sex test, the polymerase chain reaction test, not only miss steroid users, they also miss the one naturally occurring condition that does give women a "malelike" advantage: adrenal hyperplasia, a hormonal imbalance in which girls with XX chromosomes develop muscle patterns (and genitals) similar to men's. This occurs in about one in one thousand women—common enough that at marathons, for instance, a few of the runners would have this condition. According to Dr. Maria New, head of the pediatrics department at New York Hospital–Cornell Medical Center, several women who have won Olympic gold medals have had adrenal hyperplasia.[29]

The Barr body test produced false positive results between 6 and 15 percent of the time. Kirsten Wengler, for instance, erroneously failed the test in 1985 before an international swim meet. During a coed team meeting, her female teammates were handed their femininity certificates ("fem cards," they're called) but Wengler was told she would have to return to the lab for further testing. After the second test, doctors told her she might not be able to have children. "I was crying and really freaked out," she recalls. Wengler's parents arranged to have more sophisticated tests taken, and those results—four months and many dollars later—revealed that Wengler has typical XX chromosomes and no abnormalities. Only then was she granted her fem card.[30]

The polymerase chain reaction test, a purported improvement on the Barr body test, is accurate 99 percent of the time. This means that one out of every hundred women tested will be fallaciously informed that she is not female. For the Summer Olympics of 1992, that would equal 30 of the 3,008 female competitors.

Physicians worldwide, including the American College of Physicians, the American College of Obstetricians and Gynecologists, and the hospital originally contracted to conduct testing at the Calgary Olympics, have opposed sex testing, saying it is discriminatory and lacks scientific merit.[31] In a 1986 editorial in the *Journal of the American Medical Association,* geneticist Dr. Albert de la Chapelle of the Department of Medical Genetics at the University of Helsinki called for an end to testing, saying, "Eliminating screening would probably have little or no effect" on who won the championships, "and it might restore a few personal dignities."[32]

Helen Stephens approves of sex testing, saying, "I guess they have to do something to keep men out" but does not harbor any animosity toward Stella Walsh, her one-time nemesis, and does not want Walsh's eleven world records and two Olympic medals to be expunged from the books. "Most of the girl athletes had thoughts that she wasn't exactly kosher," says Stephens, "but it was an unfortunate case of birth defects."

Kirsten Wengler, who suffered the horror of a false positive test, now speaks out against the tests: "If it's a choice between possibly competing against impostors, and hurting even only a few women, I'd rather compete against a man."[33]

Maria Patino was reinstated in 1988 after sex-test opponents argued her case before the IOC. She now compares the experience to rape. "I'm sure it's the same sense of incredible shame and violation."[34]

Taekwondo world champion Lynnette Love says of testing, "It stinks. Why not test the men?"

Older athletes, especially those who have been tested many times or who have "proven" their femaleness through motherhood, don't seem to spend much time thinking about the test. Deborah Holloway, a mother and a 1988 Olympic silver medalist in taekwondo says, "It didn't bother me too much. I had no anxiety about it. They said they had to do it because there was once a man who was really a woman, or vice versa. I forget."

After extensive review, the International Amateur Athletic Federation (IAAF) in 1993 recommended abolishing all gender verification tests. An IAAF council established to consider the medical, ethical, and philosophical aspects of testing had concluded that there is no indication that men are currently masquerading as women, there is no evidence that the people eliminated by the test have any biological advantage, and besides, "The urine sample . . . required to detect illicit substances must be produced under direct visualization; thus, simple visual inspection at that time would readily suffice to exclude men masquerading as women."[35]

The IOC, however, persists in testing female athletes, "a philosophy at odds with recommendations by major endocrine, genetic, and obstetric/gynecologic bodies," says the IAAF.[36] The IOC's position, stated by Prince Alexandre de Merode, Chairman of the IOC Medical Commission, is that testing has eradicated the "denunciations, rumors, and scandals" that persisted before 1968 and were "besmirching sport and the reputation of persons concerned." Eliminating the tests would lead to "a resurgence of scandals of which sport would be the victim." [37]

• • •

To understand who exactly is being protected by gender testing, consider what happens when transsexuals (men who, through surgical, hormonal, and cosmetic interventions, "become" women) attempt to enter women's competitions. If keeping people with "malelike advantages" out of female competitions were the fundamental concern of the men in charge of such decisions, one would think they would refuse access to people who have XY chromosomes, who were identified as men at birth, and who, until recently, lived as men. In addition to male muscle mass, height, and weight, these men-who-become-women have had all the privileges of sports access that most boys and men receive: good coaching, good facilities, good school programs, and community and family support. Renee Richards, for instance, was born an unambiguous male named Richard Raskind. He attended a boy's prep school and the then-all-male Yale University, where he received athletic training from and competed against men. A New York Yankees scout expressed interest in his ability.

When, after his sex-change operation, Renee Richards announced his/her intention to play women's singles in the 1976 U.S. Open at Forest Hills, tennis's governing bodies (U.S. Tennis Association, World Tennis Association, and U.S. Open Committee) resisted, instituting a requirement that all women take a chromosome sex test. Richards refused and did not play. The next year, Richards took the case to the New York Supreme Court, which ruled that "this person is now female" and that requiring Richards to pass the test was "grossly unfair, discriminatory and inequitable, and violative of her rights." [38] Richards then competed in the women's professional circuit for a brief, undistinguished career before returning to his/her ophthalmologic practice. Other male-to-female transsexuals have been similarly protected and allowed to compete against women.

Small children sometimes believe that if a boy puts on a dress or high heels, he becomes a girl. Adults realize that this is immature, misguided thinking. Yet many adults have become convinced that if a boy ingests synthetic estrogen, has his genitals surgically altered, removes his facial hair, and *then* puts on that dress and heels, he really has become female.

What he has become, apparently, is more than a woman: a woman with more rights than a woman. He/she retains the right not to be sex tested, while no woman at the elite level retains that right.

· · ·

On September 29, 1990, a ten-year-old soccer goalie named Natasha Dennis was asked to pull her pants down. Two fathers of opposing players couldn't believe that a girl could be as good as Natasha. She might be a boy in disguise, they contended. Natasha passed the impromptu sex test.[39]

In the fall of 1989, a Union Bridge, Maryland, girl named Tawana Hammond suffered severe internal injuries after being tackled in a high school football game. Her spleen and half of her pancreas had to be removed. She was one of 109 girls who played high school football that year.[40] Girls who play football are not more likely to get injured than boys who play football. But the town mayor responded: "The feeling from a lot of the people was she shouldn't have been there [on the football team] anyway. A female playing a man's game has created a lot of hard feelings in this community."

The football coach, Terry Changuris, said, "You realize that you are at a major biological disadvantage because women are not as strong as men."[41]

No one talks about the "major biological disadvantages" of the smaller, weaker boys and men who are injured on football fields every day. No one seems to worry about the dislocated shoulders, twisted knees, broken ankles, and concussions that men commonly suffer during high school, college, and pro football games. Football causes more injuries, including deaths, per player than any other American sport. Virtually all of its victims are men.

In the 1992 season, almost five hundred players—21 percent of the total National Football League player list—endured injuries severe enough to keep them from at least one game. Seventy-eight percent of retired football players suffer from permanent disabilities. The average career of a pro football player is three and a half years; the average life expectancy is fifty-six years. Hospital emergency rooms handle 300,000 football-related injuries each year. According to the National Athletic Trainers' Association, 37 percent of U.S. high school football players were injured during the previous year badly enough to be sidelined for at least the rest of the day.[42] And each year, about eight high school football players die from football-related injuries.

Yet men say women are too weak to play football.

The truth is, *men* are too weak to play football—too fragile, too delicate to withstand the rigors of the game.

And men said that a very good ten-year-old soccer player must be male. Yet a very good ten-year-old soccer player is more likely than not to be female. In Arlington, Virginia, the youth soccer program is divided into two gender-based leagues because "boys get frustrated and discouraged with coed, so we separate them," says coach and organizer Mac Golden. "The girls are so much better."

In the 1993 Ohio Games, only one under-ten girls' soccer team (the Middleburg Diamond Football Club) signed up, so the girls played against the boys' teams. The boys resisted—"I'd rather be shot than play against girls," one said—and it soon became clear why: the girls won the title, defeating all four teams they played, three in shut-outs.[43]

What seems important to the male-dominated sports authorities is not protecting women, or protecting men, but protecting male privilege. By keeping females out of so-called male events, and by questioning the gender identity of girls and women who excel at sports, and by propagating the myth of female frailty, men cling to an antiquated dividing line between men and women. On one side are the supposedly superior athletes (who don't look so superior when women compete side by side). On the other side are women—supposedly inferior, questionably "malelike," and in need of protection by patronizing sports organizers who have yet to ask the athletes themselves how they feel about the need for gender verification.

Who gets to determine who is female and who is not? In the case of Renee Richards, male physicians performed his surgeries, male medical experts testified that Richards was now indeed a woman, and male judges concurred.[44] So a man becomes a woman with the help of other men. And men decide that certain women are not really women, not "feminine enough" to compete.

What is a malelike advantage? Did Flo Hyman, the world's best female volleyball player, have a malelike advantage? She had a genetic condition called Marfan's Syndrome, which is associated with height (she was six-five); long fingers (good for blocking volleyballs), and a weak heart (which eventually killed her). Should she have been kept on the sidelines? What is a woman?

Gheorghe Musrean, the 7'7" Washington Bullets center, owes his extraordinary height to the excess growth hormone his body produces. Should he be banned from playing basketball against men? Does his pituitary disorder somehow render him not male?

Most of us are not in the habit of wondering if gender, like eye color or skin color, could in some utopic future be largely irrelevant. But the less relevant gender becomes in business, politics, medicine, law, and child-care arrangements, the more relevant it seems to become in sports. The clearer women become about what femaleness, feminism, and femininity mean to them, the less clear the sports world becomes about these concepts, trying to ensure femininity and test femininity as if what were in question were a woman's ability to apply mascara.

Maybe that, fundamentally, is what the "amazon" labels are about, what the "women can't play football" chants are about, what the "sex control" centers are trying to control: not makeup application, exactly, but women's acceptance of the artifice called femininity. Maybe the concern is not so much that men will masquerade as women, but that *women* will no longer masquerade as women. Gloria Steinem once said, "Women are all female impersonators." What if we stopped doing that, stopped impersonating someone else's idea of how women should behave?

Female athletes, sweat soaking their muscled chests, aren't half-women, half-men. They aren't Lady Panthers or Lady Rams or Lady Cheetahs, trying in vain to catch up to Gentlemen Bulls. They're people in pursuit of perfection—a quest that human beings, in all their diversity, seem to enjoy.

5

Scoring: What's Sex Got to Do with It?

Women are mere "beauties" in men's culture so that culture can be kept male.

—*Naomi Wolf, The Beauty Myth*

OR AT least fifteen minutes in 1993, everyone knew about the Spur Posse. They were the Lakewood, California, teenage boys, mostly football players, who turned sex into a sporting contest, tallying "points" scored for each instance of sexual intercourse. At last count, Billy Shehan, nineteen, was winning with sixty-six points. Tabulations were compared to their sports heroes' uniform numbers, as in, "I'm 44 now—Reggie Jackson." Or "I'm 50 now—David Robinson." They named themselves after their favorite basketball team, the San Antonio Spurs.[1]

Several girls said the boys forced them to have sex. The girls' parents and lawyers asked that charges be brought on ten counts of rape by intimidation, four counts of unlawful sexual intercourse, one count of forcible rape, one count of oral copulation, and one count of lewd conduct with a minor under fourteen. Nine boys were arrested. The boys maintained that the sex had been consensual ("Like, you know, for example, a girl was home by herself, eight of my friends went over and each of them took their turn. And she—you know, she wanted it," one explained.) All but one boy was released. That one, sixteen, was convicted of lewd conduct against a ten-year-old and served time in a youth detention center. Declining to prosecute the others, the Los Angeles district attorney said, "Although there is evidence of unlawful sexual intercourse, it is the policy of this office not to file criminal charges where there is consensual sex between teenagers. The arrogance and contempt for young women which have been displayed, while appalling, cannot form the basis of criminal charges."[2]

The young men bragged about their exploits on everything from "Nightline" to "Dateline" to "Donahue" to "The Home Show." "I don't consider myself a normal person," one said. "You know. I think I'm a step above everyone else."[3]

The Spur Posse came from what Jane Gross of the *New York Times* described as a community "where virtually every block has its own baseball diamond or gridiron, where boys are athletes and girls cheerleaders from the age of 6 or 7 and where most fathers are part-time coaches and mothers are 'team moms.' "[4]

Don Belman is the father of three sons ranging in age from 18 to 23, including Dana, who founded the Spur Posse, and Kristopher, who was among the nine boys arrested and released. Don Belman said that Kris is "all man" and that the girls Kris had sex with were "giving it away." The girls "weren't the victims they were made out to be," he told Joan Didion in *The New Yorker*. "One of them had a tattoo, for chrissake."[5]

Dana Belman, who is enshrined in the Lakewood Youth Sports Hall of Fame for wrestling, is awaiting trial on thirteen felony burglary and forgery charges.[6]

Don Belman, who coached his sons on numerous youth teams, called them "all standouts athletically"[7] and "virile specimens."[8]

• • •

For decades at least, teenagers have talked about "getting on base" as a metaphor for sex. But doesn't it seem that male athletes and male fans are increasingly thinking of women as sex objects? While the rest of American society gradually, painstakingly becomes enlightened on matters of sex and respect, aren't things in the manly sports arena—where most boys find their heroes—getting worse?

In Texas, "topless golf" is suddenly popular. At tournaments hosted by local bars, men drive, chip, and putt. On the greens, they are greeted by female "caddies" who strip.

A T-shirt slogan, taking off on Nike's "Just do it" campaign, proclaims, "Just did her."

Stock car races now display, in prerace shows, several beauty queens: not only women but also preteens and toddlers.

The rap group 2 Live Crew has produced an obscene album entitled *Sports Weekend.*

Wilt Chamberlain proudly claims to have had sex with twenty thousand "different ladies" including "girls under five feet tall," "white girls," "Oriental girls," and "spinners, my pet name for little doll-like ladies I can just sit on my lap and spin around like tops." One time, he brags in *A View from Above,* he "got" fourteen "ladies of dubious taste" in one night.[9]

Magic Johnson said he "accommodated" as many women as he could. On "The Oprah Winfrey Show," he differentiated his one-night stands from his wife by calling the other women "floozies."[10]

On many college campuses, male high school football recruits are greeted by "hostesses." Dressed in cute, matching outfits, these college "girls," known by such names as Gator Getters, Bengal Babes, Hurricane Honeys, and Deacon Darlings, help convince prospective sports stars to attend their schools. Literal seductions are supposedly forbidden, "but it's not like you want them to know that," says one former hostess. "Let them come to the school and find that out."[11]

An annual charity event called Fight Night in Washington, D.C., features boxing matches, eighteen hundred male guests, lots of alcohol, the Washington Bullettes cheerleaders, and "hostesses" in shiny, sequined minidresses. Invitations to the three hundred dollars per ticket event, which began in 1990, read "sans spouse." Men pinch, pat, and pay (with tips) the hostesses, loudly discuss "big bazoombas," and unabashedly revel in the atmosphere of masculine athletic dominance and feminine sexual service.

"Every once in a while you get a chance to say [Expletive] it, it's a man's world," a lawyer attending the event told the *Washington Post.* "It's an old-fashioned kind of idea."

"There's a nostalgic quality to it," said the organizer, Joseph E. Robert, Jr.

"This is so un-politically correct, it's liberating," said the president of a temp service. "I'd say we're witnessing a severe backlash."[12]

Beyond the ballparks, sexism is becoming unfashionable, immoral, illegal. But in the manly sports world—which is broadcast daily throughout society—and in the women's sports world as well, misogyny is beginning to seem downright sporting. Nostalgic. Liberating.

• • •

As the only woman to play baseball through three years of college (at St. Mary's in Maryland), Julie Croteau had a unique opportunity: to watch and listen to men as they initiated other men and boys into the world of sports and masculinity.

She was horrified. Not so much by the "you bat like a girl" remarks—she had become accustomed to such "ordinary" sexism in Little League—but by how sexual the comments were, how vulgar. "You pussy." "You cunt." "You whore."

Croteau resigned at the end of her third season, charging sexual harassment on the part of some of her teammates. One time the men showed pornographic videos at a team party. Another time they read aloud from *Penthouse* while on a team bus. The article described a woman having sex with an eel. "It was a very specific degrading article about women's body parts," recalled Croteau. "I don't think they were directing it at me, but I was the only one on the bus with those parts."

Croteau also played on the college women's soccer team. There, by refreshing contrast, her teammates would "talk about guys, but not in a derogatory and potentially harmful manner," she said.

When asked about Croteau's complaints, her baseball coach, Hal Willard, defended the male players with this infamous line: "It was just guys being guys."

In the manly sports world, guys can still be guys. During televised sports broadcasts, millions of men watch, without complaint, female cheerleaders who perform lascivious dances and commercials that depict women as busty decorations. *Sports Illustrated*'s "swimsuit issue" sold 5.1 million copies in 1993, and sells more each successive year. The fact that *Sports Illustrated* (spoofed by *MAD* magazine as *Sports Titillated*) is not considered a pornographic magazine legitimizes the objectification of women. Men need not confess to consuming porn in order to drool over the images. Lusting after two-dimensional women is a normal male behavior, the magazine implies: just another sport.

Despite the protests of women and some men, men attending baseball games at Boston's Fenway Park in the summer of 1991 developed the habit of passing around and fondling plastic, life-sized, anatomically correct female blow-up dolls. As these dolls were tossed from spectator to spectator, individual men would stand, hold the dolls close, and simulate sexual intercourse. Or were they simulating rape? It was hard to tell. Other men would cheer.

"Some men were screaming, Yeah, yeah, do her! with their fists raised in the air," recalled Megan O'Sullivan, a spectator at a Boston Red Sox game. "They were touching her breasts. . . . They threw her around to each other. These are grown men we're talking about. It was disgusting. It was like an advertisement for rape." [13]

Sociologist Timothy Jon Curry recently employed researchers to record men's locker room conversations over a several-month period. He offers this as a typical example of an exchange between two athletes:

"I just saw the biggest set of ta-tas in the training room!"

"How big were they?"

"Bigger than my mouth."

The speakers were college-aged men. Such separation of human beings from their body parts is unimaginable between two, say, young female swimmers:

"I just saw the biggest weinie out by the pool."

"How big was it?"

"Bigger than my mouth."

Such talk is unimaginable for men these days in many other settings, too. Sexist comments, like racist comments, can get men fired in some circles. But not in sports. In the manly sports world, sexism is a badge of honor, a common ground, a familiar language.

Curry found that talk of women as objects took the form of loud performances for other men. Talk about ongoing relationships with women, on the other hand, took place only in hushed tones, often behind rows of lockers, and was subject to ridicule. "This ridicule tells the athlete that he is getting too close to femaleness, because he is taking relatedness seriously," writes Curry. " 'Real men' do not do that." [14]

A former college football star who asked not to be named says of Curry's research, "That's right on target. We never talked about respecting women." This man, who later signed with the Philadelphia Eagles, recalls college teammates making such sexual boasts as, "She didn't want to do anything, but I held the bitch's head down." His college teammates hosted "pig parties." The man who brought the ugliest date would win a trophy. This football star says he learned to respect women from his mother and three athletic sisters, and did not attend the parties. But he would laugh at his teammates' jokes, an act he now regrets. "I remember the first time they showed the trophy," in the locker room, he says. "I was a 17-year-old freshman in a room full of upper-class men. It was boisterous, raunchy, there was screaming and yelling. I laughed along. Men are extremely cliquish. I didn't want to be left out."

Magic Johnson, one of the world's most talented and popular basketball players, wrote that he and his teammates "speak a different language among ourselves, a language that's neither black nor white. It's a language that evolves from a group of people who share the same passion . . . that transcends race, religion, age, politics, and background."[15] With references to prostitutes, groupies, and floozies, however, this language does not transcend sexism. Johnson admits that while traveling with the Los Angeles Lakers, he had sex with women "to relax," the way others drink, smoke, or eat too much. He repeats this joke: "What's the hardest thing about going on the road? Trying not to smile when you kiss your wife goodbye." He drew the line, he says, at allowing women to spend the night. ("It just didn't feel right.") He limited the encounters to sex: "I never let myself get emotionally involved with somebody I met on the road. Sometimes you'd see a rookie do that. . . . But these things would always end badly. We tried to protect our younger teammates but a few guys got hurt anyway."[16]

In "The Myth of the Sexual Athlete," D'Youville College sociologist and former University of Buffalo football player Don Sabo confirms that among his male sports pals, "we could talk about superficial sex and anything that used, trivialized, or debased women, but frank discussions about sexuality that unfolded within a loving relationship were taboo. There was a terrible split between inner needs and outer appearances, between our desire for the love of women and our feigned indifference toward them."[17]

In _____ Oppenheimer, who documented a season with her son's high school football team _____ *Glory,* confirms, "In the crude but descriptive . . . vernacular, [the players] 'got on' girls—they just didn't get involved with them."[18]

In Little League and other youth sports, boys learn "the language of lust" and "a way of being male in which sexual desire is detached from tenderness for a person and indeed from the interest in female company except for the purposes of sex," notes Canadian sociologist David Whitson.[19]

Using women for sex is OK, but emotional attachment is "said to promote distraction, siphon energy, and erode team loyalty," write sport scholars Don Sabo and Joe Panepinto in *Sport, Men, and the Gender Order.*[20]

From the pinup "girls" on football players' lockers to the very language of "scoring," many men associate sports with male sexual virility and female passivity. Men are aggressors; women are things to be consumed, like food or drink. At times blatantly, at times more subtly, the manly sports culture equates athletic prowess—or even athletic enthusiasm—with not just sex, but dominance.

This is not true for all male athletes or fans. Some men ski or swim or play tennis with their wives or female friends, competing or just playing together. In fact, coed sports seem to engender and enhance respect between the sexes. There are men who teach their daughters how to shoot baskets, take them to see college field hockey games, and help them get fair treatment when, at school, the girls' teams are given inferior locker rooms or uniforms.

Some men, even football players, are learning how to respect, love, and listen to women. Eugene Robinson, a seven-year NFL veteran, told ESPN, "I'm learning what it is to be married. What she feel, all that." But, he added, "Most guys don't know this."[21]

Basketball star Christian Laettner told ESPN that sports teach him not to be sexually aggressive, but "how to love someone."

Houston Oilers tackle David Williams missed a key game in the 1993 season in order to be with his wife as she gave birth to their first child. Oilers management phoned him in the delivery room to try to talk him out of it, compared his action to a soldier missing a world war battle, and fined him a week's pay—$120,000. But Williams had no regrets. His wife, Debi, had lost a baby to miscarriage a year before, he explained: "my family comes first. I don't care if they fine me half a million dollars."[22]

Former Chicago Bulls basketball star Michael Jordan has said about his wife, Juanita, "She always was very independent. She knew how to work and provide for herself, which is what I loved. I love her and I never wanted to take her away from her independence. She still does what she wants, and I love for her to do that."[23] While this may sound patronizing (would it occur to a woman that to "take away" her husband's independence was even an option?) his sentiment seems sincere. But I found this quote in *New Woman* magazine. How often do any of us, particularly impressionable children, see portrayals in other magazines, newspapers, or television of manly athletes or coaches who are loving friends or husbands or fathers? How many people even know that Michael Jordan *is* a husband and father?

• • •

In the nineties, more than twenty years into the feminist movement, coaches who would be fired for calling athletes "nigger" employ with impunity such terms as "cunt." "Faggot" is another popular derogation. It refers not so much to sex between men as to weakness, timidity, cowardice—and femininity. Mississippi State football coach Jackie Sherrill, before a game with the Texas Longhorns, paraded a bull onto the field and had his players watch its castration. Get it? To defeat the "Longhorns," he implied, was to "deball" them, to emasculate them.

In response to "wimpy" performances, male coaches have been known to deposit tampons, sanitary napkins, and bras in young men's lockers. "You have debased yourself to the level of a woman," is the message. Indiana University men's basketball coach Bobby Knight has used the tampon trick. Knight also told Connie Chung, "I think that if rape is inevitable, relax and enjoy it."[24]

Knight's own son has said, "I think if I had come out a girl he would have shoved me back inside." Among men, Knight is one of the most respected coaches in the country. I've seen "Bobby Knight for President" bumper stickers far beyond his home state of Indiana.[25]

During a team meeting, Catholic University men's basketball coach Bob Valvano distributed tampons and "called us a bunch of girls," reported junior guard Tim Shockley, who justified the coach's behavior. "He did it for motivation. A lot of coaches have done that, and I guess you could say it worked. We won the next six games."[26] Catholic University fired Valvano—which was interpreted by male sportswriters as an outrageous move, justifiable only on religious grounds—but within a few months he was hired by St. Mary's University, the site of Julie Croteau's sexual harassment. "He shares the values of this college community," said St. Mary's President Edward T. Lewis.[27]

Louisiana State University men's basketball coach Dale Brown, criticizing his players after they lost to Duke and made only eleven out of twenty-one free throws, told them, "The women shoot better free throws than you do." In fact, there's no logical reason why this should be an insult; on average, college women and men shoot free throws equally well, according to NCAA statistics.

Former football star Dave Meggessey's coach described one of his tackles as "almost feminine." Meggessey writes: "This sort of attack on a player's manhood is a coach's doomsday weapon. And it almost always works."[28]

Football fans belittle the Dallas Cowboys and the Buffalo Bills by calling them the Dallas Cowgirls and the Buffalo Jills. When Rams quarterback Jim Everett began the 1993 season with several poor performances, his teammates chided him by calling him, ironically, one of this century's most successful athletes: Chris Evert.

• • •

Nowhere are masculinity and misogyny so entwined as on the rugby field. At the post-game parties that are an integral part of the rugby culture, drunken men sing songs that depict women as loathsome creatures with insatiable sexual appetites and dangerous sexual organs. Men sing of raping other men's girlfriends and mothers. Rape is also depicted as a joke. Female dismemberment and necrophilia are other common sources of humor.

Here are the lyrics to the popular "The Engineer's Song":

> *An engineer told me before he died*
> *And I don't know if the bugger lied*
> *That he had a wife with a cunt so wide*
> *That she could never be satisfied.*
>
> *And so he built a prick of steel*
> *Driven by a bloody great wheel*
> *Two brass balls all filled with cream*
> *And the whole bloody issue was driven by steam.*

Round and round went the bloody great wheel
And in and out went the prick of steel
Until at last the maiden cried
"Enough, enough, I'm satisfied."

But this was a tale of the bitter bit
There was no way of stopping it
She was rent from cunt to tit
And the whole bloody issue was covered in shit.[29]

Elizabeth Wheatley, in a masters thesis that contrasts the women's rugby subculture to men's, notes that "The Engineer's Song" reflects male fear of sexual inadequacy.[30] The song seems to transfer that insecurity into murderous sexual aggression—apparently an appealing fantasy for men overwhelmed by "liberated" women's sexual demands. Rugby songs "embody a hostile, brutal, but, at the same time, fearful attitude towards women and the sexual act," notes British sociologist Eric Dunning of the University of Leicester.[31]

Even more disturbing than the lyrics is the popularity of such songs (there are hundreds, many of which are memorized by rugby players) and the mood of festivity and hilarity in which men sing them. The songs comprise an integral part of the rugby subculture.

Sociologist-anthropologist Steven Schacht, who observed two university-based men's rugby clubs in the early 1990s, heard a coach tell a player, "Fuck you, you pussy. Just shut the fuck up, or I'll bend you over [and] fuck ya like a bitch." Code terms for plays included: "Fucked your mother"; "Your mother's a cunt"; "Gang banged your girlfriend"; and "Suck my dick."[32]

Schacht also heard this association between sexual frustration and violence: "I didn't get any pussy last night and my balls hurt real bad. I am going to kick some ass today."[33]

Which reminds me of the Navy. Just as coaches and athletes borrow liberally from the military culture, officers and soldiers borrow from the manly sports culture. The Naval Academy's admission of women in 1976 was met with an increase in several "sadomasochistic cadence calls," according to professor Carol Burke, who spent seven years teaching there.[34] These include the chant "Rape, Maim, Kill Babies. Rape, Maim, Kill

Babies, Oorah!" and a song called "The S and M Man," which is sung to the tune of "The Candy Man." Fashionable in rugby circles as well, "The S and M Man" is sung by the Naval Academy's Male Glee Club on bus trips:

> *Who can take a chain saw*
> *Cut the bitch in two*
> *Fuck the bottom half*
> *and give the upper half to you?*
>
> *The S & M man, the S & M man.*
> *The S & M man cause he mixes it with love*
> *and makes the hurt feel good!*
>
> *Who can take a bicycle*
> *Then take off the seat*
> *Set his girlfriend on it*
> *Ride her down a bumpy street? . . .*
>
> *Who can take an ice pick*
> *Ram it through her ear*
> *Ride her like a Harley,*
> *As you fuck her from the rear? . . .*[35]

According to Naval records, reported rapes in the service nearly tripled in the five years between 1987 and 1992. In the infamous 1991 Tailhook incident, Navy aviators organized a Las Vegas convention that included numerous instances of indecent exposure, prostitution, pornography, and paid strippers. Men wore T-shirts that said "HE-MAN WOMEN HATERS CLUB" on front and "WOMEN ARE PROPERTY" on the back.

Most of that was not reported in the media. We "only" heard about the sexual assaults by at least 140 male officers against at least 83 women and 7 men. Navy Lieutenant Paula Coughlin was attacked by her fellow Navy fliers in the hotel hallway. The men grabbed her breasts, manhandled her buttocks, and tried to rip off her underpants. She feared gang rape.

"For them, it was sport," she said.

For Coughlin, the experience was not sport, sporting, or sporty. It did not reflect good sportsmanship. Yet in repeated interviews after she went public with her tale of terror, Coughlin used the word "sport" to describe the men's festive, team-oriented attitude. At first, when a man at the party shoved her off-balance, "I thought I was just dealing with one or two guys," she said. "I found as I was pushed down this hallway that every man was participating in this sport." [36]

Webster's first definition of "sport" is a "source of diversion; recreation."

Its second definition is "sexual play."

•   •   •

To investigate the connection between sport and what men seem to think of as sexual play, I visited a topless nightclub on the Upper East Side of Manhattan. This particular strip joint caught my attention because it has a theme: sports. Or maybe it's a sports bar with a theme: stripped women. No matter. The name says it all: "Scores." As in, wins. As in, sexual conquests. No matter how many millions of women race onto the sporting fields, I've never heard one refer to seducing a man as "scoring." It's a uniquely male concept: sex as triumph, as victory.

This is a uniquely male place. On a mural outside the nightclub, colorful drawings show basketball, football, and baseball players in action poses. These are men: no Kristi Yamaguchi's here. No swimmers either, or gymnasts. Hard-core sports for hard-core men. No soft stuff. Until you walk inside.

Men sit self-consciously at small round nightclub tables in a cavernous room, in a cozier "champagne section" for "preferred customers," and in a private "V.I.P." room. Big men pace the floor, policing customer behavior.

One of the dancers stands on a raised platform. For the men seated at the bar, her crotch is eye level. Unlike the men, who wear suits or casual shirts and pants, this woman has virtually nothing on, her only apparel a thin gold G-string the width of a shoelace. A young, pale-skinned woman with shaved pubic hair, she undulates slowly on the small stage. Her activity doesn't resemble dancing so much as waiting: the impatient, distracted, rhythmic motions of someone whose train hasn't yet arrived.

She catches my eye and I look into the smooth face of a girl/woman, maybe college age. Maybe younger. Later she'll tell me too boldly that she's twenty-one. She stares at my two friends and me (the only clothed women in the place), her dancing slowing to an imperceptible sway.

Video monitors are everywhere, reminiscent of the television area of a department store. From each of the monitors and from a large projection screen on the main stage, two large purple-clad basketball players scowl as they stride angrily down court. They seem larger even than their actual large selves.

On the main stage a small dark-skinned woman sways—the same listless waiting dance. Close to the projection screen, dwarfed by the outsized men, she looks oddly three-dimensional and displaced, a live human being in an animated movie. To watch the game on this screen, the nightclub's customers must look at this woman, or past her.

Elsewhere, women perform what are called lap dances. Here are the steps: Seated, a man yawns open his legs. The woman stands in the triangular space where his lap used to be. Slowly, she rolls her pelvis, her timing an inadvertent caricature of the slow-motion replays on the screens behind her. Gradually she strips off Lycra and lace until all that remains is that obligatory gold shoelace. She shakes her head, letting hair fall across her face. She strokes her breasts (but not her nipples—that's against house rules). She turns and thrusts her buttocks, nude but for one strip of stretchy fabric, toward the man's face. He smiles.

More rules: he cannot touch her. To this end, the other partners in this bizarre sluggish dance are bouncers. Too numerous to count, these men lumber conspicuously from table to table. If a man touches a woman he must leave. One fleeting exception: The customer may fold a bill— usually a twenty—into the woman's G-string, at which point she immediately stops dancing and dresses herself.

This is a respectable place, others have said. The lights are on. More evidence at the nightclub tables: clean. The floor is clean, too—my feet don't stick to it.

"It's an upscale, respectable place. I bring my clients here." This from one jovial forty-year-old pharmaceutical salesman who a minute ago sniffed the discarded bra of a young woman while she stripped in front of him. He likes to watch hockey games on television here, he explains. At home it's pay-per-view, and he resents that. "But don't think men are here to watch TV," he confides, draping his arm around my shoulder. He offers to buy me a drink.

"Does your wife know you come here?" I ask a fiftyish, Pooh-bellied, uncomfortable-looking man who declines to be identified.

"She knows we entertain clients at a sports bar," he replies.

So the sports theme, combined with the clean, hotel-like furnishings, distinguishes Scores (official motto: "where sports and pleasure come together") from its sleazy strip-joint cousins. After all, "everybody," i.e., everyman, watches sports. *Ergo,* patronizing a tidy, well-lit place where sports are viewed must be respectable. Jay Bildstein, the founder and former owner of Scores, calls it "the *Sports Illustrated* swimsuit issue come to life."

For the women this is not a respectable place. They do not feel respected or respectful. "The men are gross, horrible, disgusting," says a dancer who calls herself Faith. Explaining that she "can't get money like this anywhere else," she says she's saving her $400 nightly earnings to put herself through college toward a career in dance therapy.

She's suffering and seems eager to talk to a woman. "When you spend three nights a week, twenty-one hours, gyrating—it kills you. I have no sexuality. I haven't had a boyfriend in six months. All feeling is gone."

For the women this is not a sporting place. Lucinda, another young dancer, did not know what event was being shown on the television screens behind her, though this was a semifinal game between the Portland Trailblazers and the Utah Jazz—a crucial, pivotal, high-drama event from the point of view of many men. She guessed that the sport was basketball, but was not even sure of that.

Lucinda did not come to watch sports, but to be sport. Lucinda says, "Men are children. They have to have everything—sports, girls, music, all at once. I hate them."

• • •

Most sports bars do not feature topless women. Most men who watch sports on television do not, during commercial breaks, slip bills under the G-strings of angry young women. Yet Scores is not unique, and sex-sports bars are not anomalies. They're a logical outcome of the manly sports culture, an exaggeration of the routine sexualization of women in beer commercials, on cheerleading squads, and through the lens of voyeuristic cameras panning the crowds at men's sporting events. "Upscale" topless bars are proliferating. According to *Gentlemen's Club* magazine, a trade journal for the $3 billion-a-year topless industry, about eleven hundred "quality" topless clubs now exist in forty-seven states, about three hundred more than five years ago.[37]

Sports bars, a new phenomenon, are also tremendously popular. Champions, the first sports bar designed as such, opened in Washington, D.C., in 1983. Ten years later, there are approximately five thousand sports bars nationwide, according to Michael O'Harro, founder of Champions, now the largest sports-bar chain, with twenty-four bars. When O'Harro recently surveyed twenty Washington, D.C.-area bars that did not identify themselves as sports bars, he found that eighteen regularly showed sports on TVs. "In hotels, airports, restaurants, everywhere you go now you see sports," O'Harro notes.

Jay Bildstein, an insightful investment banker, designed Scores to meet the "fantasies and leisure-time desires" of heterosexual New York men ages 25–49 who earn more than $60,000 per year. "We asked the question: What do single men gravitate to?" recalls Bildstein. "They tend to like sports. They tend to like beautiful women. Add contemporary music, good food, and alcoholic beverages that don't cost an arm and a leg and you've just about captured everything that group has an interest in."

One more factor: hierarchy. "Men are very status-conscious in their relation to other men," notes Bildstein. "As winning is important, so is winning monetarily. So we developed distinctions as to who would be in what room when, why and how." Hence the plush couches in the raised-tier section and an elegant V.I.P. room "like the sporting lounge of an upper-crust Ivy League school."

Scores offers a man "the best of all possible worlds," Bildstein says. "When he wants his women, his women are there. When he wants his sports, his sports are there. He is in the uniquely powerful situation to determine which he pays attention to when."

Like wives who complain that men watch too much football, the dancers at Scores want more male attention. They complain that sports-obsessed men lose interest in lap dances—the primary source of the women's income. Says Lucinda, "When a big game is on, the men are like, 'Not now—later.' The girls sit around waiting, then we go, 'Is it over yet? Want a dance?' "

Scores appeals to men, Bildstein says, because they can "be selfish and be little boys and cater to the id. There are no strings attached."

It's more than a lack of strings. Stripped, dancing before a man, a young woman is inches and moments away from assault, a possibility lessened only by the presence of the bouncers. Her vulnerability and his sense of power contribute to the appeal. He's not attracted to these women despite the fact that they are relatively powerless, but because of that fact.

Bildstein admits: "By the woman taking off her clothes, it gives the man a sense of predominance at that moment. Unrejectability. This woman just put herself in a deferred position compared to me. I'm in control. I'm the boss. I now have the power that I don't have when I walk into a singles bar and say, 'Excuse me, can I buy you a drink?' and the woman says, 'Get lost.' "

I learned about Scores through Michael-David Gordon, a Brooklyn stage actor. With the New York Anti-Sexist Men's Action Network, he protested the opening of Scores. An avid sports fan, the idea of the nightclub bothered him. On television he saw an interview with a Scores customer who said of the dancers' appeal: "We don't have to deal with all the yuppie questions—'What do you do? What do you think about things?' They just serve us."

Gordon says of these men: "They're avoiding the kind of conversation you have with an equal: 'How do you define yourself as a person?' The women don't ask the men, and you know the men don't ask the women."

Wendy Reid Crisp, director of the National Association for Female Executives, attributes the popularity of topless bars to men's discomfort with women's growing economic, social, and political power. "Men want to feel that they are back in control, in a relationship between the sexes that they understand. They feel extremely threatened by the issues of sexual violence and harassment. They are desperately trying to reestablish a masculinity that is familiar to them."[38]

"Part of it is homophobia," adds Michael Kimmel, sociology professor at the State University of New York at Stony Brook. "Yuppie men want to go to a bar with a bunch of other men, and the presence of women makes that experience utterly unambiguous. It gives the men the illusion that women choose to be so blatantly sexual around them, so it reaffirms the idea that women are always saying yes." He attributes this phenomenon in part to the Hill-Thomas Senate hearings. "Women have made it clear that they are tired of predatory sexuality in the workplace and on dates, and men are saying, 'Fine, we'll find a place where we can be bad boys.' "[39]

. . .

Similarly, a man watching a football game in his own living room, identifying with the athletes, acquires a sense of power and control over women that he may not otherwise feel at work or at home. Like the Scores waitresses, his wife or girlfriend may serve him pizza, potato chips, beer. Like the Scores dancers, she may try to distract him with sex or other enticements. But because of the cultural importance placed on sports, he will rarely turn off the game to spend time with his female partner. The Game—a by-men and for-men activity—is, during the broadcast, his indisputable priority, his overriding commitment.

The sex depicted in the sacred sports culture is not sensuous, playful, spontaneous, passionate, caring, mutual. The message sent in football stadiums, in sports magazines, in sports bars, and in communities "where boys are athletes and girls cheerleaders" is not just about exaggerated gender roles or "viva la difference." It's about domination. Sex as conquest. In order for men to remain dominant, to remain victorious, women must be in a subservient position. Women become opponents to defeat. Or they can be trophies: rewards for success in the intramale hierarchy. In this system women are never teammates, never idols. Sports bars, whether topless or not, show women's sporting events on television "only if nothing else is on," one bartender told me.

At a lacrosse game I attended, men in the stands cheered for their home team, American University, by chanting, "It's easy to score on the George Mason girls."

The sex-as-dominance paradigm extends beyond the playing fields. As Bildstein noted, men tend to be sensitive to hierarchies, perceiving not only sports and sex but life in general in terms of victory and defeat: who's on top? Women tend to view sports, sex, and life in general more horizontally: Who gets to play? Jean Baker Miller, in *Toward a New Psychology of Women,* says men cast relationships in terms of dominance and subordination, women in terms of care and connection. Carol Gilligan, in *A Different Voice,* writes about hierarchies and networks (or webs). Riane

Eisler, in *The Chalice and the Blade,* uses the phrases ranking and linking. Deborah Tannen, in *You Just Don't Understand,* contrasts status and connection.

These are not innate, genetic gender differences, but responses to women's and men's different access to social and economic power. Young boys learn that their success will hinge on accomplishment in a competitive world. It makes sense, in that context, to be vigilant about one's place in the hierarchy. Girls learn that to be liked is of utmost importance; in that context, concern with connection makes sense. So the group with institutional power—men—remain invested in keeping that power, and the group without power—women—learn to attach themselves to powerful people. Or to live without power as defined by men. Or to find other, internal or collective, sources of power. Or to play by the men's rules.

The media is responsible in part, but rule makers, male fans, and the women themselves also contribute. At men's pro beach volleyball tournaments, "beauty contestants" and other shaved and starved fans flock to the beach not so much to watch and admire the athletes but to be watched and admired. Randy Stoklos, who with doubles partner Sinjin Smith has led the men's pro beach volleyball tour in earnings and popularity for the past ten years, frequently signs autographs not on scraps of paper but on thighs, arms, and other body parts offered to him by eager young women. Contrasting the volleyball groupies with the more substantially clothed men's basketball "groupies," Stoklos told reporter Jack Bettridge that on the beach, "you get to see what you're going to be involved with."[40]

The women's basketball team at Northwestern State University in Louisiana donned Playboy bunny outfits to pose for their school's 1987–88 media guide. "These Girls Can Play, Boy" was the clever title. Their basketball arena, the Panther Coliseum, was called the "Lady Demon Pleasure Palace." The caption under a photograph of Coach James Smith read, "If he wasn't happily married one could easily envision the personable 39-year-old stretched out on a chaise lounge surrounded by bikini-clad babes."

Like beauty, exploitation is in the eye of the beholder. Though the bunny motif was the sports information director's idea, the Northwestern "bunnies" defended their photo when campus women's groups complained. One wrote in a letter to a member of the women's studies department: "My teammates and myself feel that women athletes are projected as too masculine and this approach gives us a more feminine image and helps to alleviate that masculine stereotype."

"What athletes are obviously trying to communicate is that although they are functioning on male territory, it's really all right because they do know, and accept, what being a real woman means," explains Jan Graydon, a lecturer at North London Polytechnic.[41]

It means, apparently, appearing to be sexually available to men.

Liv-Jorunn Kolnes, a research fellow at the Norwegian University of Sport and Physical Education, puts it this way: "You can only have permission to be this strong if you can also look this beautiful."[42]

Women's gymnastics meets have institutionalized sexiness, have made it an unwritten but mandatory part of women's routines. In the floor exercise, for example, the one event in which women and men compete, women are expected to exhibit dance elements as well as athletic maneuvers, whereas for men, tumbling is sufficient. So fourteen-year-old girls incorporate into their routines the head tosses and hip gyrations reminiscent of the "girls" at Scores. *Washington Post* writer Tony Kornheiser has called these routines "kiddie porn."[43]

Olympic breast stroke champion Mike Barrowman got a taste of what female athletes experience when appearing at a pre-Olympic meet in 1992. His experimental streamlined swimsuit, stretching from neck to groin, resembled a women's suit. One friend, upon seeing him, burst out laughing. Another said, "Looking sexy, Mike!" When he stepped onto the starting blocks, whistles filled the air. "There were probably 1,000 people here and I probably got catcalls from 900 of them," he said.[44]

Good-natured teasing about any innovation is understandable and not necessarily malicious. What's interesting is the form the teasing took. What came to mind, when people associated Mike's suit with femaleness, was not female strength or endurance or women's unique ability to give birth and nurse. No one joked that now he'd swim faster over long distances, since women win most marathon swimming races. No one called him Gertrude Ederle or Eleanor Holm. Of all the possible associations the crowd could have with women, only "sexy" and whistling came to mind. Suddenly, it was fair game publicly to taunt a man who, when dressed "as a man," never received such abuse, even as a joke.

Burt Reynolds, when he was dating Chris Evert, said that women athletes are sexy as long as they retain their vulnerability. That was years ago. But this caveat—"as long as they retain their vulnerability"—is still echoed in numerous venues, from commentators who favor small, delicate skaters over large, muscular ones, to husbands who approve of their wives' aerobics classes but not their weight-lifting sessions.

There is no positive paradigm for an attractive woman whose strength, intelligence, or courage meets or exceeds that of her male partner or partners. For a woman, being sexy *is* being vulnerable. As long as this remains true, women will never be understood to be men's peers. As long as women remain sex objects, they can't threaten the power structure. Naked women lack power. If a society can keep women, and popular images of women, in a state of undress, it can keep women down.

The experience of Lucinda, one of the Scores dancers, clarifies the equation in many men's minds between heterosexuality and vulnerability. In fact, Lucinda is a lesbian. Yet she has a difficult time convincing her male customers that she is gay. "Do you have a boyfriend?" they ask her.

"No," she says. Sometimes she says, "I like girls." The men don't believe her. Like the other dancers, Lucinda comes to Scores to work. Contrary to the men's fantasies, she is not romantically interested in them. But the men don't understand that she's a lesbian because by taking off her clothes, Lucinda makes herself vulnerable and accessible, and the patrons equate female sexual vulnerability with heterosexuality. They confuse her vocation with her desire. She doesn't want to have sex with them any more than Madonna wants to have sex with the men who watch her videos. Like Madonna, Lucinda is acting.

A woman defined by men as *not* sexy loses the popular culture's praise but gains the power to be herself. Some postmenopausal women make this discovery. A woman defined as not sexy is released from the obligation to behave in any particular way to preserve that sexiness. Not seen as pleasing to men, she becomes free to please herself.

This helps to explain why female athletes evoke anger and resistance from conservatives, and why they are associated with lesbians. Like lesbians, many female athletes indicate by their behavior that they are neither dependent on men nor concerned with how they appear to men. Like lesbians, female athletes can refuse to be controlled by the quest for male approval. Even if they initially become athletic in order to become attractive to men, they may eventually discover more important benefits. They might keep running, year after year, even if they don't lose weight.

• • •

After the Spur Posse arrests, Dottie Belman, a hairdresser and the mother of Dana and Kris, expressed shock at the "lack of respect my boys apparently have toward women." If she had it to do over again, she said, she would have steered her sons away from sports. After twenty-five years of marriage, she filed for divorce from Don and moved out of the house.[45]

Julie Croteau is doing postgraduate studies in exercise and sport sciences at Smith College and serving as assistant men's baseball coach at Western New England College. She remains a proponent of coed sport. She believes that integrated sports will ultimately reduce sexual harassment by forcing men to get to know real, three-dimensional women.

No changes loom in the men's rugby culture. But rugby is increasingly popular with women now, too, and they have written songs to reflect their own sexual thoughts, feelings, and humor. Many teams are led by women who are openly lesbian or bisexual and openly angry at male sexual dominance, as reflected in this song, sung to the tune of the *Sound of Music*'s "My Favorite Things":

> *Loose rucks and good fucks*
> *And aunts that are crazy.*
> *Girls that are horny*
> *And guys that are lazy.*
>
> *Good moves make good screws*
> *For those one-night flings.*
> *These are a few of my favorite things.*
>
> *Scrummies that tackle and backs that have hands*
> *All come together to astonish the fans.*
> *When the game's over the party begins*
> *That's when those studs think that we'll let them in.*
>
> *When the prick grows, when the juice flows*
> *When he's feeling grand*

Just fart in his face and tell him his place
And that he can use his HAND![46]

Like other women's rugby songs, this one redefines female sexuality as active, selective, and diverse. The final stanza suggests either that the man should masturbate rather than having intercourse with the singer, leaving her to enjoy instead, perhaps, other "girls that are horny," or that the woman prefers manual, rather than penile, stimulation, which "challenges heterosexual ideology through demystifying . . . how women achieve sexual gratification," writes Elizabeth Wheatley, who studied women's rugby subcultures.[47] Either way, female sexuality is redefined by women, and the singers rebut the engineer's "wife with a cunt so wide" who ends up "covered in shit."

• • •

A funny thing happened on Jay Bildstein's way to the investment bank. He noticed the vulnerability of the dancers—"the human factor," he calls it—and it upset him. He began to talk with the young women and learned that they all came from homes "where the father abandoned them, the parents are divorced, they were molested by their father, they were raped at an early age, they were molested by an uncle." He concluded that "a perfectly happy, well-adjusted functional woman who comes from a happy home with a white picket fence does not happen into a place to dance topless just for the money."

Asked if he believes such dancing exacerbates low self-esteem, Bildstein answers, "I am positive that it does. How could it not? When are women normally in a state of very little attire? Only in intimacy. And [nude dancing] is a non-intimate situation. So they're selling out a part of their intimacy, a piece of their souls."

He didn't understand the pain involved until the cash registers were singing, and then he felt "tremendously ambivalent." The men, too, bothered him: he called them "pathetic," "emotionally dysfunctional," "fundamentally lonely," "not highly evolved," and "unable to dabble in the currency of mutual respect."

He tried to lessen the exploitive nature of topless dancing, and planned to "hopefully eradicate that portion of it." He hired only women who had previous experience, thus not indoctrinating new women into the sex industry. In the first six months of the nightclub's operation, he helped five of the dancers obtain other, nonsexual jobs. He hoped to eliminate the toplessness, having the women eventually wear bikinis or "cute sporty outfits." When I pointed out to him that bikinis and cute sporty outfits still place women in the role of object, Bildstein said that perhaps the women would ultimately wear normal clothes, and the night-club could "get to where women and men can meet on equal footing, and women can understand the weakness in men's ego, and men can under-stand where women are coming from."

After about eighteen months, Bildstein sold the nightclub.

6

Men in Tight Pants Embracing

It is well that war is so terrible; [otherwise] we should grow too fond of it.

—*Robert E. Lee*

O F A pro football game that lasts three and a half hours, only about sixteen minutes are composed of actual football playing, according to an evaluation of a sample game by the Scripps Howard News Service. The rest is taken up with players' huddling, picking themselves up off of piles of men, running to the line of scrimmage, and rehuddling (one hour, fifty-three minutes); commercials (twenty-six minutes); halftime (sixteen minutes); penalties (ten minutes); injury delays (six minutes); and other delays including timeouts, official measurements, and fights. Clearly, men who love football are not wading through three and a half hours of television just to see a few spectacular touchdown passes. There must be more to it.

In the past, the sport had spiritual—and sexual—significance. "Folk football" or "mob football," the modern game's ancestor, was played during medieval times as part of a religious springtime celebration of renewal and fertility. "Any doubts about the association of the game with fertility ritual," says Amherst College professor and sports historian Allen Guttmann, "should be dispelled by J. J. Jusserand's account of the rituals at

Boulogne-la-Grasse, where 'the jour du mardi gras' included a basket of eggs and a staff at the end of which was a suspended, beribboned, leather football." [1]

Medieval football games took place between up to five hundred members of opposing villages with virtually no rules restricting violence. "Almost any sort of behavior was tolerated as long as the overt intent was to kick the ball rather than to maim other players," says Guttmann. "The game frequently degenerated into a wild scuffle, with players fighting for the ball."

Women participated—perhaps, Guttmann conjectures, because of their indisputable role in human fertility. "Peasant women . . . pushed, shoved, kicked, and frolicked with as much reckless abandon as their fathers, brothers, husbands, and sons; and they seem to have suffered as many broken bones and cracked crowns as the men did." Sometimes *only* women played, with married and single women taking opposing sides. [2]

Modern football is the quintessential manly game, worshiped with religious fervor but retaining no obvious fertility symbolism. Yet we still see, several times each game, the phallic staff—now in the form of a yardage marker—ceremoniously aligned next to the testicular-shaped football. The egg baskets are gone, unless you count the cheerleaders. The game is played not in springtime but in the fall and winter, when crops are dying or dead. In modern football, what seems to be celebrated is not woman's ability to give birth, but the male ability, when joined with other men, to hit, to headhunt, to hurt. To risk death, ultimately, in the name of virility.

• • •

A friend named John and his girlfriend, Debbie, recently attended a wedding that happened to take place on the same autumn Sunday that the Washington Redskins played the Dallas Cowboys. After the reception, the young couple had an argument over how, when, and with whom John watches sports. It was a typical football fight. Here's how John related the story to me:

"We go to the reception at the bride's parents' house. All the girls know each other. They go off together. The guys don't know each other. We say hello, hello, start looking at our watches. The Redskins are playing the Cowboys in fifteen minutes. You hear this murmuring among the men. There's more looking at watches. Then the bride comes out and says, 'This is my day. There will be no watching football.'

"I go out to my car, sit there, listen to the game on the radio. The house is on a cul-de-sac, and after a while I notice that the game is in stereo because all the other men are sitting in their cars, too. Finally the bride's mother comes out and says, 'OK, OK, you can watch in the kitchen.' So eighteen guys stand around this tiny TV in the kitchen, watching the game.

"Afterward, Debbie lights into me. 'How could you do that, at a wedding?' Debbie likes the Redskins, but she *really* likes weddings. She's very into weddings.

"I said, 'Look. There are 365 days in a year. The Redskins only play the Cowboys on two days, one home, one away. The bride could have looked at her calendar. She could have held the wedding at night. Besides, who gets married in November? Who gets married on a Sunday?'

"I won that argument."

* * *

Debbie likes weddings. She's very into weddings. She likes the idea of weddings: fidelity, security, mutual love. With marriage, a man is expected to stop seeing women as sexual conquests and start the real work/ joy of loving one person. The bachelor party, decorated with topless dancers or prostitutes, is supposed to represent the man's last fling with sexism, or at least with sexual objectification of women. To many women, a wedding represents hope that Woman and Man can actually love and cherish each other (now that the "obey" line has been deleted); that they can be friends, companions, intimates, peers. For women who are desperately seeking mutually respectful relationships with men, weddings can offer an appealing scenario.

John likes the Redskins. He's very into the Redskins. He likes the idea of the Redskins: domination, power, masculine might. He likes the fact that they often win. Watching them, he imagines himself making touchdown passes, or receiving them. He sees himself as a winner, too, albeit on a smaller scale, in disputes with his girlfriend. He argues to win—not to understand, or be understood, or grow closer—but to win. With men he argues, too, but then the arguments have a more jovial, playful quality; sometimes he'll defend an inept coach, for instance, just for the pleasure of arguing.

What weddings offer women (the prospect of bonding with men), manly sports offer men (the prospect of bonding with men). John and the other men at the wedding reception could have videotaped the game and watched it when they got home. They could have joined the women's conversation. They could have (could they have?) talked with each other.

But The Game reigned supreme. The Game took precedence over wedding festivities and even good manners. Who would be dumb enough to schedule a wedding on a Game day? In manly sports, Woman and her notions of romantic love are relegated to the sidelines, while Man and his buddies take center stage. If the male guests celebrated love on that November wedding day, it was their own love of masculine power. And of men.

• • •

Men's interest in sports begins, usually, with Daddy. A father may not bathe his son, or read stories to him, or prepare meals for him, or hold him when he cries, or listen to his concerns, or tie his shoelaces, but he will probably at one time or another play catch with his son, take him to a ball game, or quiz him about the current or past feats of male sports heroes. The fact that Dad does these things—and in most cases, despite the feminist movement, participates in few other child-centered activities—imbues Catch, or Going to the Ballpark, or Discussing Sports Statistics with special, almost spiritual significance. Men's sports, Dad says, are worthy of my attention. Athletic endeavor—particularly victory—is what will grant you my favor. Sports are the tie—often the only tie—that binds us.

Dad has power. Because Dad and other men worship them, sports have power. Sports become a son's essential, almost sacred path to his own power, or sense of it. Sports are male; to be male, and to earn male privilege, one must enter the sporting arena. A boy watches a baseball game on T.V. not because it is inherently interesting but because he is desperately seeking Daddy—if not a real Daddy, then the idea of Daddy: male authority. Televised games and box scores and multimillion-dollar contracts inform boys that male games are valued, and that they, as men-to-be, are valued. From the manly sports culture, boys (and girls) learn that men's games are valued more than women's games; that men are valued more than women. Both boys and girls enjoy playing sports for the innumerable physical, emotional, and psychic pleasures of the game. But boys seem to fall in love with spectator sports as an integral part of falling in love with the masculine privilege that their fathers symbolize.

While sports connect boys to Daddy, they disconnect boys from Mommy. They reinforce the illusion—common to many social institutions but nowhere as prevalent as in sports—that men are not only separate from but exist on a level above women. "The psychology of separation is central to the process by which men come to understand themselves as men," says sociologist Don Sabo, who has written extensively in the field of men, sports, and sexism. "One way to do that is to be nasty to women: to say, 'I don't need you, Bitch.' "

Fans of manly sports speak of women as annoyances that interrupt the male bonding process. A woman is not someone who might join you in your flag football game. She is not someone to listen to thoughtfully when she protests the brutality of boxing. Along with children and housework, wives and their desires become obstacles in men's headlong path toward The Game.

In the real world, male separation from women is no longer easy. Changing laws and mores are increasingly pressuring men not to exclude women from public gatherings, or the Senate, or even sports clubs. On golf courses, tennis courts, and softball diamonds—as well as in boardrooms and factories—men are daily confronted with women's competence, rendering sexism specious. Even in their own homes, men are faced with the growing athleticism of their daughters, who can often kick a soccer ball or hit a tennis ball more adeptly than Dad or Junior can. But at hockey or football games, male spectators can participate in an illusion of male superiority. They can root for men, for male power and might. They can peer up cheerleaders' skirts.

Organized sports provide opportunities for men to segregate boys from girls, and to indoctrinate them into their roles as members of the dominant class. Like male puberty rites in so-called primitive cultures, baseball and football training are characterized by "elders" who convey ritual to young men; the enforcement of conformity and control; isolation from girls and women; an emphasis on hierarchy and rank; and the infliction of pain.[3]

"You look at yourself as the ultimate physical male and so look at other genders differently," one former football player told researchers Don Sabo and Joe Panepinto. "If they can't compete with me, they can't be on the same level with me."[4]

In *Dreams of Glory,* Judy Oppenheimer quotes a high school player as saying, "Football makes you feel you're so awesome, you feel too good for any one girl." Football, he says, "makes you the man. Like no other sport can. It makes you feel like the man."[5]

• • •

To further understand men's relationship to sports and to each other, tune in to the blather on the increasingly popular "sports talk" radio shows. Or listen to what male sportscasters say about men. Or listen to men talk sports at work, on public transportation, at your own kitchen table. It's soap opera: speculation about who will do what; who is biggest, fastest, strongest; whose alliances are forming or crumbling. Men admire other men, gushing over their heft, their strength, their ability to "dominate" and "penetrate" and "perform." They ally themselves with the biggest and the strongest—hoping, it seems, to allay their own insecurities about being relatively small and weak.

Even if their own sports careers were limited to a few Little League at-bats, men use sports talk to establish their niche in the gender hierarchy. Sports talk is considered by men to be legitimate social and business conversation. If a man isn't "into" football, he can do what sociologist Kathryn Ann Farr calls "dominance bonding" by being "into" golf. Or baseball. Dominance bonding, says Farr, is "a process of collective alliance through which the group and its members affirm and reaffirm their superiority."[6]

Thus one appropriate answer to "What do you think of Baltimore's new stadium?" is "I don't really follow baseball; I'm into college basketball." A man doesn't have to follow baseball but he has to follow something, has to allow some form of the manly sports culture to lead him. Men's gymnastics or diving will not suffice, nor will any women's sport, but as long as a man is "into" one of the so-called major sports, he can join the dominance club, a club that accepts everyman. He doesn't need to work up a sweat *playing* a sport; all he needs to do is turn on the television. Browse through the daily sports pages. Drop some names. Utter them like incantations, with religious fervor: Jerry Rice, Riddick Bowe, Jimmy Johnson, Shaquille O'Neal, Barry Bonds, Eric Lindros, Eric Montross, P. J. Carlesimo. It becomes poetry. Mere recitation of sports names can grant you—if you are male—entry into the old boys' network. Sports talk is the *abracadabra* that opens the door.

When men talk sports, they usually do what Deborah Tannen calls report-talk: they offer information, competing to establish who is most informed. It's a verbal one-upmanship, an oral contest. This competitive conversation simultaneously establishes both hierarchy (who wins the argument; who has the most information) and unity: we are men, talking about men's interests.

"There's a very intimate relationship between sport and a man's inner sense of his identity as a male," says sociologist Don Sabo. "Part of that definition of being a man is you're supposed to be in charge, in control of the environment and destiny. Whenever your team wins, that's a verification all is right in your world and that somehow you were right. Your team came out on top."[7]

Sportswriter Frank Deford has said, "The whole essence of being a sports fan is identifying, taking sides, rooting and cheering and knowing more than the other fans."[8]

Thus much sports talk revolves around the question, "Who are you for?" Once a side is chosen, the speaker says "we," as in, "we're gonna win," or "we're gonna whip your butt," or, afterward, "we won." If a man's chosen team loses, however, he's more likely to say "they lost."[9]

More than mere vicarious victory seems to be at stake. We often hear about women's fears of male attacks, but rarely do we consider the fact that men also feel vulnerable to men. Boys grow up acutely aware of how defenseless they are against aggression by larger, more dominant males— the human equivalent of canine "alpha" males. This vulnerability seems to play a role in men's sports identifications. Men often marvel at male athletes' bulk and strength. "Now that's a big man—almost three hundred pounds," one might say with awe, even if the subject's weight is irrelevant; even if he's the coach. To affiliate with the biggest, strongest males—to "be on their side," to identify with their team—is symbolically to reduce the risk of male-on-male violence; to align oneself with the winning team is to acquire "protection"—another popular sports phrase. By taking a ringside seat in the sports-war spectacle, men and boys may obtain a sense of collective male power. They befriend the bully.

Sports also offer men a chance to play out their fear of and fascination with conflict. Almost all men's sports use military jargon. A team has a lot of "weapons," meaning strategies or players. The first team to score a touchdown "draws first blood." Winners bring back the losers' "scalps." "Fighting" takes place "in the trenches." A throw is a sixty-yard "bomb."

Introducing the first boxing match at Washington, D.C.'s annual Fight Night, former Redskins running back John Riggins said, "All right! Let's get ready for some blood and guts!"[10]

Commentator and former coach John Madden recently said of one player, "He looks like a football player now. He's got some blood on his pants. This is football."

This is also masculinity. Pro hockey player Tie Domi justified hockey fights in a *USA Today* column by equating nonviolence with femininity. "If you take out fighting, what comes next? Do we eliminate the checking? Pretty soon, we will all be out there in dresses and skirts."[11]

Describing modern college rugby, Steven Schacht says that brutality and threats of brutality, combined with misogyny, form a significant part of the game. A typical comment: "If he tries that shit during the game, I'll kick the fucking pussy's head off. The cunt should learn how to play."[12]

"The threat of violence is ever present," writes Schacht. "It reinforces what being a 'man' is all about."[13]

Martyrdom is another common theme. Playing with pain is noble, playing in agony even better. "Toughing it out" is expected. John Madden has commented, "You gotta give a guy credit when he'll say, to heck with my body, I'll run for it." Injuries are listed like accomplishments: cracked ribs, herniated disks, bruised shoulders. Rugby players even wipe their teammates' blood onto their own uniforms.[14]

Sadism is popular. A "merciless" team is admired. To play well is to "punish" the other team. "They really hurt that team" is a compliment. The late coach Woody Hayes, for whom a multimillion-dollar athletic complex at Ohio State is named, said, "We teach our boys to spear and gore.... We want them to plant that helmet right under the guy's chin.... I want them to stick that mask right in the opponent's neck."[15]

Don Sabo and journalist Joe Panepinto interviewed twenty-five former high school, college, and pro football players who made clear that sado-masochism is an accepted part of football. One player, speaking of his coach, said, "We all worshiped the ground he walked on, but he was also a huge prick. He beat the shit out of us and we loved him for it. It sounds weird now, but that's the way it was."

Another said of his coach, "At preseason camp, to sort out who was meanest, he'd stick two guys in the pit and whoever got out first was better. It wasn't really football, because guys would just punch and scratch the hell out of each other until somebody managed to crawl out."

Another reported, "If we had a poor practice, we'd run the tires until somebody puked or dry heaved, or he'd have us beat the shit out of each other in tackling drills." [16]

Phoenix Cardinals quarterback Timm Rosenbach quit pro football after the 1992 season, leaving behind a $1.05 million annual salary. "I thought I was turning into an animal," he told Ira Berkow of the *New York Times.* "You go through a week getting yourself up for the game by hating the other team, the other players. You're so mean and hateful, you want to kill somebody. Football's so aggressive. Things get done by force. Then you come home, you're supposed to turn it off? 'Oh, here's your lovin' Daddy.' It's not that easy. It was like I was an idiot. I felt programmed. I had become a machine." [17]

A former college football star now says of the sport, "I think it's barbaric. You're trained to hurt people. Taught to tear the guy's head off. When a guy gets injured, the fans will cheer. That's sick." (Yet this man still raises money for his college team, which is why he refused to be named.)

Anthropologist Douglas Foley spent a year living in a small south Texas town and observing its cultural practices, including what he calls the great American football ritual. "What the [high school] players talked about most was 'hitting' or 'sticking' or 'popping' someone," Foley writes. "These were all things that coaches exhorted players to do in practice. . . . The supreme compliment was . . . to be called a 'hitter' or 'headhunter.' A hitter made bone-crushing tackles that knocked out or hurt his opponent. . . . They talked endlessly about who was a real stud and whether the coach 'really kicks butt.' . . . Playing with pain proved you were a man." [18]

"The pain is worth it," writes Brian Pronger in *The Arena of Masculinity,* "because masculinity is worth it." [19]

Though violence is often a part of manly sports, it has a scripted, fake quality. Two basketball players swing at each other until pulled apart, supposedly, by tiny referees. Ice hockey players smash each other against plexiglass shields to the delight of eager fans. A manager and umpire scream at each other, spraying spit on each other's faces, close enough to kiss. And there's the ever-popular bench-clearing brawl. Each sport has its own style of fighting, its own unwritten rules. The anger may be real, but the expression of that anger is a deliberate choice, not a spontaneous outburst. Otherwise, why would hockey players slice each other with sticks? Baseball players don't bean each other with bats, and tennis players don't whack each other with racquets. Would a hockey player who took up tennis swat his opponent with his tennis racquet? Why not, if he's used to lashing out at people with whatever's handy? Why don't basketball coaches and referees ever engage in that spitty face-to-face drama that baseball managers and umpires do? If they're so wildly angry, why don't athletes kick each other in the groin?

Athletes are experts at emotion control; otherwise they wouldn't be able to kick field goals or serve aces under tremendous pressure. When they fight, the fighting is deliberate masculine theater, not a momentary loss of control. The decision to "lose one's temper" involves rational considerations: not losing face, trying to win games, fulfilling expectations of fans and teammates, and appearing on the evening news.

In hockey, certain players are designated fighters. Called enforcers, hit men, or goons, fighting is part of their job. Joe Kocur, an enforcer for the Detroit Red Wings, told reporter Johnette Howard, "I just look at it as a job that I'm paid to do. And my job is not to lose. I won't fight dirty. I won't jump someone from behind. But when I go to hit someone, I want to hit him in the face. I'm trying to hit as hard as I can. And a few times it has happened that someone got hurt."

Kocur explained that hockey involves more injury potential than boxing because of the skates' speed. "If you just stand there and hold a guy out and hit him, you won't faze him. But if you can pull him into you and punch him at the same time, that's when you start hurting people."[20]

• • •

I recently asked Los Angeles Raiders defensive end Anthony Smith what it feels like to "sack" the quarterback.

"It's like someone knocks the wind out of you," he said. "You don't know what happened. It's really scary. Sometimes I wake up dizzy myself, so I'm wondering what the quarterback feels like."

"Do you worry about him?" I asked.

"No. I don't worry." He laughed. "My job is to go out and hurt people, not to get hurt."

"You're actually trying to hurt him, not just bring him down?" I asked.

"Well, I get paid to take the quarterback down, but if I take him down and hit him a certain way where he's not as effective throughout the rest of the game, that's a lot better for us."

I asked: "How about if he's not so effective for the rest of his life? Would that be OK with you, too?"

"Honestly, I think it would be," he said. Then, to my surprise, he said, "My rookie year, I tore my knee up. I don't think too many people cared about me. If they'd cared more about me in that situation, I'd be more focused on just taking a player down."

I said, "It sounds like you're angry about not having been treated better when you were injured."

Smith suddenly retreated from his earlier statement, saying, "I could care less. My teammates were there with me. I didn't expect people from all over the country to say Anthony Smith's hurt. The game must go on. If I don't hit them they're gonna hit me."

The antagonistic sports arena gives men—both athletes and fans—a framework to express rage. A player can retaliate for hurt feelings through legal aggression. For a fan, another man's aggression will suffice. The aggressor can be cheered for, rooted for. Get 'em! Bring 'em down! Kill!

It doesn't assuage the aggression. The catharsis theory has long been disproved. Men who "let off steam" at sporting events gather that same steam again quickly, and let if off again elsewhere. If anything, watching violent sports increases, rather than dissipates, aggression. And playing violent sports teaches violence. People who inflict or accept pain in a "playful" setting are likely to inflict or accept pain in other settings as well.[21]

One former college football player says eight of the men on his high school football team were convicted of raping a woman. At least one of his college teammates bragged about "what sounded like a rape to me," he said. He declined his college teammates' invitations to socialize because "they were always wrecking things, getting in fights. I had enough fights on the football field. I didn't like fights."

Former college football player and *Sports Illustrated* writer Rick Telander says, "Slogans that are useful in a primitive game like football— 'Never surrender,' 'The most aggressive player wins,' 'Intimidation earns respect'—can be downright harmful in normal society where restraint, compromise, and cooperation are more typical ways of moving forward in the daily game. . . . The things players learn are not what they need to learn to be good human beings." [22]

The "sports build character" theory has been disproved, too. [23]

But the aggression inherent in football and other combat sports masks men's love for other men. In these hyper-masculine environments, men allow themselves to care about each other, to feel close. Under the guise of a mock battle, athletes touch, joke, and talk. Male spectators become free to exhibit passionate, romantic feelings for their heroes. They follow men's lives with great interest; they pore over trivia. Who do you like? ostensibly means, Who do you think will win? but it also means what it says. Who do you like? Who appeals to you?

The answer to "Who do you like?" is stated this way: "I like Michigan because of their backcourt." Or simply, "I like Boris Becker—I've got a gut feeling he can pull it off."

Gut feelings, in sports, are OK. "Emotion" is OK—it's good, even. "We need to show some emotion," a coach will say. Or a fan: "I like them because they're so emotional. I like a man who can show some emotion on the field."

Friendships are noted with awe. "Next we'll talk with Joe Schmo, a Close Personal Friend of Coach Pat Riley," a commentator will say, impressed.

Male fans will talk in reverent tones of "respect": they have a lot of respect for this player, that coach. These men also talk of trust. "I always feel comfortable when so and so's in the game," they may say. "I trust him." They may not trust their wives; they may not trust themselves or their children, but here's someone they can trust: a football player. Give him the ball.

Family is a frequent topic among both fans and players. Sitting in the bleachers of a baseball stadium on game day "is like being with family," a sixty-year-old man told me. Players say of each other, "He's part of the family," or "We treat each other like family," or, after a death, "We lost a member of our family."

Strange, mutant families are these—families without mothers. Families without sisters, daughters, wives. Antagonistic, oddly combative families. But it is within all-male families, or unambiguously male-dominated families, that many men seem to feel at ease. Deborah Tannen has noted that from an early age, boys are likely to feel most comfortable when seated side-by-side rather than face-to-face, and when discussing activities rather than feelings or thoughts.[24] Observing manly sporting contests offers a perfect opportunity for men to commune with other men.

In ordinary situations, many men feel licensed to express only a narrow range of feeling, mostly along the hurt/angry continuum. Tears are still unmanly. How many men cry, even in private? Many men don't even smile much, Gloria Steinem has pointed out, because "smiling may be seen as a sign of ingratiation and weakness."[25]

Yet fans can smile. Players, after a game, can smile. Fans and players can smile or scream (even hug each other!) without any loss of masculine face. While sport offers a man a place to worship traditional manhood, paradoxically it also offers a man a place to loosen the rigid masculine role without losing status. In sports, men can exhibit emotions for other men. They "can embrace each other unself-consciously, holding and hugging, touching and kissing without threat of ridicule and suspicion," write Boutilier and SanGiovanni in *The Sporting Woman*. "They can express fear, hesitancy, pain and doubt and be nurtured by other men. They can be irrational, cooperative, sentimental, and superstitious in the accepting presence of male camaraderie. In sum, in the absence of women, they can allow themselves to express what sexist ideology insists must be suppressed if they are to lay valid claim to being 'real men.' "[26]

Much of sport, I think, is an elaborate stage set to enable men to feel.

• • •

Some of what men seem to feel is turned on. Sports talk is laced with sexually violent homoerotic references. "Penetration" is a favorite word, as is "hole." Men "ram the middle"; "penetrate the pocket"; "jump on top of" or "get on top of" opponents; "go to the hole"; and "stuff the ball in the hole." They "get it up." They thrust, they beat. "The words for brutalized sex seem to be the same as those used for brutalized sports, and are used by athletes for both," author Paul Hoch has noted.[27]

In college wrestling there's a hold in which one man presses his pelvis into another man's bottom. It's called "the Saturday night."[28]

British soccer hooligans engage in "joyous, sexually fulfilling orgies of bully-boy bashing," one writer wrote.[29]

Chuck Cecil, a Phoenix Cardinal known for vicious tackles, was in

1993 fined twice for "flagrant unnecessary roughness involving the use of his helmet." Cecil defended the tackles as legal and told *Sports Illustrated* that a good hit is like "an orgasm. Euphoria. There is just this feeling of . . . power. For that split second of time you own that person. You are better."[30]

When the Washington Redskins defeated the Minnesota Vikings in the first round of the 1993 playoff season, a man excitedly asserted on a radio call-in show that the Redskins "ran the ball up their butt all day." Up their butt?

A football announcer recently said, "When you're 5'10", 185 pounds, and you have to put your head down and go between two of the biggest backs in the league, it takes something below the belt, doesn't it?" What would that be, that something below the belt? The implication, often repeated, is that football and other sports require a certain type of courage or fortitude that is exclusively male and somehow linked to sex.

Sexual and aggressive references in men's sports language point to a confluence, in many men's minds, between violence and sex, between dominance and sexual performance. They also point to men's erotic attraction for other men.

On the cover of *Friday Night Lights,* a book about Texas high school football, is a photo of three young men walking together. Backs to the camera, they stride onto a football field. Their taut bodies display full football regalia: helmets, neck guards, shoulder pads, black shirts and pants with white lettering. They are holding hands.

Were these same young men to hold hands in a different setting—on a city street, say, or on a beach, without their football uniforms—they would be thought to be gay. They might be taunted by other men— football players, perhaps. Yet in this picture, their handholding projects a solemn, unified sort of group power that conveys both threat and affection. It illustrates the fact that male power is based on male bonding. Together, they feel powerful. Together, they act powerful. Together, they fall in love—with power, with masculinity. They also fall in love with each other.

The frequent focus on sports violence obscures this love, this other side of the coin. The focus on violence obscures the sexual subtext— obscures it, at least, from the conscious minds of men who would never admit to admiring other men's bodies or enjoying the feel of them.

They can only admire "great hits." They can only watch those "hits"—and those post-touchdown embraces, and those close-up shots of the quarterback reaching his hands between the legs of the center, one hand touching the other man's crotch, and receiving the ball from him—over and over again. They can only relish these shrouded, armored images of male love, these curious combinations of hitting and hugging.

Since for many men, sex and power are synonymous—to be "impotent," after all, is to be without power—football players, as they parade their prowess, are sex symbols as well as symbols of aggression. They are hyper-men, caricatures of men, men exaggerated to a ridiculous extreme. Football is narcissism: a male love affair with the male gender.

Men who watch football—and other manly sports—are watching male bodies in action. Men who readily admit to objectifying women—brag about it, even—are unlikely to admit to objectifying men. Yet this is what happens. The sports spectator is riveted to the sight of male bodies. He watches them move, collide, crash, caress. The players touch. They pat each other's bottoms. Where else, except in gay bars, do men do that? The players hug each other, jump on each other, leap into each other's arms. Through their tight white pants, one can see their jockstraps.

Sports watching is voyeurism, a by-men and for-men burlesque show. The bodies being admired are not primarily those of the cheerleaders; they're the male bodies: bulky, brawny, shimmering with sweat. Fans follow with fascination every stretching, strengthening, straining action of these bodies, from weight lifting to ankle taping to the snapping of a pass with sure hands. For fifty-one weeks each year, readers of *Sports Illustrated* enthusiastically examine photographs of scantily clad, muscular men. Television watchers do the same: admire attractive images of male beauties.

Surely the ancient Greeks, who accepted male homosexuality (including pedophilia) as a natural part of life, derived erotic enjoyment from observing naked male athletes as they wrestled, boxed, ran, or engaged in other sports. Penises are prominent and detailed on Greek vases, mosaics, and figurines that depict athletes in action. Today's male athletes do not compete naked, but they tend to wear tight or minimal clothing, and visual representations of sport—in television, magazines, newspaper photos, posters—glorify male bodies, even focusing on the buttocks and genitals. With the exception of gay or bisexual men, today's sports fan generally does not accept homosexuality as a natural part of his own erotic fantasies. But voyeurism is voyeurism, acknowledged or not.

The occasional presence of women legitimizes the turn-on of sports, distracting fans from the uncomfortable fact of male athletes' erotic appeal. Female cheerleaders, topless dancers, and swimsuit models reassure men that their true lustful feelings are properly channeled not toward the men whose heroic actions and sculpted bodies so excite them, but toward women, or caricatures of women.

Peter Lyman, Director of the Center for Scholarly Technology at the University of Southern California, studied the role of sexually aggressive jokes in fraternities. He concluded that crude jokes about women's bodies, while sometimes distasteful to individual men, deflected attention from men's love and lust for each other. Jokes about homosexuality served the same function, drawing "an emotional line between the homosocial male bond and homosexual relationships." Lyman observed that fraternity men separate intimacy from sex, "defining the male bond as intimate but not sexual (homosocial), and relationships with women as sexual but not intimate (heterosexual)."[31] Surely the same could be said for many male athletes and fans. These men remain safely affiliated with heterosexuality while enjoying the prurient pleasures of sweaty male bodies.

"I've always thought part of the sports appeal for men was the subliminal seductiveness," confirms *New York Newsday* columnist Gabriel Rotello. "It's the only time straight men get to do this, look at other men's bodies. All these men in tight clothing, striking fabulous poses. As a gay man, I find it incredibly sexy. I'd rather go to a baseball game than a porno movie any day."

Elsewhere, it's primarily female bodies that are offered for visual consumption. But in sports, especially televised sports complete with slow-motion replays, broadcasters draw attention "to the male body in the only situation in which it is a legitimate object of the male gaze," writes Vanderbilt University humanities professor Margaret Morse in *Regarding Television*. The voyeuristic gaze receives sanction, and the homoerotic quality of that gaze is diffused, Morse says, because the act of men looking at men is "transformed into a scientific inquiry into the limits of human performance."[32]

Men who love football love men. Men who love hockey, soccer, baseball, basketball, wrestling, weight lifting, or bodybuilding (perhaps the ultimate male burlesque) love men. In a street-corner survey of 105 women in a northwestern city, 94 percent ranked photos of male body-builders as "extremely repulsive" on a five-point scale. The same photos shown to men netted only a 49 percent "extremely repulsive" rating.[33] Thus men seem more interested in, and accepting of, hypermasculine images than do women. Men's sport is designed to create moods and images that are appealing to men. After all, men are the primary spectators and followers of men's sports—the primary ticket purchasers, magazine readers, and television watchers.

Just as ballet, opera, and pairs ice skating offer ritualized celebrations of heterosexual love, manly sports offer ritualized celebrations of homo-sexual love. But because homosexuality is forbidden, great pains are taken to disguise the men-worshiping-men nature of the event. Sexism, homo-phobia, and violence do the trick. The dancing "girls" validate spectators' heterosexual credentials. Frequent "fag" jokes—clear indications that ho-mosexuality is on men's minds—reestablish the supposed heterosexual status of the speaker. And the blood and brutality, as Michael Messner has noted, draw attention away from the display of affection between men.[34]

Yet violence and sex are integrally connected in the vast $7-billion pornographic culture,[35] and in much of popular culture. The products of both cultures are consumed and produced primarily by men. It is men who, after victorious military battles, rape. It is men who, in the Army, sing a song in which they refer to their penises as guns. ("This is my weapon, this is my gun; one is for killing, the other for fun.") The violent element of sports such as football and boxing, while disguising a homo-erotic subtext, may also intensify men's erotic pleasure in watching these events. Blood lust.

Heterosexual love—as opposed to the desire to have sex with women—would be evidenced by true enthusiasm about women as people. Yet signs of such enthusiasm or love are oddly absent in manly sports. Instead, men only allow into the sporting arena women or images of women that represent sex or sexual domination.

Which raises the complex question: What causes heterosexuality? Why—when so many men enjoy jumping on each other and fondling each other, or watching other men jump on and fondle each other in the

name of rugby, or wrestling, or football, or boxing, or baseball, or a celebratory pile-up—do they allegedly only have sex with women?

Well, they don't, of course. Football player David Kopay, umpire
Dave Pallone, Olympic track athlete Tom Waddell, baseball player Glenn
Burke, and others have reported that gay male athletes are common.
Thousands of athletes attend the quadrennial Gay Games, including for-
mer college and Olympic champions. In *The Arena of Masculinity,* Brian
Pronger quotes scores of gay men who tell of "cruising" men in locker
rooms and even having sex there. He lists sixteen gay sports-related por-
nographic magazines, including *The Jock Book, They Grow 'Em Big,
Cocksucking Jocks,* and *Jock Fuckers.*

Notably absent from the gay male sports culture is football. Gay men's
bars rarely become sports bars, and few gay men seem to join the American male obsession with football spectatorship. Gay men don't need football, I conjecture, because they have created an alternative culture in
which they can celebrate masculinity, male bodies, and male sexuality.

But my concern is not with gay men but with the way the manly sports
culture teaches all men to love men and hate women. David Kopay said
that the question was not "how he could emerge from his super masculine
society as a homosexual, but how any man could come through it as
purely heterosexual after spending so much time idealizing and worship-
ing the male body, while denigrating and ridiculing the female."[36]

After six years of anthropological fieldwork at a major southern California gym, Alan Klein describes a culture in which bodybuilders routinely sell sex to gay men yet deny being gay themselves. In this complex
gym society—homophobic yet replete with homosexual activity—body-
builders lament, "We're everything the U.S. is supposed to stand for:
strength, determination, everything to be admired. But it's not the girls
that like us, it's the fags!"[37]

Manly athletes represent everything the U.S. is supposed to stand for:
strength, determination, everything to be admired. Part of what's admired—by men—is male bodies. I'm not contending that there are more
gay or bisexual men in sports than in the rest of society. I am contending
that in manly sports men find an avenue to express their affection for
men—and their anger at women—in a socially acceptable form. If these
men were to openly display their love and attraction for men, they

wouldn't have to camouflage these feelings with intramale violence and sexual assaults on women. Nor would they have to defend football so fiercely: they'd have other outlets in which to love men.

• • •

I was in Los Angeles recently, riding an airport shuttle bus with two men: the driver and another passenger. They began talking about the Los Angeles Raiders. They were wondering who had won that day's game with the Seattle Seahawks.

I knew. I had just come from the game. I said, "Oh, I just came from the game."

Oddly, they didn't say, "Oh, really?" Or "Who won?" They did not acknowledge my presence at all. Nothing. They resumed their talk. One said to the other that he had "a lot of respect" for Marcus Allen, that he was a "huge, huge fan" of Marcus Allen. The other said he saw Seattle's team last year and wasn't impressed. The first said, "Who do you like— Marinovich or Schroeder?"

Did I not speak loudly enough? I was sitting just a few feet from the other passenger, a businessman. I said again, "I just came from that game."

Again they ignored me. I began to understand invisibility. People who beg for money must feel this way as pedestrians rush by. I found myself thinking, too, about women who claim that by reading the sports pages and talking boy-sports at work, they gain the respect of their male colleagues. Just how begrudging is this respect? How many times are their comments ignored before men listen?

The driver and passenger were not friends; they had just met. One was black, one white. One wore coveralls, the other a tailored, pin-stripe suit. Yet they were united with each other through football. They were using sports to bond *as men,* even though I happened to know more about this particular game than they did.

These men may have excluded me no matter how I phrased my comments, but I noticed, in retrospect, that by not immediately offering them the information they sought, I had put them in the position of having to ask. Deborah Tannen notes that men often refuse to ask questions—even simple, necessary solicitations such as, What time is it?—because they perceive such a stance as neediness, and therefore a one-down position.

In this case, I suspect the men were particularly reluctant to put themselves in a one-down position to a woman.

I never did tell them who won.

• • •

Sometimes women successfully vault across the gender chasm, getting men's attention by speaking men's language: taking sides, rooting and cheering and knowing more than the other fans. But sports talk is not an open-ended discussion. There are unspoken rules. A woman can argue vociferously whether Shawn Bradley should earn $44 million for a guaranteed eight-year contract, but she can't, if she hopes to commune with her male boss or date or father or shuttle bus driver, wonder aloud why there are virtually no female baseball, football, ice hockey, or basketball coaches of men's teams. She can't hate boxing. She can't ask why Bela Karolyi, the men's gymnastics coach who surely never cartwheeled on a balance beam, was seen as qualified to coach girls, yet Pat Head Summitt, the female Olympic basketball player and coach, is not seen as qualified to coach boys. She can't propose that women, who often do a good job of balancing budgets in households, should get more opportunities to balance budgets in athletic departments (where such expertise seems sorely needed). She can't ridicule the international rifle association's decision to segregate men's from women's competitions after women won the mixed competitions too often. She might propose that more women's basketball games be broadcast on television, but even this tame opinion is risky. Women who engage in sports talk with men must play by the men's rules. Otherwise they undermine the purpose of sports talk, which is androphilial—man-loving: the worship of man and his accomplishments.

If you doubt this, try talking to a male sports fan about aerobics. Keep bringing the subject back to aerobics, to synchronized swimming, or to volleyball. If a man switches the subject to football or baseball, talk about female baseball and football players. Talk only about women. See what happens.

• • •

In a white-dominated, male-dominated culture, it makes no more sense to celebrate male bonding than it makes sense to celebrate white bonding. Exclusive gatherings of white people—or rituals designed to exalt white people—are justifiably viewed with great suspicion, not only by people of color but by whites of conscience. But male bonding is less suspect. Even some women seem to accept the idea that men need time away from women, that men need to "bond" with other men, that male worship of maleness is a worthwhile endeavor.

Whenever dominant groups segregate themselves from the mainstream, their gatherings solidify their sense of superiority, and their denigration of the underclasses. Such is the case in all-male schools and all-male military institutions, which have never been known for their enlightened views of women. It's also the case in manly sports. You don't hear most men say they're "huge, huge fans" of Monica Seles. You don't hear many men say, "I've got a lot of respect for Jackie Joyner-Kersee and Gail Devers." You rarely hear them brag that women are "close personal friends." Except during the Olympics, when indisputably amazing women are displayed on television daily, you rarely hear men publicly speak about women athletes in glowing terms—not as potential sexual conquests, but as real, admirable people.

Sportswomen disrupt the manly sports lovefest. If women can know about sports, excel in sports, coach sports, referee sports, and report on sports, then the masculinity machine itself, balanced precariously on footballs, baseballs, and hockey pucks, teeters.

So men struggle to preserve male bonding and male privilege by keeping sports as male as possible. In the early 1990s, as female athletes and coaches sued dozens of universities for equal opportunities and as judges consistently ruled in favor of the women, football coaches and administrators waged what one woman called "an offensive" against athletic feminists, claiming that women were attacking the sacred football cow.

Women weren't, in fact, attacking football. They just wanted to swim, row, play soccer, play tennis, or golf, and to coach and direct programs, as men do. They just wanted equal salaries, uniforms, travel schedules, scholarships, and facilities.

In fact, football—or, rather, male support of football and lack of support of women's sports—is responsible for much of the disparity between male and female college sports opportunities. Football "requires" oodles of athletes (108, on average, in Division 1), scores of scholarships (75, on average), excessive coaching salaries ($81,574 is the average "base"), and exorbitant operating expenses (more than for all other women's and men's sports combined).

Inevitably, if women are to have half of all sports allocations, as they are entitled to by law, football will have to change. Some schools will trim football's bloated budgets. Others will drop football altogether, as the University of Wisconsin, Superior; Wichita State; the University of Southern Colorado; and Northeastern Illinois University have already done. Others will leave football alone and add several large-squad women's sports, market women's programs to increase revenue, or find other creative ways to stop discriminating. But football defenders fear that their glory days are limited, and they blame women.

"What I'm afraid of is that somebody is trying to put a bull's eye on football's chest," said Oregon Athletic Director Bill Byrne, former president of the National Association of Collegiate Directors of Athletics.[38]

The Reverend Edmund P. Joyce, former executive vice-president at the University of Notre Dame, accused "militant women" of waging a "strident, irresponsible, and irrational campaign" against football. "Never have our football programs been in such jeopardy as they are today," Joyce said. "I think we are fighting for our lives and had better act accordingly."[39]

The fight for college football's life includes arguing that football is the cash cow upon which all the women's programs suckle, even though this is a lie. "Revenue producing"—a term often used to justify discriminatory football and men's basketball programs—is not synonymous with "profit producing." Football programs that earn money almost always spend more—not on women's sports, but on football. In 91 percent of all colleges, the football program does not make enough money to pay for itself.[40] Even in the big, football-dominated universities (Division I-A), 45 percent of the football programs lose money. In the other three divisions (IAA, II, and III), between 94 and 99 percent of the schools lose money on football.[41]

Besides, judges have ruled that "financial considerations cannot justify gender discrimination."

The fight for football's life includes arguing that football should be exempt from gender-discrimination calculations. Thomas Hearn, president of Wake Forest University, defended his school to Representative Cardiss Collins of Illinois during a congressional hearing by saying, "At Wake Forest, our athletic scholarship awards without football would approach parity, with 60 percent going to men and 40 percent to women."

University of New Haven football coach Mark Whipple has said, "Football shouldn't have anything to do with gender equity. If you don't count football, I think everyone would be happy." [42]

"I don't think football players are a third sex," Women's Sports Foundation executive director Donna Lopiano responded. The courts have agreed.

The fight for football's life includes arguing that women are being un-American, even communist, by depriving young men of their right to play football. Auburn University football coach Pat Dye has said, "To tell a kid he can't come out for college football as a walk-on because it creates a numbers problem with the women in another area, I mean that's almost like communism. That (isn't) what this country was built on, or what it stands for." [43]

University of Iowa women's athletic director Christine Grant's response: "Schools have had twenty years to think about this. It's unfortunate for the young men who get cut, but it's even more unfortunate for the millions of young women who have missed out for 100 years." [44]

The fight for football's life includes redefining "gender equity" to mean men get 60 percent, women get 40 percent. In what was hailed as a bold move, the Big Ten Conference recently approved a "gender equity" plan requiring 40 percent of its athletes to be women by 1997. Only the University of Iowa committed itself to a 50–50 split, which will make it the only Big Ten school to comply, finally, with the 1972 law.

The fight for football's life includes arguing that "progress" toward Title IX compliance is being made. In fact, if athletic directors had wanted to end discrimination during the wealthy eighties, they could have added women's programs while holding men's programs steady. Instead, over the ten-year period between the 1981–1982 season and the 1991–1992 season, for every two female participation slots created, 1.5 male slots were created. [45]

Representative Cardiss Collins has introduced a House bill called the "Equity in Athletics Disclosure Act" that would require school administrators to disclose participation rates and expenditures for male and female athletes. Football coaches and male athletic directors testified against the bill.

The fight for football's life includes contending that few women want to play sports. This is a last-ditch effort to deny women their rights based on a Title IX interpretation that allows unequal allocations if "the program fully and effectively accommodates the interests and abilities" of both sexes. Big Ten Commissioner Jim Delaney told me, "Not as many women are interested in playing sports as men. Look at field hockey versus football. Hundreds of men go out for football. It carries more status."

Collins's response: "Lower participation rates are the *result* of discrimination, and not an *excuse* for continued inequities." [46]

At the Division I-A level, only one out of 107 schools complies with Title IX. This is Washington State University (WSU), which was forced to do so by its own Supreme Court. In response to a class action suit filed by fifty-three female coaches and players, a judge ruled in 1982 that the number of WSU scholarships must be proportional to the ratio of women and men in the undergraduate student body. However, he exempted football from the count. But in 1987, the Supreme Court of Washington overruled the football exemption. The number of female athletes at WSU is now 44 percent, up from 29 percent in 1987. The female undergraduate student population is 46 percent.

"We were dragged kicking and screaming into the forefront," recalls Harold C. Gibson, Washington State's associate athletic director. People "thought the sky was falling." [47]

They still seem to think so. The College Football Association's Charles Neinas recently launched a public relations campaign with the slogan, "College football: More than just a game." [48]

In a surprisingly frank speech to his fellow football coaches and athletic directors, Neinas said, "Football may be the last bastion of male domination." [49]

Which explains a lot.

7

Sexual Assault as Spectator Sport

How can they hit us and still be our heroes?

—*Pearl Cleage,* <u>Deals with the Devil and Other Reasons to Riot</u>

DURING TWO long days at the rape trial of three college basketball players, the courtroom was packed with people leaning forward, straining to hear the graphic testimony. Sitting up front, near the judge and jury, were the woman who said it was rape and the three men who said it was sex.

This is how gang rape trials usually proceed: one woman says she was raped, and several men say no; she chose to have sex with us. When male athletes are involved, it becomes an issue not only of a woman's word against men's but also of athletic privilege. When female athletes are involved—the woman in this case also played basketball—it becomes, too, a question of teamwork: how could these men rape their sister basketball player? Why would they?

By the end of the trial's second day, the spectators had segregated themselves the way fans do at a basketball game, the woman's supporters on one side, the men's on the other. An aisle separated the two groups.

With the woman were her relatives, a few friends, and a few teammates. Many seats were empty. On the men's side the seats were filled and additional people stood. Spectators included the men's relatives, their friends, most of their teammates, and all of the assembled representatives of the college athletic department: two basketball coaches, the sports information secretary, the athletic secretary, and the "team mother." This imbalance gave the room a lopsided feel, as if the men represented a popular, successful home team, the woman an unpopular opponent from another town.

Tearfully, and in a small voice, Melody (all the names in this case have been changed)[1] told the judge and jury that the three basketball players, men whom she considered friends, chatted with her one evening through an open window of their dorm, then invited her to the side door. She went to the door but did not want to go inside. Women were not allowed in the men's dorms after 11 P.M., and it was about 11:30. But Otis, the tallest of the three men and about a foot taller than Melody, grabbed her and pulled her inside. She escaped his grasp and ran, but he and James, a second player, caught her and dragged her in. At this point she was not afraid. She thought they were playing a prank: a mock kidnapping. Like Gail Savage and other women, Melody somehow had become accustomed to being lifted and carried around by laughing men. They took her into the dorm room of Paul, a third player. Otis blocked the door with his body. She asked to be let go. Then, she told the jury, Otis and Paul held her down while James raped her. Afterward, Otis and James held her down while Paul raped her. Then Otis pointed his penis at her and said, "Suck on this." She refused, and he did not force her. Joking with each other, the men released her. As she dressed and hurried toward the door, they told her, "We should do this more often."

The next day, she tried to kill herself.

The state charged the men with a total of twelve counts of rape, second-degree rape, attempted sodomy, and abduction.

The men told a different story. Without tears and in a bold voice, Otis said, "She walked into the room on her own. She took off her sweatpants. She lay down and had intercourse with James. Then she did it with Paul."

His two friends concurred.

The men and woman all played basketball for the same university. Because the men were basketball players, they were campus heroes. Because the woman was a basketball player, she was rumored to be a lesbian, or at least bisexual. For this she was ridiculed and ostracized. For this, she believes, she was raped.

• • •

Read any newspaper and you're likely to uncover, buried somewhere deep in the sports section, the latest story of a male athlete or group of male athletes being charged with sexual assault. Unlike the news of, say, a pro baseball team winning or losing any one of their 161 games, the rape will not merit a dramatic headline or placement in the front section of the paper, nor a long story full of quotes and analysis. Unless the charges threaten the career of a money-generating star like Mike Tyson, the news will receive only one or two sentences. Unless the men are local, it will often not be reported at all. From this we can conclude that rape by athletes is not as important to sports editors as are athletes' on-field exploits. We can conclude that the men in power—coaches, team owners, athletes, editors—have not made the connection between male sports training and rape. Or that they don't think it's important.

Rape is important to women. It's important to women that "our nation's heroes," the central actors in "our national pastime," and "the role models for our children" are responsible for a disproportionate number of sexual assaults. "When football players rape they send the message: That's what real men do," says former football player Jackson Katz, founder of Real Men, an anti-sexist men's organization in Boston, and the project coordinator of the Mentors in Violence Prevention (MVP) project at the Center for the Study of Sport in Society.

Many women's sons worship these "real men." Many husbands identify with them, cheer for them, enjoy their performances so much "it doesn't matter what they do off the field." These are the men many young women long to date.

Athletes and fraternity members are the two most likely campus groups to commit gang rape, according to Bernice Sandler, senior associate of the Center for Women Policy Studies, who analyzed 150 group sexual assaults on university campuses. "It's contact team sports—football and basketball, sometimes lacrosse or ice hockey," says Sandler. "It's rarely the golfers or the swimmers."

A 1986 survey of two hundred college police departments by the

Philadelphia Daily News found that male basketball and football players were reported to police for sexual assault about 38 percent more often than their male college peers.[2]

Researchers Mary P. Koss and John A. Gaines surveyed 530 undergraduate men about their participation in a continuum of "sexually aggressive" behaviors, including whistles and catcalls; unwanted touching of a woman's breasts, buttocks, or genitals; attempted or completed intercourse by use of arguments or verbal threats; and attempted or completed intercourse by plying a woman with alcohol, threatening bodily harm, using physical force, or overcoming her with a group of men. Football and basketball players were more likely to engage in sexually aggressive behaviors than their peers, including those who played other sports.[3]

A three-year survey by the National Institute of Mental Health concluded that athletes participated in about one-third of 862 sexual attacks on college campuses.[4]

A 1991 study of more than 10,000 students conducted by the Campus Violence Prevention Center at Maryland's Towson State University found that 55 percent of all admitted acquaintance rapes were committed by athletes, though athletes comprised only 16 percent of the male student body.

• • •

A sampling from my thick file on athlete rape reads like a twisted Twelve Days of Christmas. In the past few years, the following groups have been accused of group sex crimes against women: twenty members of the Cincinnati Bengals football team[5]; five University of California at Berkeley football players[6]; five members of the St. John's University lacrosse team[7]; five West Virginia University basketball players[8]; five Kentucky State University football players[9]; four Portland Trail Blazers[10]; four Washington Capitals ice hockey players[11]; four Duquesne University basketball players[12]; four members of Glen Ridge (New Jersey) High School football team[13]; four University of Arkansas basketball players[14]; three New York Mets[15]; three University of Minnesota basketball players[16]; three Hampton University basketball players[17]; two University of Colorado football players[18]; two Oklahoma University football players[19]; and many others.

Few of these men were convicted of rape. Usually, the charges were dropped or the men were acquitted. In only 2 percent of rape cases are the men ever caught, tried, or jailed, according to a Senate Judiciary Committee report.[20] In 80 percent of the rape cases that go to trial, the men are found not guilty.[21] In a gang rape, when it's her word not only against his but against theirs, the men's version of events usually convinces the jury, the grand jury, or the district attorney that there is insufficient evidence to prove guilt.

In the case of the twenty pro football players, a ninety-eight pound woman identified in court as Victoria C. said she was "brutally and sadistically raped . . . over two hours," by twelve members or former members of the Cincinnati Bengals while another eight stood by and watched. The men were two to three times her size. She had gone to the hotel for consensual sex with Lynn James, a Bengals team member, she testified in her civil suit. When James left the room, three other players barged in and began the series of assaults. She also charged eight other men with aiding and abetting the incident.[22] (Anthropologist Peggy Reeves Sanday, author of *Fraternity Gang Rape,* cites numerous examples of the same scenario: a woman agrees to have sex with one man, then he leaves and his friends come in and rape her. Apparently this is a common modus operandi for rape.) In the Bengals case, a federal jury found in 1993 that Victoria C. was bound by a $30,000 liability-release agreement she signed in 1991.[23] In other words, she had been paid to keep quiet.

Paying women to keep quiet has become routine. One pro football player even tried to deduct as a business expense the $25,000 he paid to a former girlfriend who had accused him of harassment. Michael Harden argued that the out-of-court settlement was a legitimate business expense because in order to maintain his employment as a player, he had to keep the matter discreet. The U.S. Tax Court, noting that the relationship was personal, not professional, disagreed.[24]

In the 1989 case involving four members of the Glen Ridge (New Jersey) High School football team,[25] the teenaged victim was retarded, with the I.Q. of an eight-year-old. The perpetrators were four athletes, including co-captains of the high school football team, who knew the victim. She was outside, shooting a basketball alone in a park,[26] when the boys invited her to a nearby basement on the pretext of offering her a date.[27] The group of high school athletes did not deny ramming a miniature baseball bat and a broom handle into her vagina. She wanted it, they said. Nine other young men watched. Some cheered.[28] Afterward, they pledged secrecy by placing their hands on top of each other, the way they do at the start of ball games.[29]

The defense attorney portrayed the young men's behavior as normal adolescent sex, telling the jury, "Boys will be boys."[30] Yet Christopher Archer and Kevin Scherzer were convicted on March 16, 1993, on two counts of first-degree aggravated sexual assault, using force and coercion, and assaulting a mentally retarded person. Kyle Scherzer, Kevin's fraternal twin, was convicted of one count of aggravated sexual assault. All three men were sentenced to fifteen years in a youth detention center, the minimum term required by New Jersey law. They could be released in twenty-two months. Bryant Grober was convicted of third-degree conspiracy and sentenced to three years' probation and 200 hours of community service.[31]

Many other male athletes have been convicted of rape and other sexual offenses. Former heavyweight boxing champion Mike Tyson was sentenced to six years in prison for raping beauty contestant Desiree Washington in 1991. Former heavyweight boxing champion Trevor Berbick was sentenced to four years in prison for raping his family's babysitter in 1990.[32] Former Green Bay Packers football player Mossy Cade served fifteen months for rape.[33] Former Cowboys kicker Rafael Septien pleaded guilty to indecency with a ten-year-old girl and was placed on ten years probation.[34] California Angels outfielder Luis Polonia, convicted of statutory rape of a fifteen-year-old girl, served twenty-seven days of a sixty-day sentence.[35] Later sued by the same girl, he agreed to an out-of-court settlement.[36] Former Syracuse football player Michael Owens pleaded guilty to first-degree sexual abuse for an assault on an eighteen-year-old woman; he received a three-year conditional discharge.[37] Former Oklahoma University football players Bernard Hall and Nigel Clay are serving ten-year sentences for rape; they both claim innocence.[38] Eastern Michigan Linebacker Maurice Reed pleaded no contest to sexually assaulting a woman and was sentenced to at least sixty days in jail.[39] Oakland Raiders receiver Warren Wells was sentenced to one year in prison for rape.[40] Atlanta Hawks center Tom Payne was sentenced to ten years in prison for rape.[41] Dallas Cowboys linebacker Hollywood Henderson was sentenced to four and a half years in prison for rape.[42]

Occasionally men rape men or boys. In two separate incidents, groups of high school wrestlers allegedly raped other male wrestlers with broom or mop handles. At one high school, a fifteen-year-old said eight team-mates held him down while others spread his legs and raped him with a mop handle. He believed the attack was inspired by his coach having put him on a "wimp" list for missing practice because of illness. The coach said there was no such list.[43]

At another high school, a seventeen-year-old wrestler said he was held down by three teammates and sodomized with a broom handle after miss-ing a practice. He claimed his coach also pinched him on the penis when he did not break a hold within the allowed fifteen seconds. The coach was suspended but found not guilty of second-degree sexual assault in a jury trial.[44]

Sexual assault is my main interest here, but nonsexual assaults against women are also common. Football star O. J. Simpson pleaded no contest to beating his wife during a 1989 New Year's Day argument and was placed on two years' probation.[45] Darryl Strawberry has admitted beating his wife and pointing a gun in her face.[46] Baseball star Jose Canseco once rammed his wife's car with his car, then spat on her window. She did not press charges.[47] Milwaukee Bucks basketball player Moses Malone has been accused by his wife of physical and verbal brutality, including death threats. During his divorce trial, he insisted he never hit her or threatened to kill her but admitted having "moved her out of the way."[48] Boxer Sugar Ray Leonard admitted during a press conference that he struck his wife, Juanita, with his fists.[49] Golfer John Daly was arrested at his home and charged with assault after allegedly hurling his wife against a wall, pulling her hair, and trashing the house.[50] He pleaded guilty to a misde-meanor harassment charge and was placed on two years' probation with stipulation that he complete a domestic violence treatment program.[51]

Coaches often condone sex crimes and other crimes against women through silence, coverups, or their own abusive behavior. When Lefty Driesell was serving as head basketball coach at the University of Mary-land, he telephoned a woman and asked her to drop an accusation of sexual misconduct against one of his players.[52] At the University of Min-nesota, two men's coaches were disciplined for lying about fund-raising efforts to help a player who was charged with rape.[53] San Francisco 49ers owner Eddie DeBartolo Jr. settled out of court with a woman who accused him of sexually assaulting her at a party.[54] Former Michigan State wrestling coach Philip Parker was found guilty of raping a twenty-year-old woman while on a 1991 Valentine's Day date.[55]

"I'm going to go home and beat up my wife," Penn State football coach Joe Paterno once said at a press conference after his team lost to the University of Texas. Later he defended the statement as "just part of the sports culture, locker room talk, harmless, a joke that did not mean anything."[56]

Alabama men's basketball coach Wimp Sanderson resigned in 1992 after Nancy Watts filed a sex discrimination complaint against him. Watts, his longtime secretary and mistress,[57] alleged that Sanderson hit her as part of an ongoing pattern of physical and sexual abuse. Sanderson claimed in court documents that Watts received her black eye by colliding with his outstretched hand.[58] Watts received $275,000 in a settlement. The university bought out the last two years of Sanderson's contract for $558,454;[59] he also became eligible for an annual pension of $75,000.[60]

In *The Hundred Yard Lie* Rick Telander writes, "In my years in the locker room I have heard so much degrading talk of women by male athletes—particularly the use of women as objects to be conquered and dominated . . . that I feel certain the macho attitudes promoted by coaches contribute (perhaps unwittingly) to the athlete's problems in relating to women."[61]

Spectators also get into the swing of things. Boston Celtics fans have hung banners in the arena claiming they like to beat rival teams almost as much as "we like to beat our wives."[62]

Lenore E. Walker, a Denver psychologist and author of *Terrifying Love,* contends there is a "very strong relationship" between men who watch football and men who beat women. She studied calls to Denver's police and battered women's shelters during and after the 1988 Super Bowl. During the game, reports of domestic violence were lower than usual, but "the number of calls soared in the first four or five hours" after Denver lost the game.[63]

Women are beaten daily, but Super Bowl Sunday seems particularly dangerous for American women. Though some battered women's shelters report noticing no correlation between football and wife beating, shelters in Philadelphia, Los Angeles, and Marin County, California, have reported receiving more calls from distraught, bruised, and threatened women that day than on any other day of the year.

About 25 percent of the men referred by courts to the Domestic Abuse Center in Northridge, California, tell of at least one battering incident involving sports. "The men talk about being pumped up from the game, pumped up from having all their buddies around," says the center's director, Gail Pincus. Men get angry, she says, "when a wife or girlfriend either doesn't serve them fast enough or makes what they consider a stupid or embarrassing comment" while they are watching sports with other men.[64]

One Philadelphia woman told a counselor this story: Her husband, watching the 1980 Super Bowl, ordered her to make sandwiches and bring him beer. During a commercial he followed her into the kitchen, grabbed a knife, and threatened her with it. During another commercial she hid in the laundry room but he found her there, dragged her out, and beat her. He stopped only when he heard from the television that the game had resumed and the Eagles had scored. He returned to the game. She fled.[65]

• • •

The three basketball players were sitting in Paul's dorm room, drinking beer and, as they recall, "probably talking about basketball or sports," when Melody and two of her friends approached their open window and began a conversation with them. The three men and three women chatted, all accounts agree. After a while, James asked if the women wanted to see "the real John Holmes," a reference to a porn movie star with a huge penis. He pulled down his pants.

Soon afterward Otis asked Melody to meet him at the side door. Otis testified that he asked Melody to come to the door "because James exposed himself to her and she looked interested."

A witness testified that Otis grabbed Melody and pulled her inside, but that it appeared they were playing. Otis says he "escorted" Melody inside the building. Melody says she did not want to enter the building because of the dorm prohibition against female visitors, but was not afraid. After all, these were her friends.

Which raises the question: When a male friend grabs a woman, and drags her in a direction she does not want to go, is this play? Is this safe? Can he be trusted? About 90 percent of sexually assaulted women know their perpetrators.[66]

Once inside, Melody worried aloud about getting in trouble for breaking curfew. The men were supposed to be attending a dorm meeting, and Melody thought someone might come looking for them. "Don't worry, they never check our rooms," she was assured. Then the rape or sex began. Melody says James and Paul took turns raping her, while the three men worked in tandem to hold her down. She didn't use the phrase team effort but it sounded like that: a coordinated, strategic attack that required little verbal communication. She recalls that they said to her, "You need a real man"—a reference to her rumored bisexuality—and, "We're going to fix you."

Melody and Otis had dated several months earlier. Melody had ended the relationship. This was not supposed to be admissible in court; the judge had ruled before the trial that Melody's sexual history was irrelevant. But Melody, in a blunder indicative of her naiveté, blurted out this information while being cross-examined. The defense attorneys later used it against her.

In the men's version of events, Melody walked into the dorm room of her own volition, worried aloud about breaking curfew, then pulled down her pants.

"There was no kissing, no hugging, no fondling? She just walked into the room, laid down and did it?" the district attorney asked.

"She just laid down and did it," Otis replied.

When Melody was having intercourse with Paul, the men testified she fondled James's penis with her left hand and Otis's with her right. Afterward, James said, "Turn on the light. Let me see how pink it is." Otis turned on the light. On the witness stand he mimed the action of gently pulling apart her labia and peering in. "God dang, girl," he said he told her, "you is pink."

After Melody fled, her friends asked what was wrong. "Nothing," she muttered. She looked shaken, they said. She was unusually silent. Back at her dorm, she showered for a long time.

The next morning she ingested an assortment of painkillers and cold medicines. At the hospital, after her stomach was pumped, she filed a rape report.

In her closing arguments, the district attorney said Melody didn't tell her friends about the rape because "she didn't believe it herself—she was shocked, stunned." The district attorney also noted that Melody had been scarred by a previous experience: Melody had confided to her that her stepfather molested her at a young age, and when she told her mother, her mother did not believe her. Melody feared no one would believe her again.

The district attorney said it was ludicrous that a woman would walk into a dorm room, express a fear of getting in trouble, then "take off her pants and say, essentially, 'climb aboard.' "

In their closing arguments, the defense attorneys insinuated that Melody was lying about her stepfather as well as the three basketball players; that she had a history of false rape accusations. Pointing to Melody's admission that she'd had sex with Otis before, they labeled her "very liberal-minded."

The jury deliberated for three and a half hours. Friends, family, and members of the community waited nervously in the courtroom. People rose to get drinks of water and to talk quietly with each other. Journalists from local papers speculated on the outcome. One male writer expressed sympathy for Otis, who was charged with second-degree rape but by all accounts "hadn't even gotten laid."

When the jurors emerged, the verdicts were read, beginning with Paul: Not guilty on each of the counts against him. Then Otis: not guilty. Then James: not guilty.

Shouts of "Praise the Lord!" and "Thank you, Jesus!" reverberated throughout the courtroom, giving it a surreal, revival atmosphere. Otis's mother, shouting "Hallelujah" and crying, was so overcome by joy and relief she had to be carried out.

Melody's family formed a cocoon around her and ushered her away.

In the parking lot, James spoke of plans to celebrate the "victory" with Otis and Paul. Of Melody he said, "She's frisky. She's had sex with lots of guys. Lots of the football players has sex with her. She even goes both ways. She had a reputation of being bisec [bisexual]."

James's mother chimed in. "Yeah, she goes both ways. She do it with everybody."

I asked James, "What gave you the impression she wanted to have sex with you?"

He said, "If someone in a first-floor window expose himself to you, and you go to him, well, what is he supposed to think?"

• • •

When I tell people that male athletes are responsible for more rape than their nonathletic peers, no one seems surprised. It's not that people have seen the research—it has not been widely disseminated—nor that they're extrapolating from the few public cases, such as Mike Tyson's trial. It simply makes sense, knowing what we know.

Rape-prone societies, according to anthropologist Peggy Reeves Sanday, are strongly associated with militarism, male dominance, high male status, sex-role differentiation, general interpersonal violence, an ideology of male toughness, distant father-child relationships, and separate spheres for men and women.[67] What better way to describe manly sports? With their male-supremacist rituals, macho behaviors, systemic violence, and almost total exclusion of women, a manly sports league could be considered its own culture, and, in Sanday's terms, extremely rape-prone.

Sanday says that men in all-male groups often (1) assume promiscuous women are indiscriminate and therefore available to the population at large; and (2) punish promiscuous women. Rape is used to control women's sexuality.

This may help explain James, after the trial, calling Melody "frisky" and accusing her of having sex with "lots of the football players," as well as with women. Therefore, he seemed to be saying, she wanted/deserved sex/rape from the basketball players as well. The rape/sex could also be interpreted as a form of competition between the football and the basketball teams: if you get to "do her," we do, too.

When educating men about rape, author and psychologist Chris O'Sullivan notes dryly, "it seems to be particularly important to convey that a woman who chooses to be sexual, perhaps with several different individuals, is still sexually selective and is not available to the population at large."[68]

"Athletic teams are breeding grounds for rape [because they] are often populated by men who are steeped in sexist, rape-supportive beliefs," says Robin Warshaw, author of *I Never Called It Rape.*[69] Four common rape-supportive beliefs include she wanted it; she deserved it; nothing happened; and no harm was done.[70] According to Claire Walsh, director of the Campus and Community Consultation Service, a rape prevention program in St. Augustine, Florida, in virtually every case of gang rape, the men admit to group sex but deny that it was rape. That's the "she wanted it" myth, and the one the basketball players' attorneys used. "Why did she go to the door?" the attorney asked. "If she just wanted more conversation, she could have stayed at the window."

Many teens believe rape is justifiable (she deserves it) in certain circumstances. Robin Warshaw cites a study of 14–18 year olds in which more than half of the boys and between 26 and 42 percent of the girls say that it's OK for a boy to force a girl to have sex if (1) she is planning to have sex with him and she changes her mind; (2) she has led him on; or (3) she gets him sexually excited.[71]

The "nothing happened" myth promulgates the belief that neither sex nor rape occurred, and that women's accounts are unreliable. Unlike other assault victims, rape victims are often accused of lying about the rape, supposedly to achieve covert aims such as retaliation against former boyfriends. The false memory syndrome—the theory that many women mysteriously and mistakenly imagine that they were sexually abused as children—serves as the latest version of this myth.

While contesting the rape charges against him, Mike Tyson demonstrated the "no harm done" myth: "When I'm in the ring, I'm breaking their jaws—to me that's hurting somebody . . . didn't hurt anybody—no black eyes, no broken ribs."[72]

The "no harm done" myths are evident in the ways men define rape. "Rape is defined according to what men think violates women, and that is the same as what they think of as the *sine qua non* of sex," writes Catharine MacKinnon in *Feminism Unmodified*.[73] "Men who are put in prison for rape think it's the dumbest thing that ever happened. It isn't just a miscarriage of justice; they were put in jail for something very little different from what most men do most of the time and call sex. The only difference is they got caught. That view is nonremorseful and not rehabilitative. It may also be true."[74]

A psychiatrist who works with rapists reports, "It is becoming increasingly more difficult for these men to see their actions as criminal, as being anything more than the normal male response to a female."[75]

Kinsey Institute scholars who studied men and sexual assault concluded, "If we labeled all punishable sexual behavior as a sex offense, we would find ourselves in the ridiculous situation of having all of our male histories consist almost wholly of sex offenders. The man who kisses a girl [sic] in defiance of her expressed wishes is committing a forced sexual relationship and is liable to an assault charge, but to solemnly label him a sex offender would be to reduce our study to a ludicrous level."[76]

"Rather than 'reduce their study to a ludicrous level,' " Andrea Dworkin notes in *Pornography*, ". . . the honorable scientists chose to sanction as normative the male commitment to the use of force documented by their study."[77]

In a recent survey of 114 undergraduate men, more than 91 percent agreed with the statement, "I like to dominate a woman." More than 86 percent agreed with, "I like the conquest part of sex." More than 60 percent acknowledged, "I get excited when a woman struggles over sex" and "It would be exciting to use force to subdue a woman."[78]

Sex and rape can both involve a sort of athletic prowess, and can be interpreted as a game that must be won in order to impress other men. "The man is taught to look upon his actions on a date as carefully constructed strategy for gaining the most territory," former college student Erik Johnke wrote in his senior thesis. "Every action is evaluated in terms of the final goal—intercourse. He continually pushes to see 'how far he can get.' Every time [his date] submits to his will, he has 'advanced' and every time she does not he has suffered a 'retreat.' Since he already sees her as the opponent, and the date as a game or battle, he anticipates resistance. He knows that 'good girls don't,' and so she will probably say 'no.' But he has learned to separate himself from her and her interests. He is more concerned with winning the game."[79]

Such training "may well have the consequence of making it difficult for males to become sexually aroused in a relationship in which they do not feel dominant over the female," says sociologist Miriam Johnson in *Strong Mothers, Weak Wives*. "If one learns about sexuality in the context of being rewarded by other males for "scoring," for "getting pussy" or just "getting *it*," then this does not augur well for egalitarian sex."[80]

• • •

When explaining why male athletes rape we must note the obvious but overlooked fact that they are men. More specifically, most men were trained to act manly, were raised to develop a disdain for women, to dissociate love from sex, and to engage in various self-destructive and other-destructive behaviors that somehow, to themselves and other men, "prove" masculinity.

The testing ground by which masculinity is proved is violence. Author Michael Kaufman calls it "the triad of men's violence": violence against women, against other men, and against oneself.[81] Against oneself, violence proves toughness. Against men, violence establishes a pecking order. Against women, violence serves as the ultimate control mechanism, as Susan Brownmiller pointed out in *Against Our Will*.[82] Sports violence plays an integral role in maintaining male supremacy.

MacKinnon puts it this way: "Athletics to men is a form of combat. It is a sphere in which one asserts oneself against an object, a person, or a standard. It is a form of coming against and subduing someone who is on the other side, vanquishing enemies. . . . Physicality for men has meant male dominance; it has meant force, coercion, and the ability to subdue and subject the natural world, one central part of which has been us [women]."[83]

The tackle—the act of knocking or dragging another person to the ground—is an integral aspect of football. Illegal off the football field, assault is legal on it. The human body is used as a weapon against other bodies, resulting in pain, serious injury, and even death.[84]

In sports, a boy learns to use his body in "forceful, space-occupying, even dominating ways," notes University of Alberta sociologist David Whitson. His body becomes "an instrument of power" that enables him to "force others to do his bidding." Because these behaviors are linked to the concept of manliness, and thus to the boy's definition of self, he carries them over into his intimate encounters with women.[85]

Whether hockey fights, football tackles, or baseball brawls, intentionally hurtful acts are portrayed as natural—*for men*. Sports violence is considered appropriate. It is considered masculine. Our concept of violence is inextricably interwoven with our concept of expected, condoned male behavior. Boys are given boxing gloves as toys, whereas girls and women who attempt to join wrestling, boxing, or football teams are often ridiculed, sexually harassed, or simply barred from participation.

One implicit agreement of any sporting contest is to limit the game actions to specific boundaries in time and space.[86] When boxers take off their gloves, they're supposed to stop fighting. "Getting position" through the aggressive use of elbows and hips is acceptable on a basketball court but not in a grocery line.

Athletes have "a moral obligation to normalize relationships and lives at the game's conclusion," says University of California, Berkeley, psychologist Brenda Bredemeier.[87] Yet when games and practices conclude, relationships are not "normalized" in any sense women would consider normal. Many male athletes remain not only violent but sexually violent.

• • •

The derogatory use of the phrase "fuck you" reflects prevalent male thinking about sex: the person getting "fucked" is seen as inferior. To insert one's penis into another's orifice, or to threaten to, is to put that other person, whether male or female, in a one-down position. To "get fucked" is to lose status.[88]

The taunt "suck my dick" is also revealing. If a man were to close his eyes (or, as in the film *The Crying Game,* be fooled by makeup and dress), he would not be able to discern whether the person "sucking his dick" were male or female. But for a man to say "suck my dick" to another man is to insult him, because it puts him in the subservient role men have designated female.

Just six months after the infamous 1991 Tailhook convention, a group of Navy fighter pilots performed an obscene skit pillorying Congresswoman Patricia Schroeder. Schroeder was unpopular because she had proposed legislation that would give women access to combat assignments. In the skit, performed at a social gathering attended by five senior officers, the men "invited Schroeder to perform oral sex in a rhyming song that began with, 'Hickory Dickory Dock,' " according to news reports. The officers were eventually fired.

Author John Stoltenberg has a theory about the prevalent association between male arousal and dominance. Erections, he notes, happen to adolescent boys for no apparent reason. "Among the events or experiences that boys report as being associated with erections are accidents, anger, being scared, being in danger, big fires, fast bicycle riding, fast sled riding, hearing a gunshot, playing or watching exciting games, boxing and wrestling, fear of punishment, being called on to recite in class, and so on." Erections also occur in response to touch. But the ones associated with fear or danger "can be so distracting and disconcerting that they trigger even more panic and anxiety, which in turn can make detumescence quite impossible." So the young man eventually learns to "reproduce the erectile result of feeling threat, terror, and danger as a child simply by being threatening, terrifying, and dangerous to his chosen sex object. It works even better now, because he is in control. . . . The more dread he produces, the more 'desire' he can feel." [89]

Sexual dominance, Stoltenberg says, is what men do in order to feel manly.

Real men are aggressive in sex. Real men get cruel in sex. Real men use their penises like weapons in sex. Real men leave bruises. Real men think it's a turn-on to threaten to harm. A brutish push can make an erection feel really hard. That kind of sex makes you feel like someone who is powerful and it turns the other person into someone powerless. That kind of sex makes you feel dangerous and in control—like you're fighting a war with an enemy and if you're mean enough you'll win but if you let up you'll lose your manhood. It's a kind of sex men have in order to have a manhood.

Stoltenberg's book is called *Refusing to Be a Man.* [90]

Perhaps rape is "a violent repudiation of the female," says Joyce Carol Oates. "The supreme macho gesture—like knocking out an opponent and standing over his fallen body, gloves raised in triumph." [91]

• • •

In the manly sporting arena, misogyny and homophobia allow team members to feel close. Group rape cements that bond. Men brag about "gang bangs" and joke about "pulling train," a euphemism for gang rape; the men line up like train cars to take turns having intercourse with (or, rather, doing intercourse to) the woman. Peggy Reeves Sanday writes in *Fraternity Gang Rape,* "Cross-cultural research demonstrates that whenever men build and give allegiance to a mystical, enduring, all-male social group, the disparagement of women is, invariably, an important ingredient of the mystical bond, and sexual aggression the means by which the bond is renewed."[92]

When interviewed, rapists list these rewards of gang rape: recreation and adventure; competition and camaraderie; rapport, friendship, and cooperation.[93] Sounds fun, doesn't it? Sex, aggression, and male bonding all at once—what could be more exciting? Sanday calls gang rape "a no-holds-barred orgy of togetherness." Afterward, Sanday says, "The woman whose body facilitates all this is sloughed off . . . like a used condom."[94]

An additional motive, especially for college-aged men, "is simply the opportunity to have heterosexual intercourse," notes Chris O'Sullivan, author of the forthcoming *Nice Boys, Dirty Deeds: Gang Rape on Campus.*[95] Here that line between rape and sex again dissolves. Few women would define "heterosexual intercourse" as forced sex, yet some men seem to. Rape is an act of violence, Susan Brownmiller insisted in *Against Our Will,* and feminists have been echoing ever since. True. But it's also a sex act, both from the perspective of raped women, who experience being sexually, not just personally violated, and from the point of view of rapists. In psychologist Neil Malamuth's famous 1981 survey of U.S. and Canadian college men, one in three said they would be at least "somewhat likely" to rape a woman if they could get away with it.[96] This may indicate anger and aggression toward women, but it may also indicate that many men think of rape as one way to get sex. "We're a bunch of guys that are—I mean, better than decent-looking," said one member of the Spur Posse. "We don't have to go raping girls." [97]

Former Oklahoma football player Bernard Hall, one of the few athletes serving prison time for rape, was asked during his trial whether he did or did not rape the woman. "I certainly did not," he replied. "She is not my type."[98]

Gang rape provides the additional challenge of a public performance. Like most spectator sports, group sexual assault is conceived by and executed for the pleasure of men. "The woman is incidental," says Bernice Sandler of the Center for Women Policy Studies. "The men are raping for each other. They are showing off for their buddies, and there's a tremendous fear of losing their buddies if they don't go along."

Former Washington Redskin Sam Hamilton explains the thinking of his former football comrades: "Hey, I have no problem sharing women with my teammates. These guys go to battle with me."

So Otis asks Melody to meet him at the door, yanks her inside, then offers her to his friends, according to her testimony. If you won't have sex with me, he seems to tell her, I'll make you have sex with my friends. Three objectives achieved at once: He has retaliated for her hurting his feelings, he has asserted his masculinity, and he has offered his friends a gift.

· · ·

There are few documented cases of a man confronting other men once a gang rape begins. All men may not participate, but they rarely intervene.

One former college athlete who asked not to be identified recalls with regret a gang rape committed by his fraternity brothers, and the fact that he did nothing to stop it. The woman had agreed to sex with one man, and another dozen or so were surreptitiously planning to rape her as soon as the first was finished. A friend knocked on the athlete's door late at night and said, "So and so's pulling train. Come on over." Feeling loyal to his own girlfriend, the man declined. The next day he learned that two of the men had impaled the woman with a wine bottle and a pool stick.

One of the men who apparently participated is now a university athletic director. "I'm not sure exactly what he did—I wasn't there," says my source. "But he bears some responsibility if he was there. Even I bear some responsibility. I just went back to sleep. I wasn't interested in putting on a display for the other guys. That's what I think it is. It's the same with sexual videos. They're never just of women. The guys get off on each other."

"The peer pressure is very strong," notes Bernice Sandler. "I know men—good men—who will speak out at the first sign of racism. But when something sexist happens, there's complete silence. The fear of ridicule by other men is great. It takes great courage on the part of one man to stop gang rape."

Sam Hamilton does recall intervening in attempted rapes. At pro football parties, it would be clear that a woman was "about to be taken advantage of," Hamilton says, so he would say to the offending man, "Hey, back off." Responses varied "anywhere from fights to 'OK.'"

But Hamilton added thoughtfully: "I will tell you that in each case I've done that it's been some other athlete from a visiting team, as opposed to my teammate. I've never thought of this until we're having this conversation, but I don't know whether I was protecting my territory or protecting the individual."

So even the act of trying to prevent rape—a rare occurrence—might be motivated by male bonding, male posturing, male competition: a message from one man to another not about justice but about turf. Lay off her. She's ours.

• • •

When men rape in a group, they are performing sexual acts *on* or *in* a woman, but, experts agree, *for* each other. It's a male competition with male spectators.

But are they also performing sex *with* each other? Are they, as the college athlete surmised, also "getting off on each other"? Is gang rape a homosexual or bisexual act? Expert opinions diverge. Peggy Reeves Sanday says yes. The rapists "delude themselves as to the real object of their lust," writes Sanday. "If they were to admit to the real object, they would give up their position in the male status hierarchy as superior, heterosexual males."[99]

Author Brian Pronger agrees, saying: "If they could just give each other blow jobs they wouldn't have to rape."

But psychologist and rape expert Chris O'Sullivan disputes that theory. "It's showing off for each other. They're proving they're heterosexual, proving they're tough, proving they can exploit somebody."

In *Men Who Rape,* A. Nicholas Groth and H. Jean Birnbaum compare gang rape to group robbery or hunting: the men do not secretly want to rob or kill each other.[100] But if we think not about secret wishes but about their actions, we notice that gang rapists *are* having sex "with" each other. A woman is present (though she is often drunk to the point of unconsciousness), but these men do not look away when their peers get erections. They get aroused together. They may not touch each other, but they look. It's like a gay men's or adolescent boys' "circle jerk," except there is a woman involved to offer heterosexual legitimacy.

• • •

Why do sportsmen rape?

"As an athlete," says Hamilton, "you think you're entitled. You think, there's no reason anyone would reject me. Whatever I want, I should get." By the time he arrives at college, the manly athlete has gotten a lot. Respected community elders—coaches—have begged him to attend particular schools, camps, and universities. He has been given transportation, meal money, scholarships, sometimes under-the-table money, sneakers, wristbands, socks, uniforms, towels, soap, lockers. He has received adulation and perhaps fan mail. He has received rewards—trophies, plaques, his name in the newspaper.

He has broken lots of rules—holding, grabbing, kicking, elbowing—that are considered "part of the game." He has rarely, if ever, been punished. He has rarely, if ever, had to apologize for making mistakes, or for hurting others through aggressive acts. In fact, he has been rewarded for aggression, ridiculed for gentleness.

Hamilton likens pro football players' parties to "certain streets you don't walk down without knowing that you have to protect yourself." He likens athlete sexual behavior to a game with established but hazardous rules. "We're very freewheeling. It's clear that this is the way we behave. If you come around you're subject to the rules of that game." When women refuse to provide the sex the men feel entitled to, "it's likely to get a little rough at times."

Entitlement is a curious concept. Manly athletes have been pampered, adored, given money, cars, and even, as if slavery were still legal, women. Therefore, some feel entitled to take sex, even from women who do not offer it.

From a female perspective, this makes no sense. No matter how privileged she may be, and no matter how many gifts she may receive, a woman is unlikely to feel entitled to demand sex from an unwilling partner, or to force her sexual will upon another person.

That's because women can't rape, some would argue. But women could rape. You don't need a penis. Fingers, candlesticks, mini-baseball bats, and even crucifixes can be rammed into human orifices, as men have demonstrated. If women wanted to, they could rape. They could do it in groups. They could call it group sex.

Only certain men feel "entitled" to hurt others. Do they even think about others? How could the three college basketball players rape a "fellow" player, an athlete who ran and sweated on the same courts as they did?

Male runners, Kathrine Switzer points out, rarely rape female runners. Perhaps, she conjectures, it has to do with their understanding of what it takes to run; by running—especially alongside women—they gain an appreciation and compassion for all beings who run, and that appreciation translates to respect for women in general. Perhaps, like runners, swimmers and golfers and tennis players get accustomed to thinking of women as peers, as sister athletes. Coed sporting environments, like other coed environments, do seem to attenuate male aggression. At the University of Kentucky, the men's basketball staff includes Bernadette Locke-Maddox, the only female assistant men's college basketball coach in the country. Head coach Rick Pitino says, "Having a female in the locker room, in the huddles, gives a more dignified huddle, a more dignified locker room. Your language is much better. Bernadette is someone we all respect a great deal." [101]

But most male basketball players see, on the court, neither female leaders nor female peers. Male basketball players rarely train or compete with women. Male players are pampered, praised, and remunerated in ways no female basketball players (or male runners or swimmers) could match. At the university level, male basketball players receive more and higher paid coaches, a better travel schedule, more fans, and much more media attention than their female peers.

"Do you have a good women's basketball program at your university?" I asked Melody, the woman who accused the three basketball players of raping her.

"Oh yes," she said.

"How does it compare to the men's?" I asked.

She laughed. "Oh, well, compared to the men's—it doesn't," she said. "You know how it goes. The men have better everything."

The women male players hear about are the "cunts" and "pussies" of locker room humor; the short-skirted cheerleaders, the university "hostesses" who escort the men around campus during the recruiting process. Despite evidence to the contrary, basketball is equated with manliness. Women—even female players—become nonpeers, nonteammates, noncomrades. Even nonpeople.

The prosecutor of the three college basketball players said of the men, "I don't think they looked at it as hurting somebody. I don't think they thought of her at all."

• • •

The manly athlete becomes accustomed to having his offenses ignored. Society acts as a personal maid, following along behind him, cleaning up. Can't meet the acceptance requirements for college? No problem. We'll admit you anyway. Bad grades in college? Don't worry—we'll change them, or at least provide free tutoring. Parking ticket? We'll take care of it. Drug abuse? Help us win games and we'll look the other way.

The manly athlete knows right from wrong, but after a while such distinctions don't concern him. On the playing field, cheating isn't cheating if the referees don't see, and off the field the same rule seems to apply. Even when "referees" do see—when a player is caught using drugs, or accepting illegal payments, or breaking the law—these infractions can be overlooked.

In 1991, a thirty-seven-year-old woman accused University of Arkansas basketball star Todd Day and three of his teammates of raping her. After investigating, the university's judicial review board barred the men from basketball for a year, concluding that they'd exhibited "degrading and demeaning behavior." Yet the university president, Alan Sugg, unilaterally ruled that the woman had participated of her own will and suspended the men for only one preseason tournament.[102]

The next year, Day signed a pro contract with the Milwaukee Bucks.

A Syracuse University football player pleaded guilty to sexual misconduct for forcing a woman to have intercourse. He was sentenced to three years' probation and community service. However, a university review board ruled that he had not violated any school rules so he remained in school, retained his scholarship, and kept playing football.[103]

At Arizona State University (ASU), Jamal Faulkner was convicted of fraudulent use of a telephone credit card. He then failed to perform any of his court-ordered community service and missed numerous appointments with his probation officer. The judge told Faulkner, "It does appear throughout these proceedings that your status as a student-athlete has somehow given you the impression that you can take a casual attitude . . . toward both compliance with the law and the conditions of your probation."[104]

The presence of his coach must have contributed to that impression. Bill Frieder, who testified on Faulkner's behalf, said, "Jamal is in good standing with me. I'm not going to criticize the court system, but I still stand by Jamal." Frieder did not revoke Faulkner's basketball eligibility.[105]

Mike Tyson, sentenced to six years for rape and deviate sexual conduct, continues to receive support from men, including thousands who wear "Free Mike Tyson" T-shirts, currently the most popular T-shirt design in Washington, D.C. Just before Tyson's incarceration, Donald Trump proposed that Tyson be allowed to buy his way out of jail by giving millions of dollars to rape crisis centers. This way, he could still box. He might also go on to rape again, but that did not seem to concern Trump, nor the group of Indianapolis ministers who gathered 10,000 signatures in a petition drive to seek a suspended sentence for Tyson.

The Federal Bureau of Investigation taped six phone calls between the Reverend T. J. Jemison, head of the eight-million-member National Baptist Convention USA, and Desiree Washington's father, Donald. Jemison allegedly offered Donald Washington $1 million to persuade his daughter to drop the rape charges against Tyson. Jemison admits talking to Washington about keeping the case out of court but denies offering money. He awaits trial.[106]

If a black woman accuses a white man of rape, *Ms.* editor Marcia Ann Gillespie notes, the black male community supports the woman and excoriates the man. But the woman "who dares to speak about and hold black men accountable for the everyday acts of incest, battery, rape, domestic violence, and sexual harassment risks becoming a pariah."[107]

Pearl Cleage, author of *Deals with the Devil and Other Reasons to Riot,* notes, "Sexism is still not a word that gets used much in the black community, even though it describes a form of oppression that affects the majority population of the community—women!—and is no less virulent and deadly than racism."[108]

But are black male athletes unfairly or disproportionately accused or convicted of sex crimes? Of the few athletes in jail for rape, most are black. This might be because most pro boxers, basketball players, and football players are black. But the overall prison population is disproportionately black. Given the racist history of this country, it's reasonable to be suspicious when black men go to jail for crimes that white men commit with impunity. Yet in the case of athletes, the problem is not that too many African-American men are being convicted of rape. It's that too few men of any national origin are.

The high school boys convicted of raping the mentally handicapped girl with a broomstick and a baseball bat were all white. Their lawyer said, "The whole country is obsessed with sex. You bring them up that way, and then . . . you call them criminals? Boys will be boys."[109]

Psychiatrist Daniel Begel tells the story of how the "compulsive seductivity" of a recently retired pro baseball player, a married man, was condoned by his male community. One evening, Begel writes, this man "went with some old friends to a nightclub, where his presence was announced from the stage. From his seat he fastened a hard, predatory stare on a woman sitting at a neighboring table with her male companion." After the man stared at the woman for some time, the woman's "boyfriend rose from his chair to approach the athlete's table. Instead of the challenge that the whole gathering expected, the boyfriend asked for the athlete's autograph and shook his hand. Afterward the athlete explained his practice of compulsive seductivity as something he learned in professional baseball. The sanctioning of this behavior in the nightclub repeated a pattern that occurred many times over, in various ways, during his career." [110]

The three male basketball players accused of raping the female basketball player admitted in court that their behavior that night included indecent exposure, voyeurism, illegal drinking, and the breaking of two dormitory rules (no women in the dorm past curfew and mandatory attendance at a dorm meeting). They admitted a penchant for pornography. One player had been declared ineligible to play on the team that year due to failing grades. The other two had not yet graduated after four years of college.

Yet a juror afterward characterized the men as "pretty good kids." Despite the defendants' admissions of various broken rules and misdemeanors, and despite their admission of three-on-one "group sex": pretty good kids. She added, "The guys stuck to their story. They would. Guys do that." She smiled.

A local radio announcer trivialized the rape charges, using the phrase, "alleged hanky-panky."

A student, noting that the men accused of rape in this case were African-American, defended them as "an endangered species." Apparently seeing me as a representative of the white media, she asked, "Why don't you focus on some good things black people are doing? You're just trying to bring them down."

I reminded her that the young woman involved was also African-American. Did she extend her concern for African-Americans to the woman?

"No," she said. "I'm not a feminist."

Rape prevention expert Claire Walsh calls this community-support phenomenon "ring around the rapist." She hears people say, " 'It cannot be true. He's such a sweet guy. An upstanding citizen.' The flip side is that there's an annihilation of the accuser. Character assassination occurs."

Universities join in, prioritizing their own reputations over the safety of their female students. Congress recently passed an act mandating the reporting of campus crimes, but "administrators are going to twist every which way to redefine or discourage reporting so their universities will look great," predicts Walsh.

Administrative hearings serve as another layer of protection for college rapists. Victims are often offered on-campus hearings conducted by "judicial review boards" composed of faculty members who have no expertise in rape or legal affairs. If this board finds the woman's claims groundless, she is discouraged from reporting the incident to the police.

"It's ludicrous to assume that if a student is murdered by another student that the university would handle the investigation," notes author Robin Warshaw, "and yet they see it as totally appropriate with rape." [111]

In the spring of 1992, a coach at a major midwestern university attempted to rape a female field hockey player in her friend's dorm room. She was a 5'1", 120-pound first-year student; he was a 6'3", 260-pound, 36-year-old former college and professional football player. The young woman considered him a friend, as did her teammates, who invited him to their party. But he stayed after everyone else left, and despite her protests he pinned her on the bed, began to remove her pants, and fondled her breasts. Three of her male friends then arrived unexpectedly and interrupted the assault.

Afterward, she decided not to report the incident to police because others "might think that's betraying the community of athletes," she said. "Being a freshman, I'm not sure I have the right to cause trouble. Maybe they wouldn't believe me, would take his side. He might deny it. So I decided to work within the family."

"The family"—a representative of the athletic department—listened to the woman's story then blamed her for letting the man, who was drunk, into the apartment in the first place.

The man resigned quietly.

A filmmaker, the daughter of a pro football coach, was fifteen when sexually assaulted by a professional hockey player. She escaped, but felt responsible. "I thought, he just got cut from the team and must be in pain," she recalls. "I thought I must have done something to ask for this. I was so naive."

At the trial of the three basketball players, the athletic director, in a typical move that violated both the First Amendment and the concept of college as a center for intellectual debate, asked all students not to discuss the case. Many students complied, appearing fearful of disobeying orders.

After the trial I spoke with the "team mother," a woman in her fifties who said her volunteer job was to "create a home-away-from-home atmosphere" for the university's athletes. Throughout the trial she provided hugs and other obvious forms of support to the men and their families. She avoided Melody. Upon the reading of the verdicts, she was jubilant.

"Which teams do you work with?" I asked her.

"Football, basketball, baseball," she said.

"Oh," I said. "Only the men?"

"No, the women too," she added quickly.

"Well, you were sitting with the families of the men," I noted. "Melody's a basketball player, too."

"I have more contact with the men," she admitted. "Melody stood off by herself. She was an introvert. But they're all my children. I love them all."

. . .

Coaches used to forbid athletes to have sex the night before games. Sex dulls men's aggression, some said; it softens them, melts them, makes them mushy, romantic, cuddly. Others said sexual energy should not be wasted on women when it could be put to better use in The Game.

Maybe "regular" sex as practiced by many men is not a *distraction from* aggression but a *form of* aggression. Mike Tyson, before a boxing match, used to taunt his opponents with this telling threat: "I'll make you my girlfriend." [112] Making someone his girlfriend and beating/humiliating them were synonymous. He was threatening to fuck them/fuck them over. In his autobiography, Tyson said he likes to make women bleed; he later denied it, claiming not to have read his own book. His former wife, Robin Givens, told Barbara Walters that life with him was "pure hell."

Catharine MacKinnon writes:

Crime is supposed to be deviant, not normal. We get very low convictions

*for rape. We also get many women who believe they have never been raped,
although a lot of force was involved. They mean that they were not raped
in a way that is legally provable. In other words, in all these situations,
there was not* enough *violence against them to take it beyond the category
of 'sex'; they were not coerced enough.*[113]

I'm reminded of Jane Wagner's play *The Search for Signs of Intelligent
Life in the Universe* in which Lily Tomlin, as Trudy the bag lady, tries to
explain to her space chums the difference between Andy Warhol's paint-
ing of a Campbell's soup can and the can itself. "This is soup and this is
art. Art. Soup. Soup. Art." It gets confusing.

Three men say group sex. One woman says gang rape. This is sex and
this is rape. Rape. Sex. Sex. Rape. It gets confusing.

MacKinnon notes, "Finders of fact look for 'more force than usual
during the preliminaries.' "[114]

A lawyer for the three college basketball players said, "Her hair was
not messed up. Her clothes were not in disarray. There were no bruises,
lacerations, or contusions in her private area. She wasn't even crying!"
Therefore, they implied, no harm was done.

Unwanted sex does not necessarily cause bruises, unless the men also
beat the woman. When there are three men, there is no need to use fists
to obtain compliance. When attached to three large basketball players,
three erect penises provide sufficient intimidation so the woman usually
does not fight back. Penises, even when used as battering rams, rarely
leave bruises.

Melody "laid back and did it," the three basketball players claimed.
But even according to their account, did Melody "have sex"? Or did she
just have sex done to her? If this was "group sex," which members of the
four-person group defined the sexual experience? By their own account,
the men made no attempt to please her, to arouse her, or to bring her
to orgasm; not even to act affectionate. Even by their own account, she
got fucked.

Where did these men get the idea that a woman would enjoy having
intercourse, and fondling two men, without having her own body ca-
ressed?

"A classic male fantasy," said the (male) detective who investigated
the case.

This male fantasy is now showing at a theater (and bookstore, magazine rack, and video rental) near you in various forms of pornography. Madonna's photo book, *Sex,* offers one sports-related example of the ubiquitous rape-as-sex mythology. Shot from above, a photo shows Madonna dressed as a schoolgirl, pinned by two boys to the gym floor under a basketball net. Is it rape or is it sex?

Despite the prevalence of violent pornography, most college men have been exposed to at least rudimentary information about real women's sexuality. They should know, for instance, that for most women, intercourse is not the best part of sex. They should know that most women do not have orgasms that way, and that women crave breast and clitoral stimulation, as well as whole-body touching and hugging.

Let's consider the possibility that Melody did walk into the men's dorm, lie down and say, in essence, "climb aboard." Victims of childhood sexual abuse, naive about danger and tending to confuse sex with love, sometimes develop a pattern of being sexually abused. Repetition compulsion, therapists call it. They tend not to know how to get out of harmful situations; they tend not to cry out for help.

What would have been a responsible mature response? If men see a vagina, are they entitled to shove their penises into it? Is this what pretty good kids do?

I found two of the defendants sitting on a bench during a recess in the trial. I asked, "Did she enjoy it? Did she have an orgasm?" They squirmed. They looked down. They were silent.

Moments earlier, I had asked them about career goals, and they couldn't come up with any. "Be a free man," said Paul.

Otis agreed. "Free man."

I saw how frightened they were, how shocked, shaken, scared-to-the-bone terrified, how young. They never expected Melody to tell anyone. They never expected to be tried for rape.

They never, it appears, thought about Melody. Otis answered, "She didn't act like she didn't enjoy it." Paul said nothing.

Where did they get the idea that women like to get fucked? James' reference to porn star John Holmes may provide a clue. Pornography promotes the myth that women are willing receptacles for male sexuality and aggression. Porn promotes the myth that women enjoy gang rape. It appropriates lesbian images for male excitement. James made derogatory remarks about Melody's supposed bisexuality and told her, "You need a real man." James also exposed himself, then decided that Melody must want sex with him. This bizarre belief is also likely derived from porn: women who see naked men want to have sex with them. This is called a projection. It's men—mostly young men—who support the porn industry's images of naked women in order to become sexually aroused.[115] In a survey of thirty-two college campuses, men who admitted rape also tended to rate "very frequently" their reading of *Playboy, Penthouse, Chic, Club, Forum, Gallery, Genesis, Oui,* or *Hustler* magazines.[116] In another study, massive exposure to pornography was associated with a loss of compassion toward women as rape victims and toward women in general.[117] A federally funded study by former Surgeon General C. Everett Koop concluded that "exposure to violent pornography increases punitive behavior toward women," at least in the short term.[118]

Exposure to violent sports seems to have a related effect. Researcher Leonard Berkowitz conducted sports fan experiments using a technique from the famous Stanley Milgram experiments in which students are pressured to administer shock to another person (that person does not actually receive a shock). Berkowitz's results: "Subjects who observe films about violent sports are more willing to administer a high level of electric shock than subjects who see another sort of film [such as a travelogue]."[119]

An analysis of all U.S. heavyweight prizefights between 1973 and 1978 revealed that homicides increased by 12.5 percent directly after the bouts. After heavily publicized fights, the increase was even higher.[120]

In *Pornography and Silence,* Susan Griffin writes that watching pornography helps men to silence vulnerability in themselves, to quiet their own dread of being victimized. Perhaps watching—or participating in—sports serves the same function.

Maybe the question is not why so many sportsmen rape, but why more of them don't.

Or do they? An estimated 84 percent of rapes go unreported.[121]

• • •

As reports of male athlete rape proliferate, dozens of colleges are trying to dissuade athletes from raping women. The University of California, Berkeley, has offered rape prevention programs to its football players at least twice, though the timing is sadly ironic: once before the alleged rape of a woman by five football players in 1986 (the men said she wanted it and were never brought to trial), and once between that incident and the 1993 case in which two football players allegedly raped, robbed, and beat a woman (they also said she wanted it; the case is pending).

The University of New Hampshire is also having trouble getting the message across. During a rape awareness session for nearly seven hundred athletes, students performed a skit about date rape. Audience members laughed, joked, and engaged in behavior that was "offensive and disruptive," according to Dan DiBiasio, interim vice-president for student affairs, who wrote a six-page letter to every student on campus and to all students' parents, criticizing the athletes, detailing sexual assaults reported, and describing a new program for training athletes.[122]

More successful programs include one at the University of Maine, which has a program called "Athletes for Sexual Responsibility." Skits and discussions communicate messages about date rape, but athletes serve as teachers, not students. By training athletes to teach other students, this program acknowledges the leadership role of athletes and intimately involves them in the lessons, which emphasize dissociating masculinity from dominance, violence, and sexism.

Mandatory participation and male leadership seem to be key. When I recently gave a talk on this subject at a major university, female athletes filled almost all of the seats; few men chose to attend.

Former football player and self-described pro-feminist Jackson Katz seems successful using a gentle approach with male college athletes. In his work with the Center for the Study of Sport in Society, he trains athletes as peer educators on sexual harassment and all forms of men's violence against women. "I don't say, you're a bunch of rapists, and your culture trains you to rape women," he reports. "I ask how many have a sister or a girlfriend, and they all raise their hands. I talk about the level of terror women experience. I tell them it takes more courage to speak out against sexism than it does to play football. If you hit someone on the field, everyone cheers. If you hear a rape joke, and you say that's not funny, you'll be ridiculed. So it takes even more inner courage, but you know it's the right thing to do."

· · ·

The university attended by the three male basketball players publishes a student handbook. It specifies that students who exhibit lewd behavior (presumably including genital exposure) can be suspended. Students "discovered in a state of undress or sleeping in residence hall rooms of members of the opposite sex" can be suspended. Curfew violations result in suspensions from the residence halls. Students who permit illegal visits are subject to penalties.

Yet neither the athletic department nor the university imposed any penalties on the men. The autumn after the summer rape trial, Otis continued playing on the basketball team. James and Paul did not, but only because they had already completed their four years of eligibility. All three remained students at the university. All three continued to live in the dormitory.

Melody relinquished her athletic scholarship and transferred to a small community college.

8

My Coach Says He Loves Me

"This doesn't feel right," says the young marathon swimmer in Jenifer Levin's novel Water Dancer. She is in bed for the first time with her coach. "I'm afraid," she says.

"Want to?" he asks.

"Yes." She hesitates. "How come it's not easy?"

IN THE summer of 1991, an Oregon State University volleyball player borrowed her teammate's car. In the glove compartment she discovered a series of amorous letters that their coach, Guy Enriques, had sent to the teammate.

She took the letters and shared them with other women on the team, who read them with great interest and considerable anger. They had suspected an affair between the coach and the player. The recipient of the letters had spent time alone with the coach in his hotel room during road trips. The two of them had engaged in what appeared to be intimate conversations. "We just saw it," recalls Kristy Wing, a senior on the team. "But we never had proof." Players had even confronted Enriques, who is married and a father. But "he'd always twist it around. He'd get personal, to make you see it was your fault for asking." The players had complained to the athletic director, but he had said he could do nothing since there was no proof.

Now they had proof. They turned the letters over to the athletic department, expecting Enriques to be fired. Instead, they were told that since the letters were stolen property, nothing could be done.

The women decided to take matters into their own hands. Eight players confronted the coach and asked him to resign. This time, according to the players, Enriques admitted the affair and defended it, explaining that it was "a real relationship" between himself and the player. "They weren't just seeing each other occasionally; they really cared about each other," one player remembers him saying. The next day, Enriques resigned.

Shortly afterward, Enriques commented, "There has been some success at Oregon State and some hurt. I'd like to bury that hurt." In response to the question of whether he did have sex with the player, Enriques said, "Those are personal things and I'd like to keep it down and under."

The young woman did not deny the affair, but asked not to be named. "I don't think it's a negative issue for me," she said. "There are negative sides to it, but a coach-athlete relationship is not necessarily negative."

· · ·

Big men make a big impression on young women. A big man—that is, a man with power—who pays attention to a young woman, and who confers approval upon her, delivers in effect a message from the patriarchy itself: you are OK. Despite all the sexist remarks you have heard, despite the degrading, trivializing, misogynist photographs and movies you have seen, despite the myriad ways this culture has taught you to hate yourself because you are female, I am here to tell you: you are OK.

When the young woman is an athlete and the big man her coach; when she has physical goals that extend beyond beauty and toward strength; when she is more fascinated by her own bulging muscles than by those of her male peers; when indeed she loves sports and her own athleticism with a passion she can barely contain, an older man's approval means everything. It confirms her rejection of traditional feminine passivity, and what Naomi Wolf calls the beauty myth. It confirms her sexual attractiveness. It confirms her desire for power, her right to it.

The coach and the athlete may spend thirty hours a week together. That's more time than an adolescent will spend with any teacher, friend, or, usually, parent. During this time, the coach scrutinizes the athlete's body: the shape of it, the speed of it, the skill of it. If, as a swimmer, she wears a new suit, he notices its cut, calculating its drag in the water. If, as a gymnast, she starts to fall, he catches her. If, as a runner, she develops a cramp, he may massage her foot, calf, or thigh. If her weight goes from 123 to 126, he will notice, and may ask her to lose three pounds.

When she makes a mistake he might scream at her: "What the hell were you thinking about?" When she succeeds he might offer praise. Or he might withhold praise. Before a competition he might say, "You can do it." Or he might say, "Do it for me." If he is a control freak, as many coaches seem to be, she will be the puppet, he the puppeteer.

The young woman's gratitude for the man's attention and encouragement is often conceptualized in the only paradigm the culture has given her: A Huge Crush. She adores this man—her coach, teacher, and mentor. She admires his every move. She endeavors to please him, because pleasing him, she hopes, will lead to success in her chosen field of dreams. To please him is to acquire for herself patriarchal approval, assurance that her strong body and strong ambitions really are OK. She yearns to bring him close to her. The closer she can bring him, the more powerful and privileged she will feel.

If the coach has learned to respect women—even young women—as human beings with goals and desires that go beyond him (though they may be inspired by him), he will ignore the young woman's crush. He will continue to nurture her physical, social, and emotional development. His admiration of her young beauty will remain private, irrelevant to the task of coaching. Her crush will subside, and she will develop an enduring appreciation and respect for her mentor.

If, on the other hand, he believes he has a right to women as playthings, as ego enhancers, he will interpret the fondness and excitement between them as irresistible sexual attraction or romantic love. He will rationalize that she is a consenting adult, or at least mature for her age. He will find support for this view from his peers, many of whom have also seduced young athletes or even married them. He will also find a willingness among his peers to look the other way.

In the Oregon State case, Guy Enriques was allowed to resign "for personal reasons." Athletic director Dutch Baughman told the team not to talk about the incident to the media, three players reported. "The athletic director said, 'Be smart about this. Some things are private. It's a small affair, don't blow it out of proportion. What is personal should remain personal,' " recalls setter Kristy Wing. If the players had agreed not to talk, the incident would not have become public.[1]

Baughman countered, "All I've asked the players is to respect the wishes of the individual. I asked them not to make comments that might imply specific situations or a circumstance that could eventually be inaccurate or irresponsible. Please understand that this is a very delicate issue."

Intimacy between coaches and athletes is indeed a delicate issue. Athletic directors perceive it as delicate because the reputations of their schools are at stake. I perceive it as delicate because a woman with a male coach, like a woman with a male physician, professor, priest, lawyer, or therapist, is in a delicate position. She trusts the man to help her reach her goals. She opens herself to him. Even when she does not have a crush, she has very little power to say no to his advances. If the man seduces the woman, or tries to, or seduces her teammates, or tries to, he betrays her trust, taking advantage of her vulnerability. He deprives her of the one thing she needed (but perhaps did not realize she needed) from this teacher and mentor: nonsexual affection and respect. Since a girl in this culture has already, by the time she has reached puberty, experienced the discomfort of being talked about, treated, or touched as a sex object, the real Prince Charming is not the coach who kisses her but the coach who refrains from kissing her, from fondling her, from making sexual comments about her body.

• • •

Most coaches are men. Among women's sports teams, more than half of all high school and college coaches are men. Most youth soccer and Little League coaches are men. This is the legacy from Title IX: female athletes now get to play, but they play under male leadership.

There is no national certification process for coaches. Often, coaches receive no supervision. Anyone can coach. A coach may have no training in psychology or ethics. He may know nothing about power: how it can be used and abused. He may know nothing about women, his only athletic training stemming from his own participation. He may care nothing for women, his training in male-female relations deeply rooted in the manly sports system.

As an athlete, he may have been a star. Praised for his athletic prowess and indoctrinated in misogyny, he may feel entitled to sexual access to women.

If not a star, he may suffer from feelings of failure and emasculation. Remember: men who fail at sports are "wimps," "wusses," "pussies," "girls." A reject from the manly sports system may feel a need to prove his masculinity to himself. One way to prove masculinity is to "score" with attractive young women.

Many men who coach women do so because they cannot obtain the prestige jobs: coaching men. Thus their masculinity is threatened by the job itself, their stature among men tainted by their association with girls. To women's teams, many men bring a deep insecurity.

Sometimes they become obsessed with victory. Or they become obsessed with control, tyrannically commanding their athletes the way military generals command their troops, restricting how much girls eat, whom they associate with. Or this insecurity is expressed as a need to feel sexually attractive to the girls or young women on the team.

"The vast majority of men who coach women have not had the kind of confirmation of their masculinity and athletic prowess that they seek. It seems to me they're in a position psychologically to need this," says psychologist David Epperson, director of a week-long tournament for high school girls called the Nike Volleyball Festival. "How does a man prove his masculinity? By doing what men value: achieving, controlling, and proving he's attractive and competent—not impotent. We're not talking about something that's peripheral to gender identity. It's central."

The gatekeepers of female athletic success, male coaches may at some level feel threatened by that success, or by the increasing female social power it symbolizes. So while a coach may with one hand reach to help a woman free herself of sexist constraints through athletic achievement, he may with the other hand seduce her, thus effectively trapping her in a sexualized, dependent position.

John Pittington, the head women's and men's swimming coach at Northeast Louisiana University, says, "Most coaches at some time in their careers have gotten emotionally involved with a player. I wouldn't say sexually. The athletes put their trust in you. They're happy if they win, and they give you credit. If they lose, you console them. This person is doing what you want. Although (laughs) sometimes they don't do what you want. But if they succeed you succeed. When they fail you fail. It's a bond."

For a coach, the route to power is through the accomplishments of the athletes. He cannot win if they do not win. They are the sun to his moon: their light reflects back toward him. If their success makes him feel empowered or excited he may interpret that excitement, that sense of empowerment, as sexual. When svelte, limber, lithe young women bring trophies home to his club, and look at him with adoring eyes, and obey his every command, this can be arousing. It can feel like love.

All of this might be fine if it stopped there. Attractions are natural under intimate conditions. But often it doesn't stop until the coach has inserted his penis into a virginal vagina. Even then, often it doesn't stop. Some of the "best" male coaches in the country have seduced a succession of their female athletes. Like their counterparts in medicine, education, psychotherapy, and the priesthood, coaches are rarely caught or punished.

Some male coaches are openly flirtatious with all of their players. More often, an insecure male coach will select one young woman at a time and attempt to seduce her. Struggling with their own needs to feel attractive and loved, girls often comply.

The Boy Scouts of America have in recent years confronted and ousted pedophiles in their midst—ninety per year between 1971 and 1991, according to Scout documents. The Catholic Church has established a treatment center for priests who are recovering sex offenders. But among members of the coaching fraternity there seems to be no consensus that pedophilia—as long as it's heterosexual—is wrong. "I talk with coaches about this, and they don't like the idea of being constrained because they think they should have that opportunity to fall in love with their athletes," reports Todd Crosset, a former college swimming coach and assistant professor of sport studies at the University of Massachusetts. "That's because we've sexualized little girls. We've eroticized domination. So it's seen as normal."

What do these men tell themselves? That it's love. That it doesn't matter. That it's OK. "I never thought of you as a teenager," the coach who molested me told me recently. I was fourteen, fifteen, and sixteen.

When is a teenager not a teenager? When you're having sex with her.

• • •

We don't know how many coaches seduce their young charges. We do know that sexual seductions by priests, teachers, physicians, and therapists are prevalent, according to frequent newspaper reports and Peter Rutter's groundbreaking book, *Sex in the Forbidden Zone*.[2] Among psychologists, 9.4 percent of men and 2.5 percent of women admit having had sex with a patient.[3] Surely more commit than admit to these behaviors.

Teacher-student liaisons are also common. Between 20 and 30 percent of female college students have been approached sexually by their professors, numerous studies have concluded. One study revealed that 17 percent of female graduate students in psychology had become intimate with a professor during their training, and that another 30 percent had turned down unwelcome advances.[4]

One of the few studies regarding coaches comes from Donald Lackey, the chair of the physical education department at the University of Nebraska at Kearney. Alarmed by frequent reports of coach-athlete relationships, Lackey sent questionnaires to recently graduated high school athletes. Of the 264 who responded, ten reported knowing of a male coach who had had intercourse with an athlete. Two others knew of a coach-athlete rape. Sixteen others told of male coaches being disciplined, fired, or forced to resign for sexually harassing an athlete. Lackey believes these numbers underestimate the problem at the high school level because of girls' reluctance to report. "The girls are afraid people may not believe them, and some think they're partly at fault," he says.[5]

A landmark Supreme Court decision recently expanded the protection of such victims, ruling in a February 1992 Title IX case that a Georgia high school student who had been seduced by her teacher was allowed to sue for monetary damages. The teacher was a coach at her school.

Based on that ruling, more suits are expected. Plenty of women will have the opportunity. Donna Lopiano, for seventeen years the director of women's athletics at the University of Texas, believes a "significant number" of male coaches have had affairs with athletes or former athletes. While at Texas she fired one coach for seducing an athlete. Two others on her staff were married to former players. She told another top coach who applied—a man who had been fired from two jobs for sexual abuse—that she wouldn't dignify his application with an interview. "That would be like sending the fox to guard the henhouse," she told him.

Coach-athlete seductions are "very common," she says. "Especially when coaches go through their midlife crisis. They need to retain their virility and youth. We had to establish a policy: You don't have personal relationships with athletes."

Averill Haines, senior women's administrator at Boston University, has also had to establish a policy against coach-athlete sexual liaisons. She has fired coaches, including one female coach, for sexual misconduct. "I get incensed," she says. "It's one of the lowest forms of abuse."

Asked if he knows any male volleyball coaches who have had sex with or married their female athletes, Volleyball Festival organizer David Epperson lists, off the top of his head, twelve.

One swimming coach estimates that two-thirds of the male coaches he knows have been sexually involved with athletes or former athletes.

Michael Mewshaw, author of *Ladies of the Court: Grace and Disgrace on the Women's Tennis Tour,* says pro tennis is rife with stories of coaches who "made suggestive remarks, fondled girls, gave massages that weren't welcomed and had sex with players when they could get away with it." Mewshaw says, "It was a perfectly normal thing. For many of the girls, especially the mature ones, it was natural to form an intimate relationship with a coach. And of course many of the coaches who were older were eager to have such affairs, even though they could be very hurtful and destructive to the girls."[6]

Talk to anyone involved in women's sports. "Everybody knows coaches get involved with players," they'll say. Peter Rutter calls this the "everybody knows" phenomenon. Recently I met a former college athlete who had never heard of a coach having sex with an athlete. I commented that that was unusual. "Well, we did have an assistant coach who was dating one of the girls," she said. "But we didn't think anything of it."

While I was researching this book, word got around, and I received about a dozen calls from women who had been abused by coaches. Isolated, confused, and angry, most were seeking counseling. Some sought legal information. From these young women and from other sources I heard about the track coach for a Southern university who spent the night with an athlete, then, when confronted, justified this as "an all-night counseling session." Other examples include the basketball coach who demanded sexual favors in exchange for playing time; the baseball and football coach, a husband and father, who jumped off a bridge and drowned after being served with five felony warrants stemming from a sexual relationship with a sixteen-year-old male student; the soccer coach who molested his eight-year-old daughter's teammates at slumber parties; the coach who seduced an athlete from another college team at a hotel during a road trip; the coach who tried to seduce lesbian players to "straighten them out;" the swimmer who committed suicide after being molested by her coach.

One runner, seduced by her track coach in high school, moved away from home to college, only to have him pursue her and try to continue the relationship. When she refused, he beat and raped her. She reported him to her parents and to the high school (he had resigned), but not to the police because a college roommate had been raped in their house earlier that year, and the runner had had to testify, and she saw what a grueling, invasive ordeal a rape trial is.

Kim Carlisle, a former Stanford swimmer and a member of the 1980 Olympic team, recalls sexual harassment and statutory rape being pervasive problems throughout her high school and college careers. She watched one coach marry then divorce a player; that player dropped out of Stanford, never to return. Another of her Stanford coaches was asked to resign after having an affair with a swimmer. At a national championship, a coach and mentor came on to her, and Carlisle "flirted with" the idea of an affair. "It never got to be more than a kiss. He was walking me home. He was married, with a kid, late twenties or thirties. I could feel what was happening. It's really flattering. You don't want to turn it away. But I said, this just isn't right."

* * *

Why isn't it right? How come it's not easy? Why shouldn't a coach date an athlete, especially if they're both twentysomething? What better way to get to know someone than to watch her or him in a stressful, intimate setting? Athletes share with their coaches passion and pain, drama and dreams. "That's almost the definition of falling in love," says John Leonard, executive director of the American Swimming Coaches Association in Fort Lauderdale, Florida. "Any coach who tells you he hasn't fallen in love with an athlete, or had an athlete fall in love with him, is lying." [7]

Children's sports book author R. R. Knudson, a former athlete, is one of very few women who do not object to coach-athlete liaisons if the woman is over eighteen. Knudson says she's "furious about the abuse" if the girls are younger, but she's "a fool for love," she says. "It's so rare to find it, whatever it's attached to, it's better than nothing. At least they learn what some kind of love can feel like as a possibility." She knows of cases where a young runner's liaison with her coach inspired her to perform. "She ran faster. That's good. I take the position of a fan. As a fan I like to see the best."

Many male coaches defend coach-athlete liaisons. Coach John Pittington asks, "If people fall in love, and it's a proper situation, who's to say there can't be a relationship between a man and the woman he coaches?" It's "definitely wrong," he says, "if he's 45 and she's 16. That's taking advantage. I can see that." But "if the coach is 23 or 24, and the athlete is 21, or in some states 18, you're legislating against adults."

When the adults are therapist and client, or priest and parishioner, or father and daughter, sexual contact is considered unethical regardless of age. In most states, sex between a woman who is under eighteen and a man at least four years her senior is a felony. Many colleges prohibit sex between professors and students. The American Psychiatric Association, the American Psychological Association, and the American Medical Association all prohibit sex between professionals and patients. The psychiatric association recently made that a lifetime prohibition: no sex with patients or former patients, ever. Violators are subject to license revocation and court suit.

The United States Rowing Association, the national governing body for crew, recently issued a statement condemning sexual harassment, including sex between athletes and coaches. The American Swim Coaches Association recently instituted a code of ethics that prohibits "any behavior that utilizes the influence of the coaching position to encourage inappropriate intimacy between coach and athlete." But only another coach can file a complaint. An athlete has no recourse. And the code was watered down after coaches protested. The original wording had mandated a two-year waiting period after an athlete graduates or terminates the coach-athlete relationship. Now sex is permitted the day after graduation.

Coaches waver, I suspect, because they want continued access to the culture's prized possession: young women. They defend the relationships by pointing to "successful" coach-athlete marriages. They say the situation gets "tricky" when the young woman comes of age.

But like therapists, coaches are in a position of trust and power: trust because the athlete assumes the coach will act in her interests, and power by virtue of the coach's knowledge, his authority to train the athlete, his age, his gender, and sometimes his race. Of these, perhaps gender is most significant. Male dominance in women's sports reinforces the notion that men have the ultimate authority to teach sports; that men are the guardians of sport secrets. Access to these secrets, it can seem, can come only through intimate contact with the coach.

Many female athletes use their coaches as therapists, seeking help with personal problems. They use them as surrogate parents, hoping for love, guidance, and someone who will set limits. They venerate them as teachers and mentors.

One former coach I spoke with seduced one of his teenage swimmers, then married her right after she graduated from high school. He told me his story on condition of anonymity because, he said, "it's not one of the things I'm more proud of." He was twenty, she was seventeen. They dated openly. According to most statutory rape laws, this is not criminal behavior. The parents at his swim club, he said, never questioned him. But as he grew older, he began to understand that despite their close ages, he "was in a position of power and authority. What she respected in me wasn't necessarily what she got when we married and I was no longer in that position."

Eventually, he said, "You begin to see that sleeping with one of your players is a betrayal of them. You're gratifying yourself. If they're gratified, that's secondary. It was common in the swimming world. That's too bad. These girls don't get into sports for that reason."

Athletes are "looking for a father figure, someone to take care of them," he believes. "As a coach I wanted someone who would do what I told them to do. The only thing I cared about was winning."

Such parental-type authority is incompatible in a viable intimate relationship, he said, where "it's a two-way street. You expose your insecurities, and ask the person to fulfill your needs in return for what you do for them." Coach-athlete marriages fail, he said, because "women grow up. They realize they have their own lives. That's what happened to my ex-wife."

Psychologists agree that coach-athlete liaisons are unethical regardless of age. "I'm very concerned about male coaches getting involved with female athletes," says Mimi Murray, professor of sports psychology at Springfield College (Massachusetts) and coauthor, with Carole Oglesby and Hilary Mathesom, of one of the few academic papers on the subject, "Dangerous Liaisons."[8] Even if she is willing, and even if she's at least twenty-one, says Murray, "it's still immoral. It's not fair to the girl, and it's not fair to the team."

Psychiatrist Peter Rutter writes, "A man in [a] position of trust and authority becomes unavoidably a parent figure and is charged with the ethical responsibilities of the parenting role. Violations of these boundaries are, psychologically speaking, not only rapes but also acts of incest."[9]

Once thus victimized, the young woman "is likely to adapt to the victim role," writes Rutter, "repeating it in other relationships, each time losing more of her self-respect and enthusiasm for life."[10] Too afraid of the authority figures to become angry, she instead suffers from depression, fear, anxiety, shame, and overwhelming guilt.

"If you take an Uzi and threaten a fifteen-year-old to have sex or else, everyone accepts that as criminal," says a lawyer specializing in sexual assault cases, including coach-athlete abuse. "But this is a creeping, subtle, beguiling form of the same thing. You take a girl who is inexperienced and vulnerable and give her superficial acceptance. You prey upon her need for recognition that she's not a little girl anymore."

After almost fifty years of private practice, pioneer sports psychologist Bruce Ogilvie likens the coach to "a substitute father" who has "no right to intrude on young women his own unfulfilled sexual fantasies. The athlete wants a parent, but gets a lover. It's terribly confusing." It's the coach's responsibility, Ogilvie says, to "help the girl grow and make her own decisions. He must not allow sexual feelings to be expressed."

What if the man and young woman both insist it's true love? Ogilvie replies: "I hate to be a judgmental old bastard but I hold that relationship as suspect as hell."

● ● ●

Legendary among seductive coaches is Mitchell Ivey, a 1968 and 1972 Olympic backstroker who served as women's coach in all Olympiads since 1976. Noel Moran Quilici, a former nationally ranked swimmer, "fell in love" with Ivey, her coach at Santa Clara (California) Swim Club, and became sexually involved with him in the late 1970s. She was seventeen. He was twenty-nine. "It's like your knight in shining armor sweeps you off your feet," she says. "I grew up with that fairy tale. Some prince was going to take care of me. I thought, This is it, here he is."

They kept the liaison secret. During her first year at Stanford, they dated exclusively though she wanted to date other men "and get into the college life." But Ivey, she says, "made me feel sorry for him. Also he had a temper. I didn't want to upset him."

Ivey's intimate style, Quilici said, mirrored his coaching style: "He was in charge. I was not on an equal status at all." Even their wedding was his idea: he informed her in the car on the way to Reno, Nevada. She was eighteen.

Six months after their marriage, they separated. "He was seeing another swimmer," she says. "I walked in on them." Quilici dropped out of Stanford before finishing her first year, relinquishing her swimming scholarship and never returning though she had had Olympic aspirations and potential. But she continued to swim for Ivey.

During a brief reconciliation, Quilici became pregnant with their son. Ivey had not permitted her to use birth control pills, she says, because he feared the weight gain associated with the pills would interfere with her swimming. Three months after their son's birth, they separated again, and were divorced by the time Quilici was twenty-one.

Explaining a coach's appeal, Quilici says, "It's such an intense relationship. You travel, you're together all the time. If you're young, and this older man says he loves you . . . He was very, very persuasive and manipulative. I wish I knew then what I know now. I thought I was special to him. I wasn't. I was just another notch in his stick."

Linda Wittwer (formerly Linda Jezek), a silver-medal Olympian in 1976 and three-time world champion backstroker, began swimming for Ivey at Santa Clara when she was fifteen and quit his program when she was nineteen. "He's an excellent coach, technically and in terms of motivation," she says, "but he betrayed my trust." The betrayal came when Wittwer learned that Ivey was sexually involved with Noel, her friend and teammate. "I never even considered that that would have been possible," she says. "Not because of his age, but because of his position." The three of them had spent time together socially, and Wittwer believes she "was a cover for them. When I called him to talk about it, he basically said it was none of my business, and that I wouldn't be anywhere if it wasn't for him."

The Santa Clara Swim Club asked Ivey to resign but not without its own agonizing turmoil. "About half the parents wanted him out, and the other half wanted him to stay," recalls Earl Jezek, Linda Wittwer's father and then a member of the parents' board of directors. "It tore the swim club apart. It created very deep wounds among good friends." Those who wanted Ivey to stay, Jezek remembers, "didn't think it was so bad—Noel was almost eighteen. The rest of us felt like we didn't want a wolf in with the sheep." After Ivey's resignation, almost half of the club members left.

Another world-class swimmer reports that Ivey would make sexual jokes about the women during coed practices, "then he and the guys would all laugh." Ivey would say, for instance, "Oh, you sure can tell it's cold out," a pointed reference to the young women's erect nipples. At the time, Ivey was openly dating a sixteen-year-old on the team. "I knew Ivey had been kicked off at least two teams before, but I thought at twenty-one I was way too old for him," says the world-class athlete, who prefers to remain anonymous. "I never thought it would affect me." But Ivey also made suggestive remarks directly to this woman, she says, during her pre-Olympic training. "I was swimming unbelievably fast in practice, day after day. It was a real high for both of us. I'd never had so much attention; my other coach had been cold. Mitch and I were buddy-buddy. At one point it crossed the line and he started saying things like, 'I want to be your bicycle seat.' I'd give him a dirty look, or say, 'Oh, come off it.' "

The innuendos escalated until this woman felt "betrayed and furious. After that when I'd win I wouldn't even look at him. If I had known how much it would affect my swimming, I would have gone to another coach."

In the late 1980s, Ivey worked at Etobicoke Swimming, a swim club in Toronto. Officials there say he resigned after getting involved with his assistant coach, whom he later married and divorced.

"He has screwed up every team he coached," claims former Olympian Kim Carlisle. "It's so damaging. The trust is ruined. It destroys a team really quickly. He just went from job to job and repeated the same pattern. I think he's a good person; he's just stuck in an adolescent pattern in my opinion."

Between 1991 and 1993, Ivey served as head women's swim coach at the University of Florida, which has one of the top three programs in the country. In 1991 and 1992, he was named Coach of the Year in the Southeastern Conference. But why was he hired? Donna Lopiano, then director of women's athletics at the University of Texas, had specifically warned University of Florida administrators about Ivey's history of sexual abuse. "It was a case of a man who wanted to change and had changed," says Ann-Marie Lawler, Florida's associate athletic director for women's sports. "We knew of his reputation. Everything was discussed openly."

Ivey denied my request for an interview. On the phone, he hung up on me; in response to a letter, he wrote back, "I have no interest in talking with you in any capacity."

Florida's athletic director, Jeremy Foley, explained, "Mitch is probably tired of talking about it."

In October 1993, ESPN produced a show about coach-athlete abuse that focused on Ivey. It included interviews with two women who claimed they had been under eighteen when he had sex with them and two others who related instances of sexual harassment. Just before the show aired, Foley fired Ivey, citing "the best interests of the university." But because Ivey was terminated "without cause" (for legal reasons, Foley said), Florida will pay Ivey for the remaining two years of his contract.

. . .

Marriage seems to legitimize coach-athlete sex. Coaches who marry their athletes tend to keep coaching, even if they began dating the young women when they were underage or still in college, and even if the men bounce from one athlete marriage to the next. Some of the most powerful coaching positions in women's sports are held by men who found wives on the playing fields. Terry Liskevych, women's national volleyball team coach, married a former player. Dennis Pursley, the national team director for U.S. swimming, married a former swimmer. Bob Kersee married his former UCLA star, Jackie Joyner. There are dozens, perhaps hundreds, of others.

Is it possible for a coach-athlete marriage to work? Mike Brown, head diving coach at the University of Texas, says yes. He met his wife, Anita Rossing, when she was a diver for the Swedish national team and he was the U.S. national team coach. She was nineteen. He was thirty-one and had already married and divorced one diver. Anita came to dive for him at Texas, and, according to Mike, when she was "around a senior," she approached him and said something to the effect of, "It would be fun to get closer together and see if things could work out." She was attracted to him, she said, and they "seemed to be on the same wavelength."

He agreed. "On some level I was making the same transformation to allow that to happen," he recalls. "I told her I was attracted to her as a friend and confidante. It was a year or two after I'd split with my ex-wife. I told her some things about that relationship. That wasn't all I was feeling, but that's all I told her."

They didn't begin dating until Rossing graduated, Brown says, because "administrators and teammates would be upset."

After her graduation, Rossing returned to Texas to train with Brown's club team. At that time, Brown combined the Texas Diving Club and the University of Texas practices, so Mike Brown's new girlfriend was diving alongside her former college teammates. Some team members were "very surprised and angry," Brown admits.

The two were married in 1986 and have a young daughter. Brown says of their marriage, "It's pretty harmonious. Like any relationship we continue to work on our weak points. But I'm enjoying it."

Todd Crosset found by interviewing twenty-two athletes who had been involved with coaches [11] that "the coach was clearly in control of those romantic relationships: how far they would go, what would take place, what was deemed appropriate, who would know." In the case of coach-athlete marriages, Crosset says, "I would assume that the power dynamics inherent in the coach-athlete relationship persist in the marriage relationship and carry over into the sexual relationship."

Mike Brown disputes this. "Anita's very assertive. We're pretty sensitive to who's controlling who, or who's making moves to control. She resisted a lot of control, even as an athlete."

Rossing now works as administrator of Brown's diving camp and as a mother. Brown does not think coaches necessarily need to wait for athletes to graduate before pursuing sex with them. Such affairs can be "difficult," he says, "partially because of outside perceptions and partially because the athletes are at an age where they haven't become fully independent. There's a great tendency for adolescents to want to have relationships with adults, for adolescent reasons. It's better when they feel totally independent—which doesn't necessarily mean they have to be out of college.

"Most universities have written or unwritten rules against it," Brown adds, "but it could work."

Many point to Dennis and Mary Jo Pursley as the perfect coach-athlete couple. These two also discussed the possibility of romantic involvement before Mary Jo left Dennis's tutelage. They met in Louisville, Kentucky at Lakeside Swim Club, when she swam for him. A world-ranked distance freestyler, she was nineteen. He was twenty-eight and at the height of his coaching career; six of his swimmers made the 1980 Olympic team.

"During the coach-athlete relationship there was an opportunity to get to know one another, not in the romantic sense, but in terms of type of person, quality of character," recalls Dennis, now the national team director for U.S. Swimming. "You go through all extremes—extreme highs, extreme lows. You're reaching for a common goal. It brings out a lot."

Mary Jo recalls: "I thought he was the greatest coach. I was infatuated."

Later he accepted a position at the Cincinnati Marlins and asked her to train there with him. She did. She also swam for him at regional and national meets during her college years.

Dennis fell in love but for a while kept it to himself. "As a coach you have an ethical and a professional responsibility. It's human nature to be attracted, but you can't let that enter into the coach-athlete relationship." His feelings weren't distracting because "first, I was so intensely focused on our performance objectives, and second, I was aware of the inappropriateness, if that's the word, of pursuing any other kind of relationship. It wasn't an upfront struggle. I knew it was not realistic."

Mary Jo retired just before her senior year. Dennis "debated quite a while whether to take the risk and let her know how I felt." During her senior year at college, he visited her and "made it clear he was interested," says Mary Jo.

She was unsure. "He was nine years older. And I was even intimidated by seniors! I wrote him a letter and said, 'Not now. Let's wait until I graduate, see what happens.'"

Almost immediately after her graduation, they married. "We both knew deep down we were attracted to each other," she says. "We never really had a courtship because he was so professional. We had one date, then he was leaving for Australia to coach the national team. He wanted me to come live with him and help him coach. Being the good Catholic girl that I am, I said, 'I'll come if you marry me.' "

She didn't propose, however, without some trepidation. "I had to ask myself, is it just infatuation or am I in love? I went on my instincts."

Now in their midthirties and forties, is Dennis still in charge? Or did the power shift?

"Obviously it shifts to a degree," says Dennis. "But in our case it wasn't really relevant. If an athlete is mature enough to look beyond the infatuation that a coach can command and look to his character traits, the athlete is probably going to know the coach better than most spouses know one another."

Mary Jo says, "Especially at first, he was the dominant one, and made the decisions most of the time. I was pretty passive, let him call all the shots. We've both grown a lot. I'm now the mother of four children."

Is he still in charge?

"Yeah, for the most part. I'm not a women's libber. I've stayed home for twelve years. We're a traditional family. It has worked for us. I don't have any animosity about it."

Successful marriages arising from such relationships are rare, says Peter Rutter. Often, "the man quickly loses interest in the woman. And both of them have to face the fact that his claim of true love was spurious to begin with, either because it was a self-serving lie geared to sexual conquest or the product of temporary intoxication." [12]

• • •

Few molestation cases go to court, but from court proceedings one gets a better picture of the devastating effects of coach-athlete liaisons. A fifteen-year-old state gymnastics champion from Tennessee filed charges against her gymnastics coach, claiming he seduced her in the late 1980s. Convicted in 1991 on two counts of statutory rape, the coach was sentenced to a year in prison plus a year's probation, and was ordered to pay for the victim's counseling. The girl's gymnastics career, like Quilici's swimming career, "came to a screeching halt," said a prosecutor familiar with the case.

In 1990, at the age of twenty-six, former nationally ranked marathon runner Linda Van Housen sued her track coach, Michael Thomas Ipsen, Sr., for sexually abusing her for more than ten years, beginning when she was thirteen. She was barred from filing criminal charges because the California statute of limitations had expired.

In lieu of monetary damages, Van Housen originally asked Ipsen to apologize publicly, to seek psychiatric care, and to register as a sex offender. Ipsen refused. Van Housen then sued.

A ten-time All-American, Van Housen began running with Ipsen's Woodside Striders in 1975 and lived with Ipsen and his wife in Redwood City, California, from 1979 to 1989. After finishing twenty-eighth in the 1988 U.S. Olympic trials, she had hoped to make the 1992 Olympic team. But she suffered an emotional breakdown in 1989 and stopped running.

Almost a dozen other women came forward during Ipsen's trial in the fall of 1992, testifying that he molested them in the 1980s, when they were girls. Ipsen denied all of the charges.

Peggy and Karen Stok, identical twin runners, testified that Ipsen had sex with them in 1975, when they were fifteen. Peggy Stok said Ipsen told her their relationship was "meant to be." He loved his wife, too, "but it was OK to love more than one person," she said he told her. They engaged in sex about ten times when she was running for the Striders, she testified. He told her not to tell anyone or he would be charged with statutory rape.[13] He should know: He had been charged with statutory rape of his sister-in-law, then fourteen, in 1966. He had pleaded guilty to a reduced misdemeanor charge of contributing to the delinquency of a minor.[14]

When Peggy and Karen realized they were both being molested, they confronted him. Peggy said, "His whole reaction was, 'So what? What's the big deal?' "[15]

Van Housen says the years of molestation inflicted on her "a deep, deep, sometimes excruciating feeling of loss. The deepest part is sorrow. I was raped of my innocence." Van Housen also lost the ability to work, became temporarily estranged from her mother (who mistrusted Ipsen), and watched her Olympic dream die.

• • •

In a review of the military courtroom film *A Few Good Men, Washington Post* critic Desson Howe writes that Demi Moore's character "must surrender the romantic flag first."[16] When there is a power imbalance between the two parties—as there always is between a coach and an athlete—a woman who acquiesces to a man's request for sex/romance is in a sense surrendering, relinquishing her power. She is putting aside her own military, political, or athletic power. She is saying, in effect, "Take me, I'm yours—and no longer my own." It's a defeat.

For the athlete, this defeat can have devastating consequences. Her focus shifts from herself and her goals to her coach. Rather than concentrate on her own increasing athletic ability, she questions her attractiveness to the coach. Rather than concentrate on upcoming competitions, she wonders what the hotel sleeping arrangements will be. When listening to his advice, she gets distracted by the color of his eyes. When criticized, she wonders if he will withdraw his "love." Ordered to protect his secret, she becomes alienated from her teammates and parents.

Meanwhile, teammates inevitably intuit what's going on and experience a range of emotions from envy to anger to betrayal. "It's almost a death knell for the team," says psychologist Bruce Ogilvie.

Kim Carlisle remembers a coach-athlete affair that "devastated" her and her Stanford teammates her first year. "He was out of there pretty quick, but it was really rough on us. We all felt it. My first three years at Stanford, we had three different coaches. At that level, it really impacts performance. I think it's why we didn't win another national championship until my senior year. I attribute that to the drain of dealing with that coach. A coach is a father figure. It's about boundaries. The relationship is not supposed to be violated. You lose all respect. When you're in college, you're away from home and vulnerable. You have odd feelings of competition and jealousy. You want the support and attention—but not in that way."

Even John Pittington, who maintains that coach-athlete seductions are "not that prevalent," and that "most coaches are fairly ethical," cites several problematic cases. "Your problem doesn't lie with the individual [athlete]." The problem, he says, "lies with how the rest of the team reacts. On some teams the girls are jealous. You can give preferential treatment without meaning to. I've seen teams acknowledge that it's OK. But a lot of times, the team didn't like it. Usually the coach and swimmer leave."

Several volleyball players from Oregon State candidly discussed their disappointment and sense of betrayal after the Guy Enriques affair came to light. "I'm glad he left," said Christy Stoeckel, then a junior outside hitter. "Things were so out of hand. There was so much favoritism. It was hard to play for someone and respect him, knowing what he was doing."

"He basically was a liar," said another player who preferred not to be named. "It took a toll on the team."

Stoeckel said it was her anger that led her to disobey the athletic director's mandate not to talk. "They're trying to keep it quiet to protect him or [the young woman]; that's what they told us. I don't feel like he needs to be protected. He's made life hell for so many people. I feel really bitter towards him. I don't owe him any favors. I don't mind telling anyone the whole story. He's exploited all of us. He's a grown man. He had to know that was wrong."

Stoeckel added, "It makes you so suspicious. It's so sad that women have to think that their coach might be thinking about something besides their playing."

• • •

The coach who molested me arrived at my swim club when I was fourteen. He was twenty-five. A former football player I'll call Coach,[17] he trained us to be dedicated swimmers, offering encouragement I had never before encountered. In the evenings, after other club members had left, Coach relaxed, playing cards with my girlfriends and me. He joined us in games of Follow the Leader off the diving board, allowing us to break minor club rules: handstands off the board, running on deck. He treated us to candy from the snack bar. He listened to us, teased us, gave us silly nicknames.

He paid particular attention to me. Since I was also becoming a serious basketball player, Coach taught me a hook shot, promising, correctly, that no other eighth grade girl would have one. He taught me to play one-on-one. I still remember the feel of his firm hand against my back as I'd edge toward the basket. It seemed a forthright touch—a marked contrast to the clammy, nail-bitten gropings of the boys who in those days would ask me to dance.

That year my body came alive. Sexual feeling became a daily reality, sexual contact a remote but enticing possibility. My girlfriends began "going with" the boys in our junior high. Who do you like? was the question of the day; you were supposed to fixate on one boy, then hope he asked you out. I found some of my fourteen-year-old peers attractive, but how could they compare to Coach?

After diving contests or card games, Coach would drive my two girl-friends and me home, dropping me off last. Sitting in my driveway, we would talk, our discussions ranging from flip turns to the Civil Rights movement to God to nerdy guys at my school. Coach listened. He made me laugh. I felt privileged, special, eager for attention from this handsome man. I wrote him letters and he flattered me by comparing my style to J. D. Salinger's. He gave me a book of poetry. He gave me a poster with the Frederick S. Perls poem that begins, "You are not in this world to live up to my expectations. . . ." and ends, "and if by chance we find each other, it's beautiful."

When you're fourteen, you don't imagine that your twenty-five-year-old married coach, a father of young children, will return your affections. Or rather, you imagine it often and in detail, but you don't expect it; you don't actually think there's any chance in the world that he would fall in love back, or have a crush, too, or for any reason at all want to kiss you. If he does, it's a shock.

One day toward the end of that first summer, Coach drove me home after practice but stopped short of my house, near a cemetery. For a while, we talked. Then he put his hand on my thigh. A few weeks later he offered me my first French kiss. I did not refuse.

Statutory rape laws exist to protect girls from sex with older men. Regardless of a minor's behavior, the laws say, she is legally incapable of giving consent. A man who gets sexually involved with her is committing a felony.

We discussed this. Over the course of the next two years, we decided that the laws were stupid, that I was more mature than most girls, and that my parents, above all, would never understand. I felt indescribably flattered, wildly in love, and horribly guilty and confused.

We discussed this, too. Each time I'd raise doubts, he'd reassure me that what we were doing was OK. I was particularly concerned about hurting his wife. "It's OK to love more than one person," he told me, and, "What she doesn't know won't hurt her."

One time I asked, "If you lie to your wife, how can I know you're not lying to me?"

He grew angry. "You think too much," he said.

At age sixteen, I moved with my family across the country, abruptly ending the molestation. The next summer, one of my friends wrote, telling me that after I left, he had "fooled around with" her, too. Later I learned he had also molested another friend. I began to realize I'd been abused.

Back in my hometown for a visit, I told Coach I was angry he'd taken advantage of me. He responded with a vague letter that I interpreted as an apology. I didn't expect to talk to him again.

But in the process of writing this book, I began to wonder: what does he think about the relationship now? Does he still molest teenage athletes? Maybe out of some sense of indebtedness he'd explain his perspective. So I called him, reaching him at the high school where he now serves as athletic director. He still coaches. We hadn't spoken for almost twenty years. Over the next month we talked four times for a total of about three hours.

. . .

For twenty years, Coach claims, he has suffered from a "self-inflicted flogging." He thinks about me often—"to say every day would be an exaggeration, but I don't think three days go by that I don't think about it. Probably because of the way society has brought out the things people go through because of situations like this."

He had planned to call me, too—a coincidence, he said, but I suspect he saw me discuss his abuse on *Larry King Live*.

Before I could say much, he became chatty, telling me that my name is still on a plaque as one year's Most Valuable Swimmer. When teaching classes, he said, he mentions me as an example of a successful student-athlete. He asked about my family. He cracked jokes. He sounded how he used to sound when I was a teenager: charming.

"I called to talk about something else," I said at last.

"Good," he responded eagerly. "I need to have this conversation, too. I'm very anxious to hear this. It's a very crushing feeling to me to think that I've ever had any kind of negative impact on you. Crushing."

"You did," I said bluntly. He listened to my anger: what a burden the sex and secrecy had been, how ashamed I had felt of my own adulterous behavior, how my trust had been broken.

"I'm so very sorry," he said.

I asked him to explain how he felt about me at that time. He spoke in general terms, echoing Pittington's statements about the turn-on of being in control. "When you have someone you spend hundreds of hours with, when they give you blood, sweat, tears, their lives, you become close. You become attached to them. And it's really difficult to put parameters on that attachment. I think that's human nature, and I don't think it has anything to do with being fifty or being fifteen. It's human nature to love someone who gives themself to you."

Pressed to describe his feelings for me, he struggled. "I'm searching. It wasn't the ordinary type thing. Was there feeling? Yes. Can I one hundred percent identify that? No. Obviously there was friendship. Obviously there was a mutual attraction. Obviously there was a terrific comfort and trust level. I enjoyed your company. There were discussions, there was laughter, there was sharing. Many things were good and meaningful. Do I say, it must have been love? There was probably a fear to express that."

I told him that men who are secure, mature, happily married, and comfortable with themselves don't turn to teenagers as sexual/emotional partners.

"I can accept that," he said. "But I don't think I ever thought about Mariah the teenager. It was Mariah the person. I truly, truly believe that."

I explained: I was fourteen. I lacked the wisdom and power to say no.

Coach said, "This is why I'm happy I'm speaking with you. I thought that people could love at whatever age. But you're telling me that's not true."

"Sex is not love," I said. "Love would have been nice. Sex ruined it."

Has he had sex with other girls? I wanted to know.

He admitted the brief incidents with my two friends, but denied responsibility, saying angrily, "I was drunk!" He insisted that there had been no others. "I'm a different person," he said. "I've grown. I've gone through a lot of things, even religiously, in terms of regret."

He described letters of praise he receives from former students. "It's an irony," he said. "Thousands of kids would say to you, he's been the biggest influence for good."

In his comments I noticed a pattern: remorse interspersed with squirminess, a reluctance to take responsibility. "OK, so we made a mistake," Coach said at one point.

"You made a mistake," I corrected him.

"OK. I accept that. I made a mistake," he said. "I was chronologically older, and that's where I'm accountable. Hell, I don't know how much more emotionally mature I was than you. I don't think a whole hell of a lot. But I'm not looking for an excuse. I'm just kind of baring my soul."

For a moment we both were silent.

"Don't you think you had any responsibility?" he asked plaintively.

"No. I was a child," I said.

"OK, you're right," he said. Then, later: "It wasn't forced. It wasn't drug-induced. I wasn't trying to get you to a state where you didn't have any inhibitions. It wasn't sexual harassment."

"It was sexual abuse," I said. "Statutory rape."

More silence. Then: "You don't know how badly, if I hurt you, that I want you not just to accept an apology from me, but to forgive me."

• • •

I did forgive him, a little too quickly. The conversation shifted to how he might forgive himself. I found myself in the familiar female role of helping a man deal with his emotions. I recommended he see a therapist. He said he'd like me to come visit some time for lunch, and that he would be "very disappointed and very hurt" if I didn't come. I heard myself say that I might. I liked him again. I remembered what I loved.

After we hung up, I felt enraged. Why should I have lunch with this man? What did he want? I didn't trust him and had no desire to chat. I'd experienced a sort of second seduction, I realized. Coach had invited me to lunch to seduce me into forgiving, forgetting, and assuring him that what happened had been no big deal. Clearly, too, he was worried about my identifying him publicly. My anger barely cooling, I had rushed to take care of his needs.

This is typical, Peter Rutter writes in *Sex in the Forbidden Zone*. "Many women are so anxious to put a sexual-boundary violation behind them that at the slightest show of contrition they prematurely forgive or reconcile with the man who has injured them."[18]

So the impact of the original seduction had been great indeed. Twenty years later, after much thought and therapy, I had again become confused and angry about it.

• • •

Psychiatrist Daniel Begel writes, "The athlete-coach relationship may be among the most intimate in the lives of both parties. The intense consideration given to the functioning of the athlete's body may rekindle transferences not unlike those in psychotherapy, except that these transferences are usually unexamined."[19]

Transference is the process of redirecting powerful feelings from one person to another. These feelings "are in some ways a reexperiencing of past emotional dynamics within the family, but in other ways they look to future possibilities for developing new and healthier emotional dynamics," says Rutter. "For example, a patient trying to seduce a therapist may be repeating past injuries but is also most likely searching for a response that will discourage this repetition."

Thus the athlete who acts seductive may be reenacting past sexual victimization. When an athlete's intense feelings and desires become fixated on a coach, what she needs from him is love and respect as a person, rather than as a sexual object. How many girls receive nonsexual and caring attention from an older man? How often are women's relationships with their male mentors free from sexual harassment? To be appreciated for one's mind, one's athleticism, one's simple alive self would in fact feel healthy and healing—as long as the coach isn't seducing other athletes on the team.

If the athlete were in therapy and the coach a responsible therapist, the young woman's feelings would be discussed and analyzed. Both parties would acknowledge that despite real mutual affection, the woman's feelings don't "belong" with the therapist.

Coaches, however, usually lack the training and insight to redirect the athlete's feelings elsewhere. And some don't want to.

Even female coaches who have been on the receiving end of girls' affections admit that these crushes can be tremendously flattering. "They want to hang around in your office when they should be off with their peers," says University of Florida's Ann-Marie Lawler, who before becoming an athletic director coached high school girls' tennis and golf. "They want to be with you twenty-four hours a day. It's good for the ego. Maybe that's what happens with the men—their egos get involved."

Countertransference is when the therapist or other person in power misdirects intense feelings and desires onto the person he or she is entrusted to care for. In the case of a coach, his feelings are transferred from a parent, lover, or significant other to the athlete, and he interprets these feelings as romantic love.

Why are coaches likely to violate sexual boundaries? Besides being raised in the manly sports world and untrained in interpersonal dynamics, they lead strange lives. At the college level they spend many nights in hotels and find themselves eating breakfast, lunch, and dinner with their athletes rather than with adults. Often they have little time for peer relationships, gleaning virtually all of their social needs from their young charges. Perhaps some choose this work because their own immaturity matches that of their athletes.

Coaching styles, adopted from manly sports, are often authoritarian and all-encompassing. Athletes are taught not to question the coach. A coach might tell an athlete not only when and how to practice but when and what to eat, when to sleep, how to dress. It's the coach's job to define the rules and to say what's out of bounds, what's illegal. The coach knows best. If the coach says it's OK, it must be OK. In this way a coach creates a dominance he may not have in his family life, or may not have felt as an athlete on the manly playing fields.

Having had male coaches all of her life, the athlete may accept this strict control as normal. She may know of no other way. In the habit of acceding to numerous personal demands, the athlete who is asked for sex—even if she does not feel infatuated—may feel unable suddenly to say no to her all-powerful coach. Like incest survivors, she may feel unable to tell anyone about it. The women Peter Rutter interviewed agreed to sex "as a way of maintaining a relationship that had come to have extraordinary importance in their lives and seemed to them to open up new and boundless possibilities for the future."[20]

In sports, these possibilities may include the ability to develop her talents. If she lacks the means to train with other coaches, "rejection of their coach's sexual overtures could well mean the end of a young woman's athletic career," notes Canadian sociologist Helen Lenskyj.[21]

The very language of sports supports a dependent relationship. Athletes say they swim or run or play basketball *for* Coach X. Not for themselves, but for the coach.

Female athletes are likely to feel like outcasts. In the dating game, they are rarely the first pick of the football players—the prestige kids—nor do they attain the status of the football players themselves, though they love their sport as much and practice for as many hours. Even after decades of female athletic visibility, boys can be intimidated by girls with muscles and by girls who dedicate themselves to something besides the pursuit of men. At elite levels, female athletes live in a cloistered society, moving away from home at an early age and too busy training to engage in normal adolescent social activities. Receiving for perhaps the first time what feels like love, young women are likely to "respond in loving ways that men interpret as being sexual," says Mimi Murray. "Then the men pursue it."

But this analysis may be too complex. Mostly, coaches molest children because they can. Because no one is stopping them.

• • •

At sixteen, I did not dream of telling my parents I was having sex with my coach, although I felt confused, ashamed, and obsessed. I knew I was in over my head, but like many children, I took responsibility for the man's sexual behavior. Though my parents were not punitive people, I feared I'd get in trouble. And I feared I'd harm the man I loved.

Athletes also don't report abuse because they have been well indoctrinated into male power. "While one might expect a high level of assertiveness and mental toughness from women who are competitive athletes, there is evidence that the coach's authority, and even psychologically manipulative or abusive behavior, is rarely . . . challenged by these women," writes Helen Lenskyj.[22]

To report an incident to a coach's superior often means confronting another man. Not only are 83 percent of college athletic directors male, 38 percent of "senior women administrators"—a position created specifically for women—are male.[23] With few written policies and many unwritten sanctions of sexual abuse, many female athletes remain silent.

Male coaches and administrators who do not seduce athletes usually remain silent too, perhaps, as psychiatrist Peter Rutter suggests, because they are vicariously enjoying the sexual meanderings of other men. "Each of the hundreds of men I spoke with on this subject admitted that on some level he envied other men's forbidden sexual exploits." Many men fantasize about breaking sexual taboos, Rutter says, and "the impact of so many men sharing a similar sexual fantasy" would help explain "why even ethical men look the other way when they hear about a colleague's sexually exploitive behavior."[24]

Told I'm investigating the subject of coach-athlete relationships, David Middleton, treasurer of Toronto's Etobicoke Swimming, laughs heartily, saying "That'll be a great chapter." Why? He won't say; nor will he stop laughing. Asked about Mitch Ivey's sexual history, Middleton says, "I'm not going to say anything negative about Mitch. He's a great coach. I like the guy."

Men often cover for each other, and particularly for powerful men. Ronald W. Price, a girls' softball coach at Northeast High School in Pasadena, Maryland, was recently convicted of having sex with three female students, and was sentenced to twenty-six years in prison.[25] Price admitted having sex with seven students, two of whom he had married. But female teachers and students had reported his behavior to male administrators, including the superintendent, for seven years before Price was finally arrested.[26]

I hear from female coaches that they're "incensed" by sexual abuse on the part of their male colleagues; they're "infuriated," "enraged," "bothered," "very disturbed," and "sick and tired of it."

Many male coaches act defensive and shifty. It's "not a problem," they insist. "No more a problem than in the rest of society." "Not a problem in my sport."

Guy Edson, technical director of the American Swim Coaches Association, says that of about 10,000 swim coaches nationwide, he has heard of just four instances where a coach got involved with a minor, and another two where she was of legal age. "Swimming is a pretty clean sport," he says. "Drug use, corruption, and sexual misconduct exist everywhere in society, but it isn't as pervasive in swimming as some would have us think."

When the American Swim Coaches Association was debating its new code of ethics, "women seemed to feel stronger about it than the men, though there were men who were very supportive," reports Kris Wingenroth, head men's and women's swim coach at Rice University. She adds: "There wasn't much open debate. No one's going to stand up and say they're against ethics."

Guy Edson reports that what they did say is " 'You can't legislate morality.' You hear that phrase quite a bit."

• • •

"What about the lesbians?" Bring up the topic of coach-athlete sex and inevitably, men mention lesbians. One college volleyball coach raised the subject of lesbian seductions during our conversation about his own relationships with athletes. First he married a volleyball player from his club team (he says they met before she joined the team). Now he's married to a woman seventeen years younger than he is; he says they began dating when she was attending a junior college where he had coached the previous year. "If you're gonna look at one side, you have to look at the other," he said.

Does it happen? Do female coaches also "fall in love with" their young charges and handle their own feelings irresponsibly? Yes. Some are heterosexual. Jean-Michelle Whitiak, a twenty-four-year-old swimming coach from Fairfax County, Virginia, admitted having sex with a boy she coached for three years, beginning when he was eleven. She was found guilty of statutory rape and received a two-year sentence, all but thirty days of which was suspended.[27] Lesbians molest children, too. Joy Shamburger, former assistant basketball coach at Northeast Louisiana University, allegedly seduced basketball player Chana Perry during the recruiting process.

But when a woman is discovered, the news often becomes public, and her career ends, whereas men keep right on coaching, dating players and marrying them. Shamburger was fired, Perry's mother sued Shamburger for $500,000, and Chana transferred to San Diego State.[28] An athletic director at a southern California university tells me that she asked for the resignation of a volleyball coach who was having sex with a student; that woman, too, left the profession. I have never heard of a female coach who kept her job after it was discovered that she was "dating" a player. Nor, to my knowledge, are any current female coaches "married" to former athletes.

At Boston University, senior women's administrator Averill Haines reports that when a head basketball coach got involved with one of her players, the woman was released and "it took about eight years to remove the taint from the program." The assistant coach, it turns out, was also having sex with an athlete, but because he was a man, the taint came not from the fact of double sexual misconduct, but from the fact that one of the affairs had involved lesbians.

Men also use lesbian accusations as a negative recruiting tool, scaring parents away from lesbian "predators." "You wouldn't want your daughter to play for that team," they caution. Meanwhile, all indications are that if you want your daughter not to succumb to sexual abuse, she'll be safer with a female coach.

About 96 percent of sexual exploitation by professionals occurs between a man in power and a women under his guidance.[29] About 95 percent of pedophiles are men, according to psychiatry professor Fred S. Berlin of Johns Hopkins Medical School.[30] Yet suddenly, when confronted with their own misbehavior, men want to talk about lesbians seducing girls.

No one talks about men seducing boys. No one says, "I'm afraid to let my child play football because the coach might mess around with him." Yet such fears would not be unfounded. Stephen A. Sharp, a soccer coach and former president of the Alexandria, Virginia, youth soccer league, was sentenced in 1992 to ten years in prison for sodomizing two thirteen- and fourteen-year-old players and taking indecent sexual liberties with his own sixteen-year-old son.[31]

A twenty-four-year-old man came forward in 1991 to press charges against a popular and successful football coach named John Stuart Mackintosh. The man, whose name was withheld, said Mackintosh fondled him during weight lifting practices in the basement of a church. He was fourteen and a high school freshman football player at the time.[32]

Was this love? Often girls, too, are fourteen, fifteen, or sixteen when the relationship becomes sexual. Yet those relationships can be justified as dating and sanctified by marriage. When men are heterosexual, the perpetrators are not called pedophiles. They're often called good coaches.

What should happen when a coach and athlete have a strong attraction for each other? Terry Carlisle, Kim Carlisle's father and a swim coach with twenty-six years of experience at the college and high school levels, says he understands the temptation but controlled his behavior through willpower. He wasn't ever "in love," he says, "but maybe infatuated. I kept it to myself. I recognized the level of my responsibility and held myself to that."

For one female volleyball coach, the struggle to resist acting on her own attractions for players was more difficult, and she laments her lack of training. "When you're a young coach—twenty-two, twenty-three— they don't teach you how powerful that role is. Gee, I wish someone had talked about that in class. We talked about all sorts of other controversial issues. Why didn't anyone talk about that?"

Over three decades of coaching, she says, "there have been about ten players where I had to channel their crushes in positive ways. You struggle—you want to keep the athlete there."

In one case she, too, felt in love. "I really came close to damaging myself professionally. I ended up making the right decision. It was scary. I was old enough to know better. The chemistry was there. I should have cut her—but you don't want to hurt the student."

Lyle Nelson (no relation to the author), a private ski coach and a four-time Olympic biathlete, recently struggled in his efforts to act responsibly with one of his young athletes, Lara Burgel. Nelson's coaching style was to be "emotionally intimate with the people I train. Everyone I coach has a goal of being national or Olympic or world champion. To really understand someone, you must become emotionally entwined."

Over a period of two years, Nelson coached Burgel, a cross-country skier, almost daily. She was between fifteen and seventeen; he was in his early forties. "She's precocious," he says. "She acts twenty-five."

He once said to his own coach, Olympic ski champion Bill Koch, "I'm lucky. I don't have any sexual desire for the young women I coach."

"Don't lie to yourself," Koch replied. "You have the discipline not to act on it."

Nelson concluded Koch was right. He began to feel concerned about what he perceived as Burgel's attraction for him, and he was beginning to worry about his own behavior. Lara had a boyfriend, and when her training schedule interfered with their dates, Nelson would joke: "I'm taking his place for the night."

Nelson became concerned that such comments were "instigating some confusion." So, during a run together, he asked her, "What's your relationship with me, as you see it?"

She discussed his role as her coach. He said, "Are you sure you don't see me as your boyfriend?"

Burgel, now a Dartmouth College student with her eye on the 1996 Olympics, recalls this conversation as "strange. I didn't know how to react. He said there are a lot of problems when male coaches fall in love with female athletes. He said, 'We're going to have to be careful.' My reaction was, 'This is interesting.' I didn't know how to deal with it."

She asked Nelson something she had been asking several friends: If there were no consequences, who would you have sex with? "He said he'd sleep with all his friends. I thought that was weird."

Still, she was "infatuated," she admits, and she felt flattered. "Flattery was a big part of it. That had a lot of power. I think it's really neat but he's as old as my parents. Would I sleep with my dad? No."

She also questioned Nelson's maturity, wondering, "What in me does an older person find desirable or attractive?"

She told her boyfriend, who was "not threatened," and her mother, who was "helpful."

Months later, Burgel still feels "confused," but is "glad he brought it up." She hastens to add, "By no means did he take advantage of me."

Nelson agrees: "At no time have I thought my behavior was inappropriate." Yet after giving the issue much thought, he has concluded that "it is very risky, as a male coach, to develop an intimate relationship with a female athlete. Intimacy is just too close to sexuality to be . . . wise. If you play with fire enough, someone is going to get burned. Weak moments could arise and lead to crossing the line—even if it is only a hug that lasts a half second too long."

Based on his own experience and conversations with other male coaches, he speculates, "I'll bet every male coach has attractions to every female he coaches. Males are attracted to everything. Very few women have no sexual appeal to me. I don't know if there's any [who don't]."

"It's incredibly prevalent," he adds, "for coaches to behave in such a way as to cause confusion and mental duress."

• • •

Universities are beginning to craft policies forbidding sexual behavior between coaches and athletes. The Women's Sports Foundation, responding to recent inquiries and complaints about sexual harassment and abuse, has created a Committee on Ethical Relationships Between Sports Leaders and Athletes, which has devised policy guidelines. In England, Geoff Cooke of the National Coaching Foundation has proposed creating a national registry to record complaints and monitor coaches' careers. In both England and the United States, mandatory coaching certification programs have been proposed. Child abuse prevention specialist Cordelia Anderson of Minneapolis has written sports-related sexual harassment and abuse guidelines for parents, coaches, and athletes, published in a booklet entitled, "Keeping Youth Sports Safe and Fun."[33] She also offers sexual abuse prevention workshops for coaches, for which she says demand is increasing.

At Stanford University, frustrated students are using the media to get their complaints heard. Female soccer players, track athletes, and gymnasts have all written articles in the *Stanford Daily* complaining about sexual harassment and other forms of abuse by their male coaches. In part as a result of their pressure, the track coach resigned, the soccer coach was reassigned to a noncoaching job, and athletic director Ted Leland invited all student-athletes to tell him their stories, promising confidentiality. Many have responded.

More is needed: college, club, and high school coaches need to be systematically instructed in "concepts of human emotion, psycho-sexual stages of development, and institutionalized power, dominance, and oppression," suggest Mimi Murray and her colleagues.[34] Athletes need to be taught how to set limits and how to report abusive behavior. Murray also suggests that the entire coach-athlete relationship be restructured to give athletes more autonomy and decision-making power.

A strict code of ethics should be adopted by all coaching associations. Coaches who find themselves distracted by attractions for athletes should seek supervisory assistance.[35] And supervisors should pay closer attention and intervene when abuse is suspected, even if that means disrupting a winning season.

Quitting a job in order to pursue a relationship is often proffered as a solution to the ethical dilemma of coach-athlete attractions. Researcher Todd Crosset says, "If coaches find themselves falling in love with another adult and they want to take a shot at that, they should stop being [that person's] coach."

Most coaches seem to agree. But is it really OK to start having sex the day the coach-athlete relationship ends? Is it really OK for coaches to use their teams as personal dating services?

Peter Rutter agrees with the American Psychiatric Association: professional boundaries should remain in place for a lifetime, regardless of the changing nature of a relationship. Rutter likens it to the father-daughter boundary, which forbids sex even after the girl is grown and no longer needs a daddy.[36]

. . .

My former swimming coach now teaches ethics courses to coaches, believe it or not. What does he tell other coaches? "Anything outside of the professional relationship is wrong. Now, do I think it's difficult? Absolutely."

Why does he think it's wrong?

"Our society doesn't accept age differentials." He mentions fifty-six-year-old Woody Allen's acknowledged affair with the twenty-one-year-old daughter of his former lover. "We don't accept that."

Also, he adds, "Someone could be injured. Maybe that should be foremost." He has learned from me, he says, that I was injured from his behavior. "I pass that on," he says, concluding, "Age and wisdom have to be the better part of judgment."

Molested girls grow up. Childhood promises to keep a secret can, later, be broken. I, for instance, find myself in a different position from my innocent teenage years. I am no longer a high school athlete. I'm no longer in love with Coach. He is, as Mary Magdalene sings in *Jesus Christ, Superstar,* "just a man." No longer my coach, my god.

During our conversations he was on the defensive, justifying, explaining, and scared. "What if your mother finds out?" he asked.

"She already knows," I told him.

I assured him I will not divulge his name in this book but added that I would investigate, and if I discovered that he is currently molesting girls, or that he has molested any others in the twenty years since molesting me and my friends, I'll report him, and I'll support those who bring charges. It felt good to say that, to let him know my loyalty was no longer with my male coach, but with my female peers. It got his attention.

The Stok twins and several other runners in the Linda Van Housen case stood together and testified against the man who had abused them when they were small. It was a powerful thing to do. Whereas one woman who cries rape is often not believed, there is strength in numbers. The jury in the Van Housen case ruled that Ipsen had emotionally damaged Van Housen and that she was not at fault for engaging in sex with him. They awarded her $1.1 million.

"This is a victory for all the children," said Van Housen outside the courtroom in the fall of 1992. "It is a big issue. Ipsen is only a small part of what's out there."[37]

A year later, Van Housen feels less victorious. "I know I'm supposed to feel good, but I don't," she says. "He's a perverted child molester, and he's still walking around." Ipsen continues to coach the Woodside Striders.

Van Housen now writes "a ton of poetry," finds solace in her religious faith, and plans to return to work. She has begun running again—just fifteen miles per week, in contrast to her former one hundred-mile-per-week regimen. "I'll never get back to competition," she says. "That's another loss. I won't even watch running events on TV—I get a burning desire to go run and run forever, but then I just can't do it."

Because Ipsen did not own $1.1 million dollars, Van Housen accepted a $200,000 settlement from his insurance company, which covered only her legal fees. As part of the settlement he agreed not to appeal, but she refused to accept a proposed gag order, explaining, "There's no way in hell I'm going to stop talking about this."

9

How a Woman Is Supposed to Act

Why, in the Peking Opera, are all the women's roles played by men?

Because only a man knows how a woman is supposed to act.

—*David Henry Hwang*, M. Butterfly

A T THE 1992 Mazda Ladies Professional Golf Association (LPGA) Championship, Betsy King shot a 17-under-par total of 267, scoring 68, 66, 67, and 66 during the four-day tournament. This marked a new all-time low winning score, for women or men, at a major championship. Yet it received barely a blip on the media radar screen. Golf success is measured by low scores. Scoring the lowest total ever is not an obscure statistic. If a man had broken this record at a major championship, surely it would have received extensive coverage in sports sections, in magazines, and on talk shows. King's feat didn't.

When, that same year, the best women's college basketball teams in the country—number-one Tennessee and number-two Stanford—played each other, no television networks carried the game. The game was sold out two weeks in advance. Yet the contest only received local coverage—unheard of for a similar men's college game.

About 92 percent of televised sports coverage is of men. Just 5 percent is of women. The other 3 percent is of neutral topics, such as upcoming

Olympic sites. This is the finding of a landmark 1989 study by the Amateur Athletic Foundation (AAF) of Los Angeles.[1]

A similar AAF survey of four daily newspapers (the *Boston Globe,* the *Orange County Register,* the *Dallas Morning News,* and *USA Today*) produced this news: Newspaper coverage of men's sports during a three-month period in 1990 comprised 81 percent of the total. Women's stories made up just 3.5 percent of the total. Neutral topics made up the rest. Even when professional sports were excluded, the male-female ratio was nine to one. This represents virtually no change from almost a decade before. These papers were all named among the best ten in the country by the Associated Press Sports Editors.[2]

USA Today offered by far the best coverage, providing more women's stories, more women's front-page stories, longer women's stories (relative to the men's), and more women's photographs than any other paper surveyed. Of the 301 women-only stories, 43.5 percent appeared in *USA Today.* Even so, their women's coverage comprised only 4.4 percent of their total sports coverage.[3]

A year-long 1989 survey revealed that only 2 percent of the sports coverage at the *New York Times* and the *Indianapolis Star* focused on women. Both papers covered more women's sports back in 1971, when fewer women participated.[4]

My survey of *Sports Illustrated* covers between 1954 and 1990 revealed that only 4 percent were of women athletes. Another 4 percent were of cheerleaders, wives or girlfriends of male athletes, and models in bathing suits.

Both *Sports Illustrated for Kids*[5] and *Young Athlete*[6] feature twice as many boys as girls in their photos. On *Sports Illustrated for Kids* covers, males outnumber females five to one.

In a Coors commercial, men play volleyball on the beach. Occasionally the scene flashes to a woman in a bikini. Each time a woman is pictured, a male voice says, "hot little number."

No one cares about women's sports. That's the rationale. When organizers of women's pro tennis tried to attract sponsors and media coverage in the seventies, male corporate honchos and media managers said no one wants to watch women because the women can't hit the ball as hard as the men can.

They should have known better. Women's Olympic sports, including track and field and swimming, have always drawn large audiences though male Olympians swim and run a little faster, throw a little farther, and jump a little higher. By the early 1990s, women's tennis had become at least as popular as the men's. During the 1991 U.S. Open, the women's finals received higher Nielsen ratings (6.1, with 5.62 million households watching) than the men's finals (5.5, with 5.07 million households watching.) In 1992, the women's French Open finals drew larger television audiences than did the men's. Though pro football ranked first among Americans' favorite sports in a recent survey, women's and men's gymnastics and skating claimed six of the top eight spots.[7]

The more women's basketball is broadcast on television, the more popular it becomes. Sales of television rights to first- and second-round NCAA championship games more than doubled from 1992 to 1993. Ticket sales for the 1994 championships sold out nine months in advance. Increased reporting of women's games on ESPN (the all-sports network) contributed to the greater interest. "For people who don't normally watch women's basketball, that gave it some legitimacy," said Regina L. McNeal, NCAA assistant director of communications.[8]

Seventy percent of ESPN viewers are men, ESPN reports. For overall sports broadcasts, according to Nielsen ratings, about 61 percent of viewers are men. According to a Miller Lite survey of more than 1,100 Americans, about 78 percent of "ardent" sports fans are men. But when asked what events they would like to watch, 70 percent of respondents reported that they would be equally interested in watching women's and men's competitions.[9] Seventy percent is a sizable majority. Even without daily familiarity with women's sports events and personalities, most spectators are equally interested in women's and men's coverage.

• • •

When female athletes are depicted, they're usually wearing short skirts or smiling. Commentators say approvingly, "She's really strong *but still feminine.*" The word "but," linguists explain, negates what came before. Commentators openly approve of petite bodies that move gracefully and disapprove of large bodies that push each other around.

Most critically, writers and broadcasters minimize female strength by sexualizing it. They tell women that they are not getting strong for themselves. They're not playing basketball or baseball because they love the process, the power, the joy of playing with other women. They're not lifting weights so they can back up the defensive threats they make to their boyfriends, and to aggressive strangers on the street: hit us and we'll hurt you. Male muscles symbolize strength and power; female muscles symbolize sexual attractiveness. Beauty. Display.[10]

Jockey Julie Krone won the Belmont Stakes in June 1993. Though Krone had already won more than 2,700 races, this was the first time a woman had won a Triple Crown event. Reporters asked her afterward: How does it feel, as a woman, to win?

She responded, "I don't think the question should be genderized."

Good word, genderized. Even if she did make it up. Krone wanted to talk about how it felt to win, period. She didn't want to frame it in terms of being female any more than she wanted to frame it in terms of being white. Her breasts, her genitals, her ability to give birth—none of this seemed relevant as she steered her horse, Colonial Affair, toward victory.

This is what male reporters often don't seem to understand: Women feel like people. We don't think constantly about being women. It's natural for us. We can even forget about it for long stretches of time.

For years, men tried to keep women out of certain sports altogether. They still try, at the college level in particular: athletic directors moan that providing women with equal opportunities will "hurt football" or "hurt men." But court rulings are increasingly in women's favor, and the floodgates of women's sports participation will not close.

So men scramble to retain some power by framing women as special athletes: female athletes. Through both text and photographs, sociologist Margaret Carlisle Duncan has noted, women tend to be depicted primarily as women[11]—genderized—while men are depicted as brave, successful, tough, admirable human beings.

How does it feel, as a person, to be continually placed in the category of Other? Why are there so few female jockeys when the ideal jockey weighs only about 100 pounds? Since few men are so small, aren't women better suited for this sport? Aren't girls notorious horse-lovers? What's keeping more women from entering this sport and succeeding? From gender-conscious reporters, these might have been good questions.

The myth used to be that athleticism would masculinize women; that female athletes were ugly to men; that female athletes were incapable of attracting men; that we were "a bunch of dykes." You still see that in the media, but less often. There are too many of us now. Almost two million high school girls play organized sports; sixteen million women play softball. They can't all be lesbians. Could they? What if they were? A world populated by lesbian amazon athletes? Too horrifying. So the myth has changed. Now our athletic bodies have been appropriated as decorative objects for male pleasure.

Except when feminist messages—such as pleas not to "genderize"—sneak through.

• • •

Allida Black, a history professor, watches football on television because it reminds her of the past. As a child, she played football with neighborhood boys and attended college games with family friends whom she adored. At home, her parents force-fed her femininity; she remembers having her hair brushed and "wearing organdy dresses that itched." But at football games, whether playing or watching, she "could scream and carry on and act outrageous and no one would get mad at me." She dreamed of playing quarterback for the University of Alabama.

Recruiters never called. So now she watches and reads about football. Scanning the sports section, she'd "be happy to read about women, too, that would be fabulous," but the *Washington Post,* her local paper, covers women only sporadically.

So, opening the morning paper, Allida Black doesn't get to read about the women she admires: those who do play football, baseball, basketball, lacrosse, soccer, or golf. Nor can she read about women like herself: would-be athletes whose ambitions were stunted.

In a Perry Ellis Fragrance ad entitled "Life is How You Change it," a woman catches a football. But she looks absurd: she's barefoot on a beach, wearing an ankle-length cream-colored dress.

I remember reading the *San Francisco Chronicle* in the late seventies, when I was a Stanford basketball player. Perusing the paper during breakfast each day, I'd rant. That's an unpleasant way to start the day but I couldn't help myself. I'd scrutinize the sports pages, hoping to see something I could relate to, something relevant to my life. I almost never did. As an athlete, I cared about sports, but I couldn't make that leap to caring about men's sports, not when my heroes and indeed my own sports achievements were summarily snubbed. Frequently I saw headlines with the heartening words, "Stanford Basketball." It took many disappointments before I realized that they always, always meant Stanford *men's* basketball.

What about us? I'd think. What about Stanford's nationally ranked women's swimming and tennis teams? What about its crew team, struggling to raise money for a shell, when the men already had three? What about the professional women's basketball league, just starting up then, or the professional women's softball league, whose games I attended, or women's pro golf or tennis? What about the hurdles women have to jump over before they can even get to the track, as they try to convince administrators that they, too, deserve opportunities? Aren't these sports stories?

I wondered why the sports pages ignored the Pacific Ocean rough-water swims, which attracted hundreds of eager participants, both female and male, and the coed surfing competitions, which drew skilled competitors from around the world. I've always been an athlete, and I've always enjoyed watching other athletes, but the sports pages have consistently told me that the sports I participate in don't count as sports, and the sports I like to watch don't count as sports.

"First females" now make the news, especially if they interact with men and especially if they have to take their case to court: the first female to referee a men's pro basketball game, the first NCAA president, the first girl to wrestle or box or play high school football. What we don't hear about are the second female, the twenty-second female, the countless females who enjoy sports as a matter of daily fitness or fun or fanaticism. Women don't receive the status of ordinary, daily heroes. If a college women's team wins a national championship, that might make the local news, but viewers won't learn how the team is progressing during the season: the regular, routine coverage granted to men.[12]

We can read, on a daily basis, stories told by men about men: male strength, male bonding, male power and struggle and sweat. Imagine how the world might seem if we could also read, on a daily basis, stories told by women about women: female strength, female bonding, female power and struggle and sweat. What if, in the sports pages, we could read how a friendship is challenged and strengthened when two women compete for one position? Or how a crew team develops muscle—and trust? Or what sort of intimacy can develop between a softball pitcher and catcher?

What if we saw, on a daily basis, female athletes in action, muscles taut, faces intent on victory?

As it is, we don't even learn much, really, about the life of Monica Seles and Steffi Graf, the best tennis players in the world, or JoAnn Carner, a Hall of Fame golfer still competing in her mid-fifties, or Sheryl Swoopes, the Texas Tech basketball player who scored forty-seven points in the championship game of 1993. No research has been conducted to tell us if female athletes are less likely to stay in abusive relationships than nonathletes. We don't learn just how empowering women's sports can be.

"Revving Up for Ladies' Drag Racing" appeared in the *Washington Post*'s style section recently, even though all-male drag racing stories appear in the sports section. Why, when women do it, is it no longer considered sport? Aerobics, cheerleading, marathon swimming, company softball, mountain biking, in-line skating—why don't these things count as sport? Might women be more interested in reading sports sections if they did?

Instead we hear men's stories, which are largely stories of dominance, violence, potency. Who, among men, is the greatest? Who is toughest, meanest, biggest? *Who has the biggest penis?* They don't say that, but I think that's one metamessage, alluded to through daily reiteration of words like performance and penetration, end zone and hole and huge and humongous and massive and immense. Who is the most manly means who is the most violent and the most sexual.

A billboard ad for a Phoenix health club shows a picture of a man flexing his arm. The caption: "Get hard, stay hard."

"Look at that hit!" announcers say excitedly. When a player is paralyzed, suddenly everyone speaks in hushed tones about "tragedy." But the everyday tragedies of men crunching each other's bodies into oblivion are considered great entertainment.

Fights are what get replayed on the evening news. It's part of an overall media fight pattern: After the stories about foreign wars and terrorist attacks and congressional "battles," and before the evening sex-murder dramas, viewers watch a player strutting over to another player, puffing his chest. Or a team of twenty or thirty players emerging from the bench to defend their pitcher, who has just beaned a batter with the ball, then gotten clobbered by the batter. Or thousands of happy male fans looting and vandalizing a city after a pro football, basketball, or hockey championship.

Football players bang their helmets together (this passes for affection; a Portland State coach recently broke his nose when excitedly "head-butting" a helmeted player) and hockey players pummel each other's faces with fists (this passes for "part of the game") and male reporters cheer. On one NFL ·highlight film, as men tackle or smash into each other, a soundtrack plays car accident noises. Before each Monday Night Football game in the 1992–1993 season, ABC computer graphics depicted two helmets, head to head, colliding and splintering into hundreds of pieces.

Announcers say, "Let's replay the hits, the hurts, the tackles." Commentators' synonyms for "tackled" include hit, drilled, buried, upended, attacked, pounded, gang tackled, sacked, wrapped up, put down on one's face, hammered down, knocked down, ridden down, wrestled down, and hunted down. Former Oakland Raiders coach John Madden has commented, "When something bad happens to you, you don't let it bother you. You go do something bad to the other guys."

Magic Johnson, commenting on the Phoenix-Chicago NBA playoffs in 1993, seemed disturbed at that fact that the two teams had dined together at Michael Jordan's restaurant before the fourth game. "You've got to have some kind of fear—not hate, but dislike—if you're gonna win this championship," he told the television audience. "When I was playing, I never went out to dinner with any of the guys. I felt they had to be the enemy." Later, when Jordan yelled at Danny Ainge and Ainge grabbed Jordan's shirt, Johnson said, "There was too much friendship earlier. Now they're going at it the way a championship is supposed to be."

An ad run in *Sports Illustrated* shows an unsmiling, leather-jacketed man sitting on a motorcycle, thumb hooked into his jeans pocket. "MEN ARE BACK," it announces. Then, below, a picture of aftershave and the phrase, "Brut. The Essence of Man."

The sports media offers paeans to male strength and male violence. They rarely offer descriptions or images of female strength and almost never describe female violence,[13] even in self-defense. Strength and violence are the province of men. Televised hockey, baseball, basketball, and football define men to men and to impressionable boys, equating thuggery with masculinity and depicting men as dangerous, combative creatures with uncontrollable tempers (but, inexplicably, infinitely controllable jump shots). The sports media also defines male violence and male dominance as natural.

Everywhere we turn, we see men banging into each other's bodies or cars while smaller, older, balding men excitedly discuss the athletic men's "exploits." In a fascinating analysis of football instant replays, Vanderbilt University humanities professor Margaret Morse points out that "the most memorable shots are the ones shown in slow motion, where violent force and speed are invested electronically with grace and beauty."[14] Massive male bodies knock each other down over and over again, metamorphosizing brutality into beauty. Violence becomes attractive, graceful.

"Feel the power. In the ring. On the field. On the court. Only on video." In a magazine ad for *Sports Illustrated* videos, one boxer has already pummeled his fists into another man's body so hard the other man is falling down. "Feel the power."

As commentators admire violence, so they admire men. An athlete is a "very likable guy" with "a terrific personality." Commentators say, "I'm his number one fan." They say, "You have to respect him."

"You have to admire a guy who goes out there . . ." John Madden ends that sentence different ways on different occasions. It doesn't really matter what that athlete goes out there and does. You have to admire him. He's a man, you're a man, and there he is, going out there and getting hit, or hitting, or affectionately patting another man's behind. Whatever. Madden gushes: "It doesn't get any better than this."

Players are discussed with a degree of passion many women wish men would offer them. "Mark Rypien can break your heart, then make your heart beat with sheer joy," a sportscaster said during a Redskins-Vikings game in 1993.

Accompanied by footage of athletic forefathers, commentators almost tearfully recount past heroes and past contests. Such "great moments in sports history" provide a sense of continuity, reminiscence, nostalgia. These flashbacks serve to ritualize sport, to establish the current contest as an important link in a historical trend. Networks even provide great moments in men's sports history during women's events. NBC interrupted its own broadcast of the 1993 LPGA Championship to air a seven-and-a-half minute reminiscence about Johnny Miller's 1973 U.S. Open victory.

Men's sports are staged as meaningful. The winner goes to the play-offs, or these two teams haven't met since 1990, or these two coaches have a vendetta against one another, or it's the halfway point of the season, or something, always something. You can see commentators struggle to create meaning—it's difficult to do for each baseball team's 161 games—but they always try. It's always going to be a great game, a decisive game, a close contest, a tough battle. The players are always courageous, big, strong. The fans are always expectant, eager, numerous. The commentators act excited—not because they necessarily feel excited, nor because in their professional opinions the event is actually important in any scheme of things—but because they are essentially advertising the game.

Sports talk radio, directed toward men between the ages of twenty-five and fifty-four, is increasingly popular. As of July 1993, there were at least fifty-one all-sports stations nationwide, twice as many as there were eighteen months before. The editor of *Radio Business Report* predicted another doubling or tripling in three years.[15]

The Washington, D.C., sports talk radio station, WTEM, bills itself as "the team." Callers are greeted with, "Hello, you're on the team." Few women call. When they do, they are likely to be told they have sexy voices. The hosts rarely interview female athletes. They do interview Bul-lettes, the young women who dance at Washington Bullets games. Rich Gilgallon, who hosts the "Kiley and the Coach" show with Kevin Kiley, once introduced two of these women as Madeleine and Carla, as if they had no last names. He seemed primarily interested in their sexual avail-ability: "So, are you single?" One replied that she had a boyfriend, the other a husband. Gilgallon persisted. "Would you dump him? If someone else came along?"

After a commercial break (the station frequently runs commercials for impotence services and products), Susan O'Malley, president of the Washington Bullets, called to tell listeners about a toll-free number. Gil-gallon lamented that O'Malley refused to date him. He had tried on sev-eral occasions to get her to go out with him, he said, and then at the last minute "she has to wash her hair or something."

Carla defended her boss. "She's busy," said Carla. "She's a professional girl—I mean, I started to call her a girl, a lady, but she's a woman. She's very busy."

There ensued a several-minute conversation about why Gilgallon can't get a date.

The traffic reporter, Janet O'Connor, joked that she'd get more air time if she'd "dance around with pom-poms."

Though there is a female traffic reporter and an occasional female host, women can't really be "on the team." Male hosts refer to women as "girls" or "the fair sex" or "the opposite sex." Of female athletes, one WTEM host said: "I want to go to the ice skating world championships. I want to go sit in the lowest possible seat, front row, so I can look up the skirts." Another said that women's basketball would sell more tickets if the players wore fishnet stockings and lingerie.[16]

• • •

For most women, the heroes of the sports media are not our heroes. Their dramas are not our dramas. Men who escape the drugs and violence of the city only to succumb to drugs and violence in one National Manball Association or another: this is not our experience. Male sports stars slam basketballs through hoops, grab other men and throw them to the ground, punch each other in the face. This does not excite us. On national television, baseball players yank at their crotches. This does not seem heroic.

"Who won?" is not women's primary concern. Women tend not to be trivia buffs. They tend not to compete over who has more information. After interviewing athletic women for more than a dozen years, I've only met one (former UCLA and Olympic basketball star Denise Curry) who memorizes sports statistics. When women discuss sports, they tend to talk about their own achievements, fears, passions. They mourn opportunities missed. They admire virtuosic performances, comparing basketball to ballet, hockey to ice dancing. They delight in close, exciting contests, whether between men or women. They enjoy the community or school spirit that can accompany a team's success. And they bemoan the lack of women's media coverage.

When they do see images of strong, graceful, successful female athletes, women are moved, sometimes to tears. The Women's Sports Foundation produces vivid videos that include montages of women skating, shooting, sprinting, rowing, running, and riding.[17] One woman races across the finish line in a wheelchair, her arms raised in victorious salute. Another leaps to snatch a basketball, body extended like a cheetah's. I have seen these videos repeatedly at conferences. Every time, there are women in the audience who are so enthralled they cry. They applaud, too, cheering for women, for themselves.

During Olympic competitions, when television broadcasts feature proud, muscular women slapping batons into each other's eager hands, and proud, muscular women twirling and hurling themselves off unbelievably high platforms, American women are enraptured. They inhale the newspaper's sports section, curious about their new heroes. They organize evenings and weekends around Olympic broadcasts. They talk sports, admiring Nancy Kerrigan, Janet Evans, Gail Devers, Bonnie Blair.

Then the Olympics end and men's sports again pervade the daily coverage, a recitation of which man defeated which other man and how.

When women's sports are covered, they are often subtly sexualized, trivialized, treated as Other, or otherwise devalued. Women's accomplishments are compared to a male standard and found lacking. The event is framed as less historically significant than a comparable men's event. The technical production is inferior, with fewer camera angles, fewer graphics, fewer slow-motion replays. There's talk of weakness, failure, luck, and mental mistakes. The women are called girls,[18] the way African-American adults used to be called girls and boys. And the stories tend to appear at the end of broadcasts or newspaper copy, as if women were an afterthought.

A woman and man, dressed in sports clothes, drive to a basketball game together. Surprise! It turns out to be her game, not his. The man sits in the stands and cheers, but as women run up and down court, the camera focuses on bouncing breasts. A fan holds a sign saying "GO MOM." An off-camera voice says, "It's a whole new game," and, "When you really love to play, the game takes on a whole new flavor. Introducing grape-flavored Gatorade. It's a little different. It's a whole lot wilder."

Though women receive serious coverage more often than they did in the past, women are still portrayed as silly, sexy, uncoordinated, or unlikely athletes. Actress Cheryl Ladd, wearing a low-necked red minidress, posed with a basketball on the end of her long fingernail on a recent cover of *TV Guide*. Ladd's show, "Changes," would "compete" against CBS's Men's Final Four basketball telecast; hence the cute ball trick.

Two inside photos showed Cheryl looking equally dorky, wearing a shorter white dress and again supposedly spinning a basketball. "Cheryl's on the ball," the copy read. The article reported that Ladd, who would play the part of "a beautiful TV reporter who has to choose between her glamorous, fast-lane job in New York and her love for a handsome heart surgeon on the West Coast," is an eighteen-handicap golfer but a "self-confessed ex-tomboy." So, although she golfs, she's not an athlete. An athletic childhood is something women have to grow out of, and then confess to, like juvenile delinquency.

Real female basketball players wearing real uniforms don't grace magazine covers, though on *TV Guide* that would be appropriate, since an increasing number of women's college games are broadcast on TV: fourteen on ESPN in the 1993–1994 season. (That's still a far cry from the two hundred men's games ESPN broadcast that season, but it's a significant advance from the two women's games ESPN broadcast ten years before.) But basketball and women are a safe combination only if made absurd. Cheryl's dainty spin technique made the idea of female athleticism seem hilariously implausible.

Lauren Wolfe, one of about two hundred female high school wrestlers on otherwise boys' teams, recently appeared on a Detroit TV show called "Kelly and Company" to discuss her wrestling experiences at Okemos (Michigan) High. Other guests included a boy who played with dolls and a girl who refused to wear dresses. The program became "a freak show about tomboys and sissies," Wolfe told *Sports Illustrated*. "I don't think of myself as a tomboy. I think of myself as an athlete." [19]

Margaret Carlisle Duncan and Cynthia Hasbrook, University of Wisconsin-Milwaukee professors, analyzed running events, surfing events, and women's and men's basketball broadcasts in 1985 and 1986 and concluded that the physical skills of the women were virtually ignored and that the emphasis on physical features subtly undermined the women's achievements. "The basketball broadcasts described the women as 'fun to watch' and 'very pretty,'" write the authors, while commentators described the men as "great" and "powerful." Camera shots of the surfers focused on their breasts, bottoms, and faces. Even Grete Waitz, winner of nine New York Marathons, was identified as "someone who cooks, sews, and washes clothes just like most wives."[20]

Cooking seems to come to male commentators' minds often. During the 1987 Pan Am Games, CBS's Dick Stockton and Billy Packer had this conversation about United States basketball player Jennifer Gillom:

PACKER: Doesn't Gillom remind you of a lady that someday is going to be a great cook? Doesn't she look like that? She's got just a real pleasant face.

STOCKTON: Maybe she'll open a restaurant.

PACKER: I bet her momma can cook.

Nine women in a magazine ad are "playing basketball" wearing stockings and Easy Spirit pumps. I put "playing basketball" in quotes because one can tell by the way the women are standing—arms askew, legs too close—that they are not athletes. Only legs and buttocks are visible—no heads. One woman dribbles; the others crowd around the way children do, before they learn to play the game.

"To prove a point, we asked women to play basketball in Easy Spirit Dress Pumps," the copy says. "Not just for a few minutes. But for hours. They played hard. And they played to win!"

In the male version of the ad, we see Wilt Chamberlain wearing a business suit and dress shoes, leaping toward a basket with ball in hand. We are not asked to believe he "played to win!" in Easy Spirit dress shoes (or pumps).

Broadcasters and journalists take great pains to remind viewers and readers that Nancy Lopez, for instance, is a "female golfer," and that what women play is "women's golf" (or soccer, or tennis) as opposed to (real) golf, soccer, or tennis, which men play. It's the "lady doctor," "poetess," "woman driver" phenomenon: feminine qualifiers modify the noun, shape it into something unusual, something different.

It's called "gender marking." It becomes sexist only when it's done asymmetrically, with the women's gender being noted, the men's not. In tennis, matches are usually referred to as "men's finals" or "women's finals." This makes sense: viewers might want to know. These parallel markings make the games seem equally important.

But in most other sports, only women's gender is marked. During the 1989 Final Four college basketball championships, broadcasters marked the gender of the women's event ("women's championship," "women's game") an average of twenty-six times per game. The men's games were called simply "The Final Four" or "the NCAA National Championship."[21] Because women's teams continue to use the "Lady Tiger"-type monikers—another sore point with many fans—viewers were actually reminded of the players' gender almost sixty times per game. "As a result, the men's games and tournament were presented as the norm, the universal, whereas the women's were continually marked as the other, derivative, and, by implication, inferior to the men's," conclude the authors of the AAF study.[22]

"What's life like on Planet Reebok?" The female version of a commercial answers itself: "No limits, no pain, no fear . . . no fat, no beauty pageants . . . no old-boy networks, no winners, no losers . . ." Not bad. But Reebok's top eight corporate officers and ten of the eleven directors of their board are male, which may explain why the men in their ads seem to live on a different planet. In one, decathlete Dan O'Brien lifts weights and runs; the ad reads, "On Planet Reebok you can be all-powerful and run the world."

During the 1988 Olympics, swimmer Janet Evans, who won three gold medals and set an Olympic and a world record, was described as "a small wonder, "a tiny tiger," and a "kitten-sized tiger."[23] She was thinner than many swimmers, but she was 5'6", two inches taller than the average woman. Are men—even 4'11", 100-pound jockeys—ever "kitten-sized"? Though male tennis players have relatively small bodies compared to other prominent male athletes, they are routinely described as "big" guys with "big" forehands who play "big games."[24]

After her infamous collision and fall during the 3,000-meter race in the 1984 Olympics, Mary Decker Slaney was described as "a crying distraught woman-child." She was twenty-five years old. Her rival, Zola Budd, then eighteen, was called a "woman-child perfectionist," "a slender shy girl" and "a frightened little deer."[25]

During the quarterfinals of the 1993 French Open, ESPN commentator Barry Tompkins said of Mary Joe Fernandez, "Mary Joe is not a big person physically, but she's got a heart the size of Brazil." Fernandez is 5'10", 140 pounds. That's not big? Compared to whom? How big must a woman be before her body is bigger than her heart?

Washington Post writer William Drozdiak also belittled Fernandez. Writing about her three-and-a-half-hour upset of Gabriela Sabatini, Drozdiak said, "Despite her almost frail appearance, Fernandez said she did not suffer from the extended rallies under the bright sun of the warm spring Paris day." Clearly she was not frail and did not suffer; she came back after losing the first set and being down 1–5 in the second to win 1–6, 7–6 (7–4), 10–8. Afterward, Fernandez hugged Sabatini rather than offering the traditional handshake. Yet Drozdiak said Fernandez "collapsed in Sabatini's arms at the net as they shared a hug."[26] I saw the match and replayed it on videotape to be sure. Fernandez did not collapse. She graciously hugged her opponent.

So female athletes appear frail and not very big and they collapse. They are kittens and tiny tigers, girls and woman-children. They are surprisingly small, even when they are not, and young, even when they are not. The implication: only big people (i.e., men) are or should be athletic. Female champions are not superwomen, but little girls.

Women are further subordinated by being called "Steffi" and "Martina," while men are rarely called "Boris" or "Ivan." Female tennis players are referred to by first name about 53 percent of the time, men about 8 percent of the time. This is what bosses do to subordinates and adults do to children. It's a matter of status. First names infantilize; last names confer respect. Are female tennis players mere teenagers, while men are older? No: the women average 24 years to the men's 22.8 years.[27]

During the prelude to a recent world figure skating championship, viewers saw images of girls in bed sleeping, interspersed with footage of young women skating. The implication: little girls dream, wake up, and magically become champions. Boys, too, dream of becoming sports heroes. But try to imagine a televised introduction to a men's basketball (or skating) championship that features small boys in bed clutching teddy bears, dreaming of turning pro.

• • •

If women can't be kept "in their place"—whether in the back of sports pages, or in the back of the pack behind male athletes, or in predictable feminine, skater-gymnast roles, some male reporters get upset. Tom Callahan, in a *Washington Post* article entitled "The (Lesser) Games Women Play," criticized Olympic basketball players as "faking along and pretending to be near-men." He wrote that they "walked like men. They slapped hands like men. They played like junior high school boys. No, to be fair, like high school boys: the junior varsity."[28]

How should women walk? How, if at all, should they slap hands? These women seemed to offend Callahan by reneging on a social contract to act ladylike. Callahan castigates them for trying to be "near-men" then ridicules them for failing. Apparently women will never be like men— never as good as men—and they shouldn't try. They can't achieve athletic excellence as women, either, for excellence is male. Basketball is male. Slapping hands is male. Walking without high heels is male.

In a Dare perfume magazine ad, Lynn Hill uses impressive shoulder and arm muscles to hoist herself up a steep mountain. "Lynn Hill, world champion rock climber," reads the caption.

In a second photo, she lounges on her side wearing full cosmetic costume: bare-shouldered evening attire, makeup, long pearl earrings, moussed hairdo. Yet she still grips her coiled, pink and black climbing rope, as if she plans to use it during the evening's events. Caption: Lynn Hill, Daring Woman.

Margaret Carlisle Duncan, who has done extensive research on sports, gender, and the media, has noted that when referring to women, newspapers and magazines often use pairs of contradictory modifiers, such as powerful and cute, courageous and vulnerable, skillful and manipulating, all within the same story.[29] Duncan explains the "far-reaching ambivalence" this way: "Many people perceive female strength as threatening, as inappropriate, or as unbecoming." It is "easier to accept female assertion, ambition, and success by casting it in terms of weakness."[30]

Steffi Graf, for instance, has been called "the wonder girl of women's tennis." Basketball players have been described as "big girls" with "little jump hooks." Of one player, a commentator said, "She's tiny, she's small, but so effective under the boards."[31]

In a Coors magazine ad, Olympian Valerie Brisco sits, folded almost pretzel-like. The caption says, "Funny, she doesn't look like the weaker sex." Yet because of her strange position, she does. Large muscles are visible, but she's seated in an impotent posture. The subtext: the triple gold medalist looks funny, weak, and sexy.

During the 1992 U.S. Olympic trials, one American gymnast spit on her hands then rubbed them together while waiting to mount the uneven parallel bars. Gymnasts commonly use saliva to improve grip. It was not an unusual act for an athlete. But the commentator, apparently seeing *female* more prominently than *athlete*, was shocked. "This is something you don't often see!" he said.

At that same event, a fourteen-year-old young woman wearing only a white, legless leotard sat on the floor icing her calf. Her knees fell open, thighs spread—the most convenient position, apparently, for applying the ice. This was something you don't often see either: a girl sitting casually, unself-consciously, influenced by neither womanly shame nor womanly seductiveness. Neither hiding nor displaying her body. It was an exceptional moment of unadulterated innocence, remarkable for its rarity. How often, in the media, do we see images of women with their legs casually, thoughtlessly apart?

Instead we see a self-conscious sexuality, both in the seductive dances of gymnasts and skaters and in the commentary provided by male broadcasters and writers. Olympic gold medalist Mary Lou Retton was called "a calculating coquette." Of Romanian gymnast Ecaterina Szabo, Tom Callahan wrote, "little Szabo looks like she would sooner fall off the balance beam than neglect eye shadow."[32]

During the 1993 French Open, commentator Barry Tompkins misspoke, saying, "This is the men's quarterfinals," then laughed and corrected himself: "Excuse me. The women's quarterfinals. Especially with these two, I should know the difference." "These two" were twenty-three-year-old Argentinean Gabriela Sabatini, praised by male reporters for her glamorous good looks, and Mary Joe Fernandez, an attractive American twenty-one year old. So pretty women are "especially" female, extra female, so female that a male commentator "should know the difference."

Dick Enberg, during the 1993 Ladies Figure Skating World Championships, described Ukrainian Oksana Baiul, who eventually won the competition, as "flirtatious . . . that glorious combination of maturity and vulnerable fragility makes her irresistibly attractive." In the 1988 Olympics, Dick Button said of American skater Caryn Kadavy, "She is so lovely. You know she really has a vulnerability that makes your heart warm to her." Jim McKay agreed: "It fits her personality. A very appealing and vulnerable person."[33]

Male commentators seem to like that: vulnerability. They find it attractive—*in women.* Not in men, whether skaters, gymnasts, golfers, or hockey players. Fragile, vulnerable, flirtatious, and attractive are female words, gender markers to remind us that this person is not only female but feminine, cast in a childish (subservient) and sexy (available to men) position.

In an ad for Russell sporting goods, a woman lifts a large (perhaps a fifteen-pound) weight in a biceps curl. But instead of focusing on what she's doing, she glances over her shoulder toward the (presumably male) viewer. Her mouth is drawn into a pout.

I offer college audiences a slide show called "Pretty Powerful: Images of Female Athletes in the Media." Exhibiting a variety of photos from articles and ads in magazines and newspapers, I ask students, Is this an honest image? Do athletes really look like this? In the course of training or competing or simply living, do they actually get in these positions? Or are they posing for a male audience?

Photos of Olympic swimmer Dara Torres appeared in the premier issue of *Men's Journal.*[34] No other women appeared in this issue, unless you count the fishing article, in which the author asserted that fishing trips are more fun if wives are left at home.

In each of three full-page photos, Torres wore a leotard—not a gymnast's leotard, but the kind one might wear under clothes, with a built-in bra and adjustable straps and a hint of lace. In other words, she posed in her underwear. But it's subtle. Perhaps one could argue that it is a bathing suit. Surely it's not a racing suit, not the kind Torres wore when she won medals on the 1984 and 1988 Olympic teams, nor when she qualified, at the age of twenty-five, for the 1992 Olympic team, shortly before the magazine appeared.

In none of the photos is Torres swimming. In the first she gazes dreamily, hands behind her head, elbows wide open, inviting. In the next she stands on the dock of a lake, arms gracefully extended skyward as if to begin a back dive, except she's not a diver. In the final one she laughs, hands again trapped behind her head, chest thrust forward. This time she is dripping wet. Rivulets of water meander toward her cleavage.

They are beautiful photos. Artistic. Pleasing to the eye. But posed and false. Dishonest. Shapely in the new, muscular definition of the word,

Torres presents an alluring, extraordinary form (the photo essay is called "Return to Form") but we see no substance. No action.

If we think about her as a swimmer at all, we might think that she spends hours each day face down in a pool *so that she can look like this,* wet and muscular and stretched open and laughing. Not the reverse: that she has become stunning incidentally, because of her commitment to athletic excellence. There's a big difference. On the contents page, she is referred to as "Dara Torres, Olympic swimmer on a pedestal." Female athletes have not attained the earthly stature of human beings. They are toys, objects, art, statues. Especially considering that the rest of *Men's Journal* celebrates male bonding, readers could surmise that women are good for only one thing, and that's not Olympic swimming.

Often women appear in unnatural positions eerily reminiscent of pornography. In 1988, triple-gold Olympic runner Florence Griffith Joyner posed on the cover of *Life* touching her toes, nearly bare buttocks in the air. She was doubled over again for a two-page spread inside captioned "Hot Numbers." This time, both top and bottom of the shot were cropped so the viewer saw only a confusing assemblage of body parts: the back of a bare thigh, an inverted face, two muscular arms, and of course all ten painted fingernails.

You've probably seen the headless Special K woman/body emerging from the water in a white bathing suit. Nordic Track ads crop women's heads. Decapitation is also popular in pornography. Without a head, a woman becomes a nonperson, a body that can't object to the reader's stares or imagined assaults because she can't even see. She can't speak. She can't say no.

Photos become pornographic, according to Duncan, when "they highlight women's hips, thighs, buttocks, breasts, crotches (signifiers of sexuality), when they offer viewers voyeuristic thrills by showing "forbidden" sights, or when they show female athletes with certain facial expressions signifying sexual invitation."[35] Many current images of female athletes fit this bill.

This is perhaps the most disturbing trend: the appropriation of women's sports images as sexy, as seductive. The richer and more powerful women athletes as a group become, the more often they are made to resemble prostitutes.

A magazine ad shows a photograph of a man's pelvis. All you see is the area from his waist to his upper thighs. He wears tight jeans. Squeezed into his front pocket is a Casio mini-television. The copy reads: "GET THE ENTIRE USA WOMEN'S HOCKEY TEAM IN YOUR PANTS."

When Ron Martin, editor of the *Atlanta Journal-Constitution,* surveyed his own paper, he found that in 1991 it had used these words to describe women: babes, belles, beauties, bimbos, blonde bombshell, broad, bubble-headed blonde, chicks, coeds, dame, fishwife, gal-pal, girls, hags, harpie, hussie, little lady, nymphette, sex goddess, sex kitten, sex siren, spinster, tart, temptress, tomatoes, vamp, wench, and woman person.

So sexism is not limited to the sports pages. But nowhere are women as under-represented as in the sports pages, and nowhere are women so systematically thrust into feminine, sexualized roles.

• • •

When the Women's Sports Foundation recently asked thirty-four champion female athletes what changes they would like to see in sports, the most frequent response was "more media support/respect." [36] Yet many athletes, eager for fame, endorsements, or an acceptably feminine, heterosexual image, collude in sexual portraits. Ironically, they seek the money that will enable them to keep participating in sports that could, if portrayed honestly, earn them respect. But they understand that for women, sex sells faster than world-class athletic achievement. In order to acquire sponsors, female athletes increasingly must succeed at what Norwegian researcher Liv-Jorunn Kolnes calls gender performance: presenting an image not only of health, vitality, or physical attractiveness, but of feminine beauty and obedience to traditionally feminine standards of behavior. [37]

They may also be motivated by "love." The promise of appearing "beautiful" may especially appeal to women whose large, muscular bodies have been subjected to ridicule and rejection.

In any case, we often see athletes adopting what they think are sexy poses. *People* magazine named skater Katarina Witt and pro volleyball player Gabrielle Reece among "the 50 most beautiful people in the world" in 1992. Reece, who also works as a model, posed for the shot splayed in the sand. Wearing only a bikini bottom, her tangled, sandy hair falling over her face, she clutched a hot-pink volleyball to her naked bosom.

When Steffi Graf posed for *Vogue* in 1990, two photos were "swimsuit" shots. In a third photo, dressed in a low-cut dress, Graf leaned over, her breasts nearly falling out as she struggled to strap a black high heel on her foot. Thus one of the world's greatest tennis players offered the absurd impression that she lacked the coordination to dress herself. Her father explained, "I want a totally different image for Steffi, a feminine image because she's more woman than tennis machine. She's a multitalented girl with terrific modeling possibilities. She could do anything—that's why this new image is so important."[38]

* * *

A woman lifting a heavy weight but pouting seductively is not a woman who would defeat a man in a race. Or, even if she can run or swim faster, if she remains a sex object she remains enfeebled, subordinate. By highlighting her sexuality, the media conceals her strength.

With men, the opposite happens: their strength is highlighted, and their sexuality—at least when it involves criminal behavior—concealed. For instance: When former Washington Bullets basketball player Bernard King and his coach, Wes Unseld, shoved each other at practice one day, the altercation received extensive front-page sports section coverage. But when former Alabama men's basketball coach Wimp Sanderson slugged his longtime secretary/mistress, the news was related in tiny stories on the back pages (near the one-paragraph reports of rape by male athletes.)

So violence between men is exciting, a sporting contest in itself. Male violence against women is noteworthy only if the woman sues—which Sanderson's secretary did—and even then, it's not particularly newsworthy. If covered at all, it's likely to be minimized or joked about. The media seems most interested in male violence against women if it interferes with men's ability to "perform" or if it threatens to draw attention away from "sport."

In 1992, after a woman charged twenty Cincinnati Bengals with rape or aiding and abetting rape, ESPN host Roy Firestone asked Bengals coach Dave Shula how he was managing to focus on the upcoming game without being "distracted" by the allegations. During ESPN's "first American sports awards," called "ESPY's," presenter Gary Busee used the issue of domestic violence jokingly, to impugn the manhood of hockey players: "It's not like it used to be," he said. "There's a bunch of sissies on the ice now. Eric Lindros, the only fights he has are with a woman."

Often both rape and battery are blamed on alcohol. When John Daly withdrew from the PGA tour in 1992, it was to seek help "for an alcohol-related problem," the *Washington Post* reported. The withdrawal followed an "alleged brawl" that resulted in his "arrest on charges of third-degree assault after allegedly attacking his wife, Bettye," but the attack was not mentioned until the sixth paragraph; alcohol appeared in the second.[39]

USA Today also framed the story as an alcohol problem—"Daly Leaves Tour to Enter Rehab"—discussing alcohol in the first paragraph. It's not until the seventh and eighth paragraph that we learn Daly was arrested for "allegedly throwing his wife against a wall" after he had been drinking at their Castle Rock, Colorado, home. Bettye said he also pulled her hair and "destroyed the house." Deputies found broken liquor bottles and broken glass all over the house.[40]

University of Southern California sociologist Michael Messner and Rutgers University journalism professor William S. Solomon analyzed all of the Sugar Ray Leonard-related news stories and editorials in three newspapers in the nine days following Leonard's admission of having physically abused his wife and also having overindulged in alcohol and cocaine. They found that the media framed the story as a "jocks-on-drugs" tale of sin and redemption, minimizing or ignoring Leonard's violent acts toward his wife.[41]

Juanita Leonard testified in divorce court that Ray often punched her with his fists, threw her around, and harassed her "physically and mentally in front of the children." He threatened to kill himself with a gun, she said. He threw lamps and broke mirrors. Leonard denied none of this and spoke of having struck his wife with his fists.

Yet headlines referred to cocaine use, "cocaine abuse," and "drug use"—without mentioning Juanita. Beatings became Juanita's "allegations" and "claims." Threats with a gun and punches became "physical mistreatment." Leonard stated at a press conference that he and his wife "fought, argued," and "grabbed each other," but that "that was in our house, between us."

Within a week, the story was "simply another stage in a heroic career," Messner and Solomon write. *The National* ran a column headlined,

"This Is the Truth About Sugar Ray: He's Not Perfect, but then, Who Is?" Wife abuse was not mentioned. In a *Los Angeles Times* column entitled, "Act of Courage Didn't Involve a Single Punch," Leonard was applauded for his "courage" at the press conference "under the most difficult of circumstances, when he admitted he had used cocaine." The word courage was used nine times, the word bravery three. Wife abuse was not mentioned.[42]

Two years later, I watched Roy Firestone spend a half-hour interviewing Ray Leonard on ESPN's Up Close. Firestone asked about Leonard's infidelity, drug use, and absentee fatherhood. He indicated that he received prior approval from Leonard for these topics, and seemed unusually solicitous, eager not to offend. At one point Firestone asked, "Is it because you didn't have anything in your life that you needed the drugs, and the parties, and the alcohol?"

Leonard said, "I think . . . especially people of high profile, you cross a certain bridge and the people there to greet you, you should not be companions with, you know?"

Thus Leonard's past problems were cast as other people's fault. This led to Leonard discussing his "inner child" and how he had found ways to nurture it.

"Shake that body, shake that body. Baby let me show you how to do this, do that." Several young, thin women wearing boxing trunks, boxing gloves, and sports bras hit punching bags, toss their long blond hair, and throw their arms around Sugar Ray Leonard. The words "full, full" and "sexy, sexy" appear on the screen. It's a commercial for Revlon Mascara, and it's showing now, in the middle of this ESPN interview. We hear a woman's voice saying, "Lashes that are three times as full are three times as sexy."

Back at the studio, Leonard and Firestone comment on the commercial. "Tough work," says Firestone, laughing. "How long did you work on that?"

"Not long enough," Leonard jokes, laughing. He mentions that he has produced an exercise video for women called "Boxout." The interview concludes with talk about Leonard's boxing career—maybe the best boxer ever, Firestone says. He thanks Leonard for his honesty. Wife abuse is never mentioned.

• • •

Why are reporters so schmoozy with male athletes? Editors, writers, producers, and advertisers are primarily white, wealthy men. Sports coverage reflects their interests and their attachment to the status quo, University of Colorado sociologist Jay Coakley has noted.[43] To acknowledge a possible link between punching men in public and punching women in private would interrupt the ongoing celebration of male violence. To acknowledge women's growing physical power would reveal that the jock emperor wears no clothes. To acknowledge that sports don't have to be about combat or dominance would upset the entire discourse.

So reporters cover primarily male events and make men's achievements sound important, historically significant, fascinating, impressive. "Success is described in terms of dominance over others rather than the dynamics of the game itself," Coakley writes. In contrast to countries such as England, where broadcasters downplay the importance of "competition, dominance, and final scores," United States broadcasters "emphasize success through competition, hard work, assertiveness, dominance, and obedience to authority. The idea that success could be based on empathy, autonomy, personal growth, progressive changes, or the achievement of equality gets little or no attention."[44]

Women, similarly, get little attention, unless they have big breasts and jiggle them in the baseball stands.[45] By watching sports we can surmise that what men do is more important than what women do; men have the "necessities" to lead, comment, command; men are better athletes than women are; men are naturally aggressive; and women are naturally sex objects for men. These values appeal, apparently, to male viewers. At least, that is the assumption of most male advertisers and media decision makers. They keep reinventing the same wheel of fortune: selling male violence and female sexiness to a male audience. They don't seem to think about a female audience.

Even women's publications are beholden to the desires of male advertisers. When I worked at *Women's Sports* magazine, advertisers threatened to withhold ads if we covered bodybuilding, weight lifting, basketball, softball, or other "dykey" sports. The publisher soon transformed the magazine into *Women's Sports and Fitness,* which now primarily features photos of thin, pretty women who are not necessarily athletes.

Increasingly, the media doesn't cover sports so much as it sponsors sports. Television in particular plays a marketing role. It enables sports to exist at their current levels. By offering multimillion-dollar deals for the rights to broadcast games (NBC agreed to pay $456 million for the rights to the 1996 Olympics), television producers become invested, literally, in those games being portrayed as fascinating entertainment. They showcase events rather than report on them. Rarely do broadcasters raise indelicate issues like rape or battery. Rarely do they risk alienating their primary audience—men—by depicting strong, aggressive women playing team sports. Those million-dollar investments come from advertising revenue: a projected $11.5 billion by the year 2000 from sports ads.[46]

Reporters who criticize or even question male athletes, coaches, or owners can find themselves locked out of the locker room. Anger him, and an athlete may refuse to talk. Reporters who hope to establish ongoing access to athletes have to keep those athletes happy by not being too harsh, too judgmental, or too honest about the athlete's off-field exploits.

But often, reporters don't feel critical of the athletes anyway. Most reporters are fans, and they tend to adopt the views of the people they cover. Most sports reporters are men who grew up collecting baseball cards. They were mesmerized by sporting events long before they got paid to watch. They feel privileged to converse with "great athletes." If they feel critical, it's often born of snobbery (these men aren't too bright) or jealousy (these men make too much money).

Former Mets manager Jeff Torborg, speaking to a group of female sports reporters, responded to their criticisms of his team this way: "If you're not fans, if you don't love the game, why cover it?" Political writers are not expected to love politics. Business writers are not expected to love business. But sportswriters are expected to be fans.

And most of them seem to be. Television in particular is uncritical of male athletes, but newspapers and radio also soft-pedal sexism (as well as racism and homophobia). Instead they fill pages with "controversies" such as who owns the rights to the image of Michael Jordan's face.

Most reporters also seem to be fans of violent masculinity. A recent survey of 207 sportswriters and broadcasters found that 90 percent believe hockey would be "less exciting than bowling" without the fights.

Sixty-eight percent said they watch the Indianapolis 500 to see an accident.[47]

It seems safe to assume that most male sportswriters and editors are not feminists. When covering men's sports, they are not thinking about the effect on women of the culture's worship of male violence. When the men in the locker room joke about the cheerleaders or female reporters, male reporters tend to laugh along.

In a recent conversation with a male reporter, I asked, "Why don't you cover women's sports?"

He said, "No one goes to women's games, so why should we?" Coaches of women's teams are achingly familiar with this rationale.

"If you go," I explained, "readers will know the games are happening, and how exciting they can be, and they'll consider attending, too."

"Oh, we wouldn't want to do that!" he said immediately. "We're not social change agents. We're just here to report the news."

He was wrong. Reporters do not simply follow the public's interest. They create interest by discovering and reporting on interesting people, events, and trends. But his attitude was typical of many reporters and editors. They see themselves as reflecting and maintaining the status quo.

The public issues its own demands for laudatory journalism. At KIRO-TV in Seattle, one reporter who was not, apparently, ensconced in the athletic supporter role quit when the station killed a controversial story about the 1991–1992 Washington football players. The planned broadcast would have reported that several Huskies failed to respond to outstanding arrest warrants on charges ranging from traffic offenses to assaults.

Station president Ken Hatch explained that he did not want "to spoil some of the beauty of the season" because "the whole region is just thrilled with their Huskies."

The story had been the second in a two-part series. The first, about poor graduation rates among the players, had been criticized by viewers and university officials.

• • •

Despite all the glorification of men and obfuscation of women, we're beginning to see a few chinks in the armored images of male athletes, along with some serious, respectful treatment of female athletes. Such as: muscled men holding babies. Tom Hanks and Geena Davis in *A League of Their Own* having a simple nonsexual conversation on the team bus. Hall-of-Famer Kathy Whitworth, winner of eighty-eight tournaments, offering golf advice to hundreds of *USA Today* readers, male and female.

In a Kodak ad, a woman with huge arm muscles lifts a large weight in a biceps curl. She is not pouting. She is looking at the weight, concentrating. Her yellow muscle shirt glistens with sweat. The caption: The Color of Power.

Responding to pressure from Fairness and Accuracy in the Media, NBC ran a thirty-second public service announcement (PSA) decrying domestic violence during the 1993 Super Bowl's pre-game show. In the PSA, a man wearing a shirt and tie sits unhappily in a jail cell. "I can't believe this is happening," says a narrator. "We were just having an argument. I didn't mean to hurt her. . . . I didn't think you'd go to *jail* for hitting your *wife*."

NBC spokesman Curt Block told the *Washington Post* that the network decided to air the antiabuse message "because their cause is a good one," and denied any link between football and violence against women.[48] But journalists at media outlets from the *New York Times* to *Good Morning America* discussed the correlation between football and male violence against women in the home. Backlash ensued: a few newspapers refuted any correlation between the Super Bowl and domestic abuse. Yet hundreds of women responded to the ad's 800 number, and people who saw the ad or read newspaper stories began to think and talk about male sports and male violence against women in a new way.

In an ad for Moving Comfort, the women's athletic clothing company, the owners state, "We believe that a physically fit woman is a powerful woman. And we take pride in making clothes that encourage a woman on the path to fitness and power."

Power. Advertisers are starting to take risks with the revolutionary concept that women want power—or already have power—to be used at their discretion. Not the power to be sexy, to attract men. Power to do whatever one pleases.

John Papanek, managing editor of *Sports Illustrated for Kids,* was once asked why his magazine covers depict a preponderance of male athletes. His response: "It is reasonable to think that a cover that features only females will be repugnant to those people who are most likely to buy the magazine."[49] The awful truth is, he may be right.

But the more boys see female athletes, the less they seem to feel that way. Several young male friends of mine decorate their bedrooms with posters of Michael Jordan *and* Dawn Staley, Pete Sampras *and* Monica Seles. I've overheard boys at college basketball games excitedly, reverently discussing the abilities of Sheryl Swoopes and other female athletes, and bragging that in their own leagues, they wear the same numbers that their female idols wear. At the high school where I coach girls' basketball, many members of the boys' basketball team enthusiastically watch televised women's college games. If some boys still can't relate to female athletes, it is in large part *because* of what has been in essence a media boycott of honest images of those athletes. When they receive access to those images and to those actual women, they no longer seem to feel repulsed.

"THE CLASSIC STORY REALLY," begins a Nike ad. **"Boy meets girl. Boy falls in love with girl. Boy and girl run out of things to talk about. Girl resents boy's patronizing tone. Boy doesn't understand. Girl grows distant. Boy doesn't understand. Girl takes up running. Boy doesn't understand. Girl tells boy to buzz off. Girl wins major outdoor road race. BOY FINALLY GETS IT."**

Legend has it that Nike insiders once dubbed a shoe "The Vagina" because it "looked like hell but felt good once you got inside."[50] Fact has it that Nike is a male-dominated company that endorses primarily male athletes and coaches. But in the past few years they've decided to reach out to a "women's market." They now sponsor hundreds of female athletes and coaches, and they have published some innovative ads written by women for women.

"BOY FINALLY GETS IT" is one of these ads, in what they call their "Empathy" campaign. Another begins, "All your life you are told the things you cannot do." Another begins, "You do not have to be your mother." Another: "This isn't P.E. class." Another: "You are not a goddess." The poetic prose speaks to ordinary women who are discovering the extraordinary exhilaration that comes with athletic effort. It addresses women's anger at unattainable beauty ideals and at men who have tried to thwart their ambitions. It addresses women as real people with dreams and desires and a history of athletic humiliations and roadblocks. The campaign boosted Nike's sales, generated 100,000 appreciative letters in the first eighteen months, and led to widespread media attention, including a feature on the "Oprah Winfrey Show."

What's most important, say the female executives, copywriters, and art directors who are creating the new real-woman ads, is to respect women. Apparently this is a new concept.

> Jockey's "real people" campaign features Olympic swimmer Nancy Hogshead, a three-time gold medalist, and also photos of a truck driver, a physician, and a makeup artist; the women are Asian, Hispanic, and "queen-sized." "We have a sign on the wall here: "Most women would rather be comfortable than sexy," says Gail Compton-Huff, Jockey's vice-president of advertising, adding that the campaign has been "very very very successful."

Good intentions sometimes go awry. Readers came across the Hogshead ad when flipping past pictures of busty nonathletes in the 1992 *Sports Illustrated* swimsuit issue. Hogshead, president of the Women's Sports Foundation, called the models' photos "degrading" but said she felt "very comfortable" with her ad and its placement, in part because revenue from sales of a poster of the ad directly benefited the Foundation.

> A few commercials now mock masculinity and men's egotistic association with sports. Some offer alternative images of women—strong, self-assured, amused by men's macho posturings. They give viewers a chance to laugh at men in a good-natured way. In a Subaru commercial, a woman dressed in jeans and a work shirt looks under her car's hood, checks the oil. She says, "Every guy I've ever known thinks he knows everything about cars, and everything about the '69 Mets. They walk around the car, and lift up the hood and say, 'This is where the engine is and this is where the oil goes.' What would I do without 'em? . . . This is what I did. I bought . . . the new Subaru Impreza with a horizontally opposed engine and ABS brakes. And after I explain to him exactly what that means I say, 'The '69 Mets? . . . The Cubs choked. Yes, they did. They choked.' "

In the late eighties and early nineties, a few male writers began to take a feminist stance. In *The Hundred Yard Lie,* Rick Telander described college football's systemic corruption, including sexism. In a *Sports Illustrated* column called "Not a Shining Knight" Telander criticized Indiana University basketball coach Bobby Knight for numerous sexist incidents, including his infamous "If rape is inevitable, relax and enjoy it" line. Phil Taylor, in another *Sports Illustrated* column, proposed that female basketball coaches should be hired to coach men.

> **One more commercial. I forget what they're trying to sell this time, but we see three men standing on a golf course, lamenting the fact that their buddy had to stay home and help his wife clean the garage. "Poor Bob," they say. The camera shows us that Bob is not, in fact, cleaning the garage, but playfully, tenderly beginning to make love with his wife. Back at the golf course, the men say to each other, "So what shall we do tonight? Talk about cars?"**
>
> **We laugh at the men. Women still represent the extremes of household drudgery or sex—Bob's wife was not, apparently, invited golfing—but it's male sports bonding that's being ridiculed.**

Advertisers are not dumb. They know that most men are not fierce football players, not tooth-breaking hockey players, not baseball brawlers. They know that many men are feeling pressure from the women in their lives not to demean women in large or small ways. A few advertisers—perhaps pointing toward a trend?—are cleverly offering self-parodies that ease some of the cognitive dissonance men may feel between their sports-watching lives, in which they celebrate violence, and their personal lives, in which they admit, however grudgingly, that they must change.

10

The Looker Room

Women have faithfully kept male secrets, have passionately refused to speak on the subject of men—who they are, how they think, how they behave, how they dominate.

—bell hooks, *Talking Back*

ON SAN DIEGO'S Mission Boulevard, two businesses sit incongruously side-by-side: Acapulco Joe's, a bar with sidewalk seating, and Movin' Shoes, a sporting goods store for runners. Some of the region's top female runners shop at the sports store. Frequently they borrow shoes, run around the block to try them out, then find themselves sexually harassed by rowdy patrons of Acapulco Joe's.

Kate Callen, a freelance writer and former UPI sports editor, was on her way to investigate increasing tensions between patrons of the two stores when she herself was harassed. She had parked her car and was carrying her young niece across the street when she heard a man whistle and shout at her from his table at the bar: "Hey baby, that's a cute baby you got and you're cute too!"

"What kind of sleeze would whistle at a woman carrying a baby?" she thought.

It was not the first time she had been harassed. A runner, she had heard sexual taunts during training runs and even competitions. But she'd never before been carrying a purse with pen and paper. This time, she walked over to the man and interviewed him. A bartender, his name was named Ted Lewis. "He was dumb enough to give me his full name," Callen said later, "so I wrote it down."

Lewis admitted that he often yells at women as they pass by, and that his remarks include obscenities, but he maintained that his comments are "totally friendly." If women don't like it, he said, "there's something wrong with them."

Callen recorded his answers in her notebook. She later interviewed sexual harassment experts and Cori Brown, a local runner who was angry about repeatedly being harassed. Callen's story, "Friendly Fire: Men Call It Flirting, Women Call It Insulting," appeared on the front page of the *San Diego Union*'s Currents section in July 1991. In the following month, the paper received sixty-five letters on the subject, mostly from women with harassment stories of their own to tell. Ted Lewis telephoned the paper's ombudsman to complain that Callen had made him "look bad."

· · ·

Most women don't have the opportunity to make men look bad. Journalists do. Filmmakers, authors, and radio and television reporters do. They can record male behavior and disseminate their observations and interpretations to large audiences. They can name names. They can interrupt a daily discourse that tells readers and viewers how heroic men are.

There are fewer women writing about sports than any other popular media subject. Few women write about women's sporting experiences— including sexual harassment—and few women write about male athletes and their varied "exploits." When women do write about sports, they can offer an alternative perspective on male behavior. They can interject soprano voices into a discourse long dominated by the bass.

This explains, I believe, why editors have been reluctant to hire female reporters. Women might attend a sporting event and bring back a different story than a man would tell: a female perspective, a feminist perspective. Women might ask, "Why are all the coaches and umpires men?" They might ask, "Why are baseball players always tugging at their crotches?" They might say, "These fights look as fake, and as silly, as 'The Three Stooges.' " They might say, "Hey, these guys aren't gods! They're ordinary people!"

Female reporters might insist on covering women's games, on describing female strength, on honoring the athleticism of female skaters gymnasts, and synchronized swimmers. They might publish or broadcast the names of men who hassle them on the street, and the names of male athletes and coaches who sexually assault or abuse or molest them. For many women, these would be interesting sports stories to read.

After her harassment article was published, Kate Callen received obscene phone calls, some on her home answering machine. One man called her a bitch; he said that to write such a "biased, bullshit" article she must be fat, ugly, and unable to attract men; he told her to break up with her vibrator and "taste sperm"; and he vouched for sperm's good taste because he said he and his friend routinely lick it off "girls' boobies." He concluded by threatening to "come over at four in the morning and fuck you up the ass."

Melanie Hauser, reporter/columnist for the *Houston Post,* says her appearance in pro baseball and football locker rooms over the past eighteen years has been greeted with comments of "fresh wool" and "nice cunt." A player on the Buffalo Bills once came up behind her and whispered, "Hey baby, don't you dream about this at night?"

The first time Michelle Kaufman entered the Miami Dolphins' locker room along with several male writers, she was a college junior. She began to ask questions of a player, then, she recalls, "All of a sudden everybody was laughing directly across from me. I knew there was some joke going on." She later learned that one naked player had stood behind her, gyrating his hips as if thrusting his penis inside her. Mock rape or mock sex? In either case, "it was a terrible experience," recalls Kaufman. "It was disturbing that none of the writers told him to stop. You would think someone would have done something."

After being propositioned by a married All-Star baseball player whose wife had just had a baby, Johnette Howard said, "I talked to other writers. They said, Everybody knows he's a wild man. I said, Then why does he have this reputation as a 'great guy'? You know, you always hear that these are 'great guys.' But the people who have been constructing these images are guys. I bet if the women made up a list, it would be completely different."

"And shorter?" I asked.

"Much," she said.

Sexual harassment is as familiar to female journalists as the scent of sweat. Everybody's got not one story, but many, many stories. Talk to women who cover men's sports on a daily basis and you hear about players who walk past, deliberately brushing their genitals against your arm. Coaches who say, "Oh, you must know which guy has the biggest thing." Male reporters who joke about tennis matches being "lesbo" events. Editors who say, "You look as pretty as you write."

The Equal Employment Opportunity Commission defines sexual harassment as any behavior "for the purpose or effect of unreasonably interfering with an individual's work performance or creating an intimidating or hostile or offensive environment." Estimates of the frequency of sexual harassment of sportswriters vary. *Detroit Free Press* reporter Michelle Kaufman says that during her two-year tenure covering the Tampa Bay Buccaneers for the *St. Petersburg Times,* she was "hassled every single day"; Claire Smith, of the *New York Times* says she's only had one "bad day" in more than a dozen years of sports writing. But harassment is clearly pervasive. At the 1992 Association of Women in Sports Media (AWSM, pronounced awesome) convention, various women stood to testify to their experiences of sexual harassment. President Tracy Dodds added her own stories, then asked, How many of you have had problems like these? About sixty out of seventy-five women raised their hands.

"What would happen if one woman told the truth about her life?" poet Muriel Rukeyser asks. "The world would split open."[1] Women who have access to the media have the power to split the world open.

There aren't many of us yet. Only 8 percent (about 800 out of 10,000) sportswriters and broadcasters are female. Only about a dozen women write regular columns in the sports pages;[2] only four women serve as top sports editors. Nor do women have many opportunities to publish sports stories in women's magazines, which tend to encourage women to lose weight rather than gain strength. Women who do work as sportswriters are often beholden to male bosses who demand booster business as usual, albeit with a female byline. They don't want the world split open. Nor, it seems, do many male readers and fans.

The public dialogue over female reporters has focused not on their opportunity to tell their truths but on the propriety of their presence in the locker room. The locker room always means the men's locker room. In fact, women have locker rooms, too, and male reporters sometimes interview female athletes there. (Using common sense, the women keep their clothes on until reporters leave.) Male athletic trainers enter women's locker rooms. Male coaches give pregame and postgame talks in women's locker rooms. Male coaches have even been known to molest female athletes in their own locker rooms. Yet there has been no outcry about male intrusions into women's "sacred spaces."

In *A League of Their Own,* the baseball coach played by Tom Hanks stumbles into the women's locker room drunk, pulls out his penis, and urinates. He urinates for a long time, as if marking the territory as his. Because of the authentic sound effects, it's a humorous scene.

What if a female coach barged into a men's locker room, drunk, and urinated? Could that be amusing? Or would we fear for her safety?

Male locker rooms are shrines to masculine might. Traditionally, women have entered only as men's fantasies and fabrications, as body parts. A man might say he "needs some pussy," or that he "fucked her brains out last night." A man may call another man "my bitch" or a "wuss." A two-dimensional woman, breasts bulging out of a bikini, may be pinned to a wall. This is not a place where men boast of their wives' successful careers. When mentioned at all, women tend to be discussed in derogatory and often sexualized terms.[3]

When a real woman does enter this shrine, she automatically challenges the male bonding process. Having defined masculinity as sexually aggressive and not feminine, many male athletes seem to feel they must subjugate this woman to an inferior role. In order for them to continue feeling like men, she must become Other.

If she can be defined as a wife or a girlfriend, that takes care of the problem. But a reporter has no sexual relationship to the men. She enters their locker room not to be seduced but to ask questions and to report those answers, along with her own assessments, to the public. She becomes what University of Minnesota scholars Mary Jo Kane and Lisa Disch call "an authoritative critic of male performance."[4] As such, she presents a threat unless the men can successfully sexualize her—asking her for dates, showing her their penises, commenting on her physical attractiveness—all of which they do.

• • •

"Whenever I go somewhere, I'm asked, 'How did you get into sports writing?' " says *Detroit Free Press* writer Michelle Kaufman. "Male reporters never get asked that.

"I say, 'I like sports and I like to write.' What other reasons could there be?

" 'But why sports?' They always say that."

"I say, 'Why not?'

"Finally it comes out that they think my ulterior motive is going into the locker room."

I get asked about "the locker room" everywhere I go. I could be on the radio talking about girls' basketball. I could be on a television show or at a public forum discussing football players and rape. It doesn't matter. Inevitably I'm asked, "What do you think of women in the locker room?"

Women never ask. From this I conclude that this is not a burning issue for women. Women do not harbor fantasies about men's locker rooms. They do not seem curious about them or interested in questioning women who have been there.

In fact, it's men who want to rub shoulders with their heroes, congratulate them, high-five them, bask in their reflected glory. In fact, far from private sanctuaries, locker rooms are often deluged after games with male celebrities, groupies, and "wannabes." *Washington Post* reporter and columnist Johnette Howard says of the Los Angeles Lakers' locker room, "I've seen O. J. Simpson, Arsenio Hall, and Dudley Moore in there. There are millions of guys in backwards baseball hats saying " 'Yo, Man.' "

"Be in the locker room before the game," an NFL video promises. They're not talking to women. It's boys and men who adore male athletes, who paste their posters on their walls, buy their biographies, memorize their batting averages, watch their highlight films.

The men who protest women's right to be in the men's locker rooms may be envious of the athletes' entitlements: unimaginable sums of money and a supposedly endless queue of sexually available women. But more importantly, they seem jealous of women's ability to get close to these powerful idols, and to see something they themselves are curious about: How big are these men's penises? Accusing women of "looking," male fans want to look for themselves. It's men, not women, who express fascination with penis size. Speculation about penis size, measuring one's own penis size, and racist stereotypes about penis size are common male preoccupations. One recent *Playboy* cartoon featured an African-American man asking a hotel clerk for a shoehorn so he could cram his huge penis into a trembling white woman's vagina. Male reporters (most of whom are white) frequently discuss which pro athletes (many of them are African-American) are "well hung" and which are not. Whether this reflects a racist obsession with penis size or just a male obsession with penis size (or a combination of both) is difficult to tell. In any case, "the guys often talk about how well endowed someone is, whereas women never do," says Johnette Howard, a sportswriting veteran of more than thirteen years.

During a lovemaking scene between Kyra Sedgwick and Campbell Scott in the movie *Singles,* Sedgwick asks Scott, "What are you thinking of right now?" The camera reveals he's imagining conducting a locker room interview with his sports hero, Xavier MacDaniel. Perhaps it's not incidental that Scott has this fantasy during sex. Perhaps for men, a fantasy of interviewing pro athletes as they undress is on some level a sexual fantasy.

Gay men admit this. Before entering the Los Angeles Raiders' locker room myself, I asked several people for advice. One was Brian Pronger, a gay man and the author of *The Arena of Masculinity: Sports, Homosexuality, and the Meaning of Sex.* "If you were planning to go into the Raiders' locker room after a game, what would you want to ask the players?" I inquired.

"I'd just want to see what their bodies look like," he said. "I'd be too busy looking to ask questions."

• • •

Women don't go into the locker room to look, but to listen. *Washington Post* writer and columnist Christine Brennan, the only woman to have covered the Redskins, says, "The locker room is the place where writers interview athletes. It's not exciting or sexy or tantalizing. It's cramped and steamy and messy."[5]

CBS sports commentator Lesley Visser has called it "the least sensual environment I've ever been in."

The first time Michelle Kaufman entered a men's locker room, for a football game between the University of Miami and the University of Florida, she was a college sophomore, writing for the *St. Petersburg Times.* "I was scared. I was grossed out," she recalls. Of the seventy-five members of the media, she was the only woman. "I was shocked that the men weren't dressed. You see old men—coaches—walking around naked.

The offensive linemen have all these zits on their backs and behinds. There's a bloody trail of tape on the floor—it sticks to your shoes and you have to peel it off with your fingers. There's a bin where they're supposed to put jockstraps. They shoot them like slingshots. Half don't make it to the bin."

Kaufman says that men always tell her, "I don't think I could interview Gabriela Sabatini naked. I wouldn't be able to do the job."

Her response: "Well, women can. I've said to athletes, I hate to burst your bubble, but I'm not interested in seeing your schlong."

Is it really appropriate for a nineteen-year-old college sophomore to be interviewing her nineteen-year-old peers while they dry their naked bodies with towels? In tennis, swimming, golf, track, and the Olympic Games, reporters meet athletes in interview rooms, where everyone remains dressed. In women's college basketball, the women remain dressed until the reporters leave the locker room.

But men's pro team sports, which are nothing if not tradition-bound, have two traditions dating back to the days when all reporters were male: reporters conduct locker room interviews, and athletes lounge in the nude. There is a belief among most reporters, male and female, that it makes sense for reporters to interview these men while they dress. Reporters need to obtain quick notes to meet their deadlines, and athletes are notoriously reluctant to talk with the press, especially after defeats or poor performances. While they can avoid interview rooms, it's harder to escape the locker room.

Strangely, few team administrators insist that the men *get dressed* during the ten-minute-or-so "cooling off" period after a game and before reporters are permitted in the locker room. Coaches, owners, union representatives, and even commissioners also act peculiarly impotent to convince these million-dollar men to refrain from harassing women or to stop by an interview room to speak to the media. Former Mets manager Jeff Torborg says, "I know there should be a conference room. But you can't get the guys to go into a conference room. You can't even get them to go on a post-game TV show and they get a gift for it."

NFL commissioner Paul Tagliabue says the players' representatives have told him, "You give my players a three-dollar per diem and they will agree not to flash reporters."

Donald Fehr, executive director of the Major League Baseball Players Association, told a group of female sportswriters, "Nineteen-year-olds are going to act like nineteen-year-olds. You can't get away from that. There's a lot of things that ought to go under the category of, Can't you [reporters] have a thicker skin?"

Female reporters have tried not to rock this bizarre yacht. "We just want to be treated equally," they maintain, insisting that they "don't mind" interviewing eighteen- to forty-year-old males in various states of undress or "don't mind" waiting a few extra moments while a man gets dressed and that they can accomplish this "professionally." I've only heard one, *San Jose Mercury News* writer Annette John-Hall, state the obvious: "It's ludicrous to conduct business in a place where men are not dressed."[6]

Even physicians don't do it: they ask their patients to wear gowns. A system that "worked" when all reporters were men was intrusive and undignified then, too, but it is more so now that women report on men's sports. The system should be changed. But as minorities, female reporters have not proferred that perspective. They want to fit in, to be accepted. In an odd stalemate, male administrators and players also refuse to budge much, first denying women access to the locker room, then begrudgingly allowing them access but not relinquishing their right to lounge in the nude.

Pro football, baseball, and basketball have had equal-access policies since the mid-1980s. Some, like the Dallas Cowboys, use an interview room. At the college level, there is no national equal-access policy, so some schools now allow male reporters inside but close the locker room to all reporters if women request interviews. Occasionally colleges still allow male reporters access to the locker room but expect women to wait outside. That doesn't work. "These are not the most articulate guys in the world," explains Claudia Polley, the first woman accredited (in 1974) with the Indy 500's top credential (a Silver Badge), and the first woman (in 1975) to broadcast network TV sports. "Once they've said what they were going to say after a game, they aren't going to say it again. Their minds are on partying."

Female reporters continue to demand equal access, whether in locker rooms or interview rooms, but they don't seem to feel entitled to say,

"Now that we're here, and we can all see how ridiculous nude interviews are, let's change the system." They are pioneers, but only to a point. They have the power to split the world open, but don't seem to know that yet.

• • •

Women have been writing about sports in America since at least the 1920s, when Lorena Hickok, an Associated Press journalist, wrote about baseball, football, boxing, and other sports for the *Minneapolis Morning Tribune*. Hickok, who covered Franklin Delano Roosevelt's campaign in 1932, also reported on Eleanor Roosevelt and later became her friend and lover. It was Hickok who suggested to Roosevelt that she permit only women to cover her news conferences, a policy that forced many papers to hire women.

Mary Garber has worked as a sportswriter for the *Winston-Salem Journal* for almost fifty years. During World War II, she served as sports editor for an "all-girl" staff. After the men returned from the war, she lost her editor's position and resumed writing. Rosemary Carron of Philadelphia also wrote about sports for her daily paper during World War II. None of these women entered locker rooms. Nor were they allowed to sit in press boxes.

During the 1970s, as the second wave of the feminist movement gained momentum, a few more women began to be hired to cover sports. The late Anita Martini, the first woman to enter a men's locker room (in 1974 at the Houston Astrodome), co-broadcast a Houston sports talk radio show for thirteen years in the 1970s, 1980s, and 1990s. Phyllis George appeared on CBS's "The NFL Today" from 1975 to 1984. NBC's Gayle Gardner was the first female football anchor to appear weekly on a major network.

A turning point came in 1978, when the New York Yankees refused *Sports Illustrated* reporter Melissa Ludtke access to their clubhouse (locker room). Ludtke sued, claiming that she had been excluded on the basis of her gender, which violated the Fourteenth Amendment. Baseball Commissioner Bowie Kuhn responded that he needed to protect the "sexual privacy" of players and "to protect the image of baseball as a family sport."[7]

New York Federal District Court Judge Constance Baker Motley ruled in favor of Ludtke, ordering that women not be excluded from the

Yankees' locker room unless male reporters were excluded too. The men's privacy could be assured by the use of towels, a separate interview room, or curtains, she noted.[8]

During that year's World Series, Kuhn appealed to the Second Circuit Court of Appeals for a stay of Motley's order, which was denied. Judge Walter Mansfield, responding to the "baseball is a family game" argument, remarked, "The last I heard, the family includes women as well as men."[9]

• • •

Recently, women have gained some authority. In 1993, the Associated Press Sports Editors (APSE), with more than five hundred members, elected its first female president. Sandra Bailey, a former *New York Times* deputy sports editor who now edits for *Sports Illustrated,* dedicated her tenure to improving working conditions for women and minority men. That same year, the first two women—Melanie Hauser of the *Houston Post* and Nancy Gay of the *San Jose Mercury News*—were elected to the Pro Football Writers Board of Directors. When San Diego State University officials pulled three female reporters out of its locker room after the USC game in 1992, APSE and AWSM pressured the university to change its policy and guarantee equal access, which it did.

A few women, including Nanci Donnellan of Seattle and Ann Liguori of New York, host sports radio shows. CBS recently assigned two female reporters, Andrea Joyce and Lesley Visser, to major-league baseball play-offs. Visser, a former sportswriter for the *Boston Globe,* has worked the men's NCAA Final Four and is a regular on CBS's "The NFL Today" show. Mary Carillo, who broadcasts tennis and other sports for ESPN and CBS, was the first woman to cover championship-level men's tennis. The *Washington Post*'s sports section has a male editor, George Solomon, but two of the three editors directly below him are women.

Yet membership in the American Society of Newspaper Editors remains 97.5 percent white and 90 percent male. Fifty-one percent of newspapers hire no minorities. Female broadcasters are especially scarce: about fifty women broadcast sports at the 630 network affiliates nationwide.

Overall, female journalists earn only 64 percent of what male journalists earn. In the top jobs, women receive from $3,400 (newspaper) to $9,000 (TV) less than men doing the same work, with the same experience, according to a study by Jean Gaddy Wilson of the University of Missouri.[10]

Despite increasingly open men's locker rooms, these women face difficult working conditions, from minor annoyances to pay inequities to verbal and even physical assaults. Not only are they confronted with virtually all male colleagues and bosses, the athletes they are assigned to cover are usually men; so, too, are the coaches and owners; so, too, are most of the people who read or listen to or watch their work.

The work itself is arduous: extensive travel; incessant tight deadlines; young, uneducated interview subjects; and, frankly, many dull games that must somehow be made to sound interesting. Live television reporting can be particularly tough. Kathrine Switzer, perhaps best known for being the first woman officially to run the Boston Marathon, has broadcast marathons and other major road races for ABC, PBS, and local stations since 1978. "Doing broadcasts from the back of a motorcycle is harder than you could believe," she says. "You can't hear what's said in the studio. It's freezing-ass cold. As you talk, they're telling you to shut up. You start explaining something, and a voice in your ear says, 'Wrap it up in ten,' and they start counting ten, nine, eight, seven—and you can't finish your thought."

When male coaches, colleagues, producers, readers, and athletes are uncooperative, seductive, or abusive, it makes the work trickier. An NBA coach repeatedly tried to kiss *Washington Post* reporter Johnette Howard and invited her to dance with him. Howard patiently explained, "If you kiss me, the fifty other reporters are going to think that's the only reason you're talking to me, because I let you kiss me." He stopped trying to kiss her. He also stopped talking to her. "He didn't seem to be able to figure out another way to relate," Howard says.

When Michelle Kaufman joined the sports staff at the *Detroit Free Press* she got tested, literally, by a reader who sent her a ten-question quiz. "These are things you should know if you're going to be a sportswriter," he wrote. Kaufman showed the quiz to the male reporters in her office. None of them knew any of the answers.

Readers have told Kaufman that she can't write about football because she didn't play it. "Most male writers haven't played football," she reminds her detractors. "They've never played ice hockey or boxed, either, and they write about those things."

Even women doubt her competence. A reader recently called the newspaper and asked to speak to "someone who would know the answer to a question about pro basketball."

Kaufman said, "I'm a sportswriter, ask me."

"I'm looking for a writer who would know," said the woman.

Kaufman said, "Ask me."

The woman lobbed an easy question. Kaufman answered it.

The woman said, "Are you sure?"

Frank Deford, one of the country's most celebrated sportswriters and the former editor-in-chief of *The National* sports daily, said during a talk at the 1990 AWSM convention that when he was covering pro football, Gayle Gardner's press credentials were frequently questioned, while his and Bob Costas's were not. "And we probably know one-tenth of the things Gayle knew about football," he said.

Yet he said: "I know you struggle . . . and the reason you have to is we men are pigs. It's nothing to be proud of, but that's us. We [men] think we need you for procreation and recreation. But we don't need you for sports. [We're] trying to keep you out and we're going to make it tough on you." Deford advised the reporters not to be advocates for women's sports and not to be afraid to flirt with male athletes.

Fortunately, he was ignored. Female reporters seem increasingly interested in covering women's sports, and few besides ESPN's "Downtown" Julie Brown (a former MTV dance-party host who openly flirted with athletes during the 1993 Super Bowl media day) and former *Sacramento Bee* reporter Susan Fornoff (who admits to being flirtatious in her book, *Lady in the Locker Room*) have found flirtation wise or useful.

Sometimes it's hard to tell for sure if one is being discriminated against. After ten years of serving as ABC commentator for the New York Marathon, Kathrine Switzer was replaced with Mary Ann Grabavoy, who had never before done a major broadcast. Nor is she a runner. "Gorgeous. Young. Blonde," Switzer says. "I'm certainly aware of getting older and having wrinkles and needing to tint my hair. Recently I found a tape of me doing the New York marathon about ten years ago. I looked very swishy. I thought, oooh, I wonder if that has anything to do with it. If television were my be-all and end-all, I'd go get a face-lift."

• • •

The most publicized case of locker room harassment involved five New England Patriots football players. On September 17, 1990, *Boston Herald* sportswriter Lisa Olson entered the Patriots' locker room to interview cornerback Maurice Hurst. Olson had requested that the interview be conducted elsewhere, but Hurst insisted that she meet him at his locker— a fact that later made Olson suspect that the incident had been planned. When she began the interview, she heard other players complain loudly, "She's in here again."

According to Olson's testimony and that of several players, tight end Zeke Mowatt then walked toward the bench where Olson was seated and stood next to her, naked. Other naked players joined him. One told Olson to "take a bite" of his penis. Others said, "Make her look" and "Is she looking?" Mowatt said, "You're not writing, you're looking." Several paraded past, displaying their genitals. In Olson's words, they "positioned themselves inches from my face and dared me to touch their private parts." [11]

The encounter became known as "the Lisa Olson incident," defined by her victimization rather than by their assault. Had Olson remained a victim, or had she used verbal aggression, clever comebacks, or other tactics practiced by her female colleagues, the episode would not have gained nationwide attention. But instead Olson left and reported the incident to her editor, Robert Sales. She asked Sales "to handle things diplomatically and quietly. I did not want to become the story, not because I wanted to protect the Patriots' reputation, but because I wanted to be able to continue doing my job."

Alas, things did not remain diplomatic or quiet. The *Boston Globe* first reported the story, beginning a furor that has yet to die down. Patriots owner Victor Kiam told Sales that he was "asking for trouble sending a female reporter to cover the team. Why not stand in front of her [naked] if she is an intruder?" Kiam also called the incident "a flyspeck in the ocean compared to the wider issue of football." [12] Three male reporters heard Kiam call Olson "a classic bitch." [13] The National Organization for Women threatened a boycott of Remington, Kiam's company.

After hiring a public relations firm, Kiam bought $100,000 worth of newspaper ads in which he denied calling Olson a classic bitch and wrote, "Rape—physical, mental, threatened, hinted at or joked about—

is something I will not stand for." Yet four months later, invoking the popular penis-as-weapon metaphor, Kiam joked at a dinner presentation that both Iraqi soldiers and Lisa Olson had "seen Patriot missiles up close." He later apologized."[14]

In newspaper reports and columns, much mention was made of the locker room being "male turf." "Her mother should have told her that if she stepped into a men's locker room, she would be entering a man's world," wrote former pro player Dave Butz.[15]

"Everyone knows that some professional athletes are not exactly Lord Chesterfields," wrote Jeffrey Hart in an article for the *Norristown (PA) Times Herald,* entitled, "No Matter Athletes Behavior, Women Out of Place."[16]

Melvin Durslag of the *Los Angeles Times* called Olson "a pain in the hip, now reacting out of proportion to the stimulus." He added, "Traditionally, vulgarity is part of the locker-room scene. It isn't to be recommended, but if one isn't tough enough to brace oneself for the crudeness one is apt to encounter there, one should cover tea dances."[17]

One man who seemed to "get it" was the *Washington Post*'s Tony Kornheiser. In response to the "wives don't like women in the locker room" rationale, Kornheiser raised the subject of widespread athlete infidelity, writing, "Better they should be concerned with who's seeing their husbands naked in private than in front of 150 people in a locker room."[18]

NFL commissioner Paul Tagliabue appointed Harvard Law professor Philip Heymann to investigate. Heymann concluded that he was "unable to determine exactly what happened, but that Olson's version that she was harassed was most credible."[19] He wrote, "Mowatt's account of the same period is not credible."

Tagliabue fined Mowatt, Robert Perryman, and Michael Timpson a total of $22,500, but the fines were never collected. Later, asked about the noncollection of fines, he said, "At some point, enough is enough," apparently referring to the players' suffering.

The Patriots were fined $25,000 and ordered to pay another $25,000 for materials to instruct players on "responsible dealings with the media." The new ten-page "NFL Media Relations Playbook" explains, "When female reporters are in your locker room, they are there in a professional capacity. It is not a sexual experience. Women have earned the right to perform all kinds of jobs once restricted to men, including football writer. Please respect that right."

In April 1991, Olson sued Kiam, the three players, and other Patriots personnel. She asked for unspecified monetary damages for sexual harassment, civil-rights violations, intentional infliction of emotional distress, and intentional damage to her professional reputation.[20] The following February, the parties reached an out-of-court settlement for a reported $250,000 that Olson said she would use to establish a journalism scholarship at her alma mater, Northern Arizona University.

Reaction from the male public was venomous, even beyond the degree of hatred expressed toward other women—Anita Hill, Desiree Washington, and Patricia Bowman—who have recently charged powerful men with sexual abuses. Olson received hate mail, death threats, threats to throw battery acid on her face, rape threats, and suggestions that she should kill herself. Her apartment was broken into twice. "Classic bitch" was spray painted on the apartment house. All four tires were slashed; a note on her windshield read, "Next time it will be your neck." Michael Avery, one of Olson's lawyers, said, "I do a lot of civil-rights cases, so I've seen things that have gone through the mails, but this was the worst stuff I've ever read. The sexual references, the obscene drawings. Things that make you sick."[21]

Olson tried to continue sports writing by covering Boston's pro hockey and basketball teams. Male fans heckled her, poured beer on her, and demanded that she show them her breasts. From the luxury boxes, the only seats above the hockey press box in the Boston Garden, fans spat on her. For protection, she wore a hat.[22]

Playboy invited her to do a "pictorial layout."[23]

Olson found herself trying to tread water in a media whirlpool, defending herself on such shows as "CBS This Morning" and "NFL Live." She was tentative on television, disorganized and, worst of all—for a woman—angry. Johnette Howard recalls, "She was too emotional. You have to be unemotional, because you have to be aware how women are stereotyped and dismissed as hysterical, even when anger is the appropriate emotion."

Olson now regrets the media appearances. "My editor told me we were at war. I didn't think I could say no. But it was bad advice to do television interviews then. I was so blinded by anger that I came across as a very angry young woman. And that's because I was a very angry young woman."[24]

The *Boston Herald* offered Olson a stint in its international program and gave her a choice of living in London, Hong Kong, New Zealand, or Australia. She chose Australia "because it was the farthest away." She now writes features for Sydney's *Daily Telegraph-Mirror.* She is homesick, but a recent incident rudely reminded her that male athletes would not exactly welcome her back.

On December 27, 1992, when the Miami Dolphins traveled to play the New England Patriots, former Miami wide receiver Mark Clayton screamed to a locker room full of reporters, "Close the door, and keep Lisa Olson outside! Make sure to leave that dick-watching bitch outside!"[25]

Only three reporters, all from Florida, reported it. Olson was nowhere near the Patriots' locker room at the time. She was flying back to Australia after visiting her ill father in Arizona.

Almost two years after the incident, the *Boston Globe* devoted a month of research and another five full pages to the issue, employing no female writers in the vast project. They focused on Olson's reputation as "a looker," questioned inconsistencies in her story, accused her of wearing Bermuda shorts at training camp (which is what male reporters wear there), and challenged the veracity of her resume.

• • •

What do men fear? What do they hate? If they want to get dressed privately, why don't they?

Sometimes, the locker room is just a place to change clothes. But often, beginning in about junior high school, it is a place where men work out their feelings about being men. It is what sociologists calls a "highly gendered space," a space where the athletes and coaches are acutely aware of gender and "appropriate" gender-role behavior.

The men's locker room culture condones long periods of nakedness. In this way, men grant themselves many opportunities to "look"—to observe each other's genitals and to display and compare their own. For teens, "looking" may assuage or exacerbate fears of abnormal development. For young men, "looking" may provide a rare voyeuristic opportunity to appreciate men's physical attractiveness.

But that can't be openly acknowledged. To admit homosexual feelings would be to take a great tumble off the social ladder. The avowed heterosexual man who spends hours in locker rooms looking at penises and exhibiting his own penis for other men to see must somehow deny the obvious subtext of this behavior. So he asserts his heterosexuality by talking about women or women's body parts.

Theoretically, a man could claim heterosexual status by speaking lovingly about his wife or girlfriend. But according to male reports of male locker room conversation, this is not usually how it happens. Instead of indicating mutual interest in a woman or women, he brags about sexual dominance. Using language such as "hounding the beef," "catching snatch," "fucking her brains out," "making her bleed," and "keeping it wet," he defines women as pornographic playthings, claiming his own role as that of a successful sexual predator.

But "proving" heterosexuality through sexual dominance talk is still not enough. Since bisexuality exists, the man in the locker room must also deny his attraction for men. To this end he mocks gay men and uses gay epithets (faggot, queer, fairy) as put-downs. Fag jokes serve a double purpose: they mock both homosexual men and all women, because usually what is being ridiculed is feminine attire, feminine mannerisms, or feminine sexual subservience. The terms "kiss my ass," "suck my dick," and "cocksucker," common locker room jargon, all point to a disdain for a person, male or female, who provides sexual pleasure to men.

In this way, male athletes enjoy men's naked company without losing their heterosexual dominance. They stand, walk, shower, joke, and even play cards naked with other naked men, yet they distance themselves from the frightening possibility that this is a sensual, sexual activity.

Then, in walks a woman.

A real, live, breathing woman, not a pinup. Not even a wife or a girlfriend. That in itself gives her power: she is not in any sense the sexual property of any of the men. This particular woman has additional power because she is a journalist. She has entered this arena not to serve as a sexual plaything, but to gather information so that she can inform the public about these men's behavior—on the field but also off the field. And she has caught them with their pants down.

Consider, for contrast, the most acceptable woman to appear consistently at men's sporting events: a cheerleader or dancer. She provides a literal sideshow. At the high school level she sings and cheers, but as she ages, like the title character in *The Little Mermaid,* she stops speaking and singing. At the college and pro levels, she entertains men with her beauty and her dancing alone. She loses her voice.

The female reporter has a voice. She can comment on what men are doing. She can reveal the truth—her truth; she can interpret male behavior from her own point of view. The female reporter has the power to make men look bad.

What might she see? What might she say?

She sees men without their armor—football players without their padding, baseball and basketball and hockey players without the authoritative air that uniforms provide. Because some men insist on lingering nude, she also sees men's nakedness. She sees the softness, the fleshiness, the scabs and the pimpled buttocks that these men and their corporate sponsors do not choose to share with the general public. She sees vulnerability. She smells the pungent odors of male exertion. She hears the quivering voices of defeat. She sees tears.

She also sees penises. Who sees penises outside the privacy of a bedroom? Our culture offers Washington Monument-style phallic symbols, but penises are not icons the way breasts are; we don't see gigantic images of penises blinking neon when we drive through any part of town. The power of the penis is in its veil: men protect penises the way they used to protect sacred languages, maintaining mystery by denying public access. Yet the female reporter sees penises. How small they are, or skinny or fat, crooked or mottled or semierect. How exposed they are, how defenseless. Not intimidating symbols of power. Just dangling flesh.

And what does she do with this grand opportunity, this rare privilege to observe men's private parts?

She looks away.

· · ·

Lisa Olson was tagged by the players as a "looker." The word, which rhymes with hooker and has some of the same connotations, is used by male players to express their opinion that a particular woman stares at their genitals too much. In psychological terms, this would be called a projection, an attribution to others of one's own feelings or desires. Large numbers of women have never expressed interest in looking at men's genitals. If women were so interested in penises, they would be delighted when flashers expose themselves; instead they report them to the police.

It is men who look at and loiter nude with men in locker rooms.

It is men who look, to the tune of a $7-billion pornography industry, at images of female breasts and genitals. A woman can be acceptable as "a looker" when the connotation is that men look at *her* body. But woman as "looker" becomes problematic when women are doing the looking, men being looked at.

As the "gaze in the military" debates made clear, straight men fear the stares of gay men. The "gaze in the locker room" debate makes clear that they also fear women's stares. They fear the prospect of being sex objects. They fear rape. They want to be the looker, not the looked upon; the actor, not the acted upon.[26]

Los Angeles Times writer Melvin Durslag wrote of the Patriots case, "the way some tell the story . . . three members of the team, familiar with Olson and deciding she was a 'looker,' meaning one who tended to peek excessively, chose to teach her a lesson."[27]

A pair of professors (political scientist Lisa Disch and sport sociologist scholar Mary Jo Kane of the University of Minnesota) are writing an entire academic paper on that phrase, "peek excessively." A woman is "supposed to peek, because that indicates interest," explains Kane. "But she's not supposed to peek *excessively*." If she peeks excessively, she takes on the role of subject, and makes men the object of her stares. Because the right to look—to stare at another's naked body—is a right men have claimed for themselves and have defined as male, Disch and Kane maintain, the female sportswriter who peeks excessively is "feminizing" the men, putting them in the traditional female role of object.

But for all men's protestations, female sportswriters actually don't stare and are not particularly curious. Remember: these are women who express disgust at slingshot jock straps, zit-covered backs, naked male coaches, bloody tape. They use words like messy and gross. They are professionals on deadline, eager to "get quotes and get out of there," as many phrase it.

Which leads to another, perhaps better explanation of men's obsession with women's "looking": that women aren't looking at all. That they don't care, aren't interested, aren't impressed. That, presented with the athlete's prized possession, they yawn. The sportswriter "emasculates men if she does look at them, and she also emasculates them if she does not," write Disch and Kane.[28]

• • •

I made my first foray into a men's locker room in the fall of 1992. After a game between the Los Angeles Raiders and the Seattle Seahawks, I found myself being swept along toward the Raiders' locker room in a river of players and reporters. Somehow I ended up in the front of the procession, walking next to defensive tackle and fourteen-year veteran Bob Golic. Fans, mostly adolescent boys, leaned over the railing, shouting Golic's name as we passed. "Bob! Bob! Golic! Golic!" Like girls at rock concerts, these boys were wild with enthusiasm, leaning so far over the railing I thought some might tumble onto the pavement below. They would have given their favorite football posters to be in my shoes, walking almost hand-in-hand with huge Bob Golic.

Other players passed us. My hand brushed against someone's body, perhaps a forearm; I touched sweaty tape, an arm hard as oak. A taped tree. A male reporter commented excitedly on the blood cascading from someone's nose. We reporters waited ten minutes, then entered the locker room.

Immediately a bare behind greeted me as a player leaned over, fishing for something in his gym bag. As I turned away, another naked man emerged from the showers and strode quickly toward his locker. These men were clearly rushing to get dressed, and I felt my own presence as an intrusion.

I approached quarterback Jay Shroeder, who stood fully uniformed in front of his locker, really just an open cubicle. He informed me politely that he was going to shower and dress first, then meet all reporters in a conference room. That made sense.

The rest of the men weren't planning to do that, apparently, because they were talking with reporters, sometimes having to move a bouquet of microphones out of the way in order to slip shirts over their heads. The Raiders' other quarterback, Todd Marinovich, also remained fully dressed but seemed shy, moving backwards as he spoke. In response to my female-reporters-in-men's-locker-rooms question, he said, "I don't mind," which, as it turned out, was what most players said first. Then, as with most of the players, he expressed discomfort. "I don't know how correct it is to be in a men's locker room. It makes me uncomfortable. I think it makes them [women] uncomfortable too. I'd rather meet in the conference room."

Defensive lineman Howie Long said, "I don't think my wife likes it. It would make me uncomfortable if my wife was naked in a locker room and men were reporting in there. It'd make me more than uncomfortable. I'd be flat-out pissed. I wouldn't allow it!"

He added, "I think they should supply bathrobes."

There were now about forty reporters (including three women) in the locker room, along with a few P.R. men, running back Marcus Allen's father, two small boys (an official's sons) asking for autographs, and about ten of those guys in backwards baseball hats saying, "Yo, Man." It was crowded. As I made my way from one locker to the next, I tripped on gauze, bloody bandages, and white tape in the shape of large ankles. It looked like a messy prosthesis factory.

A British camera woman walked by, maneuvering her equipment between two hefty players. "We have nothing like this in England," she told me, smiling conspiratorially. "My eyes are watering." Which I took to mean her mouth was watering. Although I've never heard this from an American reporter, here I did see evidence of the men's worst fantasy: that they would be objectified.

Defensive end Anthony Smith answered my inquiry with, "I think she [female reporters] should be allowed in." Then Smith, who is African-American, added, "Being a minority, I can't be prejudiced about too many things."

Heisman trophy winner Tim Brown began, "I don't object." Then he said, "I think women don't look like they come in to report. Come in here with their shades on, and look like they're sneaking a peek. But if they enjoy that, so be it. I don't have a problem with it at all."

"Are you talking about particular women?" I asked.

"I don't have a clue," he said. "And I wouldn't say if I did know."

I persisted: "What percent of women coming in here are not legitimate reporters?"

"Actually," he said, "I only saw one lady do that."

"How long ago?"

"I don't remember."

"Have you ever seen a man sneaking a peek?" This question took him by surprise.

"I don't think anybody ever pays attention to that," he said at first, then, "If somebody saw something like that going on, you'd all know about it 'cause it'd probably be in all the papers."

"What do you mean?" I asked. "What would happen?"

"What are you trying to do?" he said, angry. With an open hand, he pushed me on the arm, not hard enough to make me lose my balance, but hard enough to make an impression. Then he walked away.

• • •

Tim Brown may have felt harassed by my question about men looking at his naked body. "Oh, they hate the gay thing," Johnette Howard told me afterward. But I felt intimidated by Brown's anger and his shove. I didn't know how to respond. Shove back? Argue? Ask more questions? Joke?

Over the years, women who cover men's sports have had to figure out how to respond to such situations and to considerably more offensive ones. Usually, fearing that athletes will ostracize them or that editors will reassign or fire them, female reporters bear abuse quietly, devising individual solutions. "An overwhelming number of female sportswriters do not go public with their sexual harassment," says *Austin American Statesman* sports editor Tracy Dodds, who began writing about men's sports in 1973. If you report harassment, she says, "you are a strident bitch."[29]

Houston Post reporter and columnist Melanie Hauser says, "If you cry the first time someone calls you a fucking cunt, you won't survive. You learn to deal with assholes. Profanity is part of the business. It's a macho world. If you just keep working, you'll gain their respect. The best compliment I've gotten is, 'You're one of the guys—and don't take that the wrong way.' "

Detroit Free Press reporter Michelle Kaufman says, "There are going to be jerks in just about every locker room. If you can't deal, you shouldn't get into the business. It's unfair, but that's how it is."

You can hear, in the voices of these women, their anger and their weariness. They're tired of getting asked about Lisa Olson everywhere they go, tired of seeing "locker room access" and "sexual harassment" on the agenda of their own convention year after year.

Back in the seventies, pioneer sportswriter Melissa Ludtke says, "we arrived with a basic strategy: We would try to fit in and flourish in an environment that was created for and by men by proving that we could transform ourselves into better men! We buried our female sensibilities at the door and tried, as best we could, to talk and act and move around as our male colleagues did." [30]

Right away, this was problematic. While male reporters show up at stadiums in polo shirts, jeans, and sneakers, women knew they wouldn't be taken seriously in that attire. Nor could they wear skirts: That could be interpreted as too flirtatious.

In *A Spy in the House that Ruth Built,* a documentary about a female filmmaker's relationship with baseball, Vanalyne Green describes resentfully donning "the standard uniform of the female sportswriter: khaki pants, loose-fitting blouse—white but definitely opaque—that goes up to the neck and down to the wrists. Sexless. While 6'5" gods stride on the fields spraying their sex in all directions." [31]

Nor have female reporters felt entitled to "act exactly as male reporters do," Ludtke says, "which often meant lingering around the locker room or conversing in a friendly fashion with the players" for fear of being accused of either flirting or "looking." They have to be careful not to sit while a player is standing so that they don't inadvertently position themselves, in Michelle Kaufman's words, "at genitals height."

Vanalyne Green describes "old male cronies . . . chatting so nonchalantly with each other while I worried that a simple misspoken word would get me kicked off the field or that my misplaced banter would leave me the butt of players' jokes about women and women's bodies." [32]

New York Times writer Claire Smith says, "You could take a bum off the street, shave him, clean him up, and put a pad and pencil in his hand, and he could walk into a clubhouse [where] I have worked for five years, and be instantly accepted in a way . . . I will never be." [33]

Christine Brennan writes, "Let's face it. I'm an outsider in the players' domain. I have to learn to laugh when Dexter Manley shouts out, 'Hey Chris, come here. I've got something to show you.' I can't take that seriously." [34]

Women often find a way to diffuse tense situations through humor. When Johnette Howard approached massive Tony Mandarich about steroid rumors, Mandarich replied gruffly: "Why should I talk to you?"

"Cuz I'll beat you up if you don't," Howard told him. She punched him playfully. He laughed and granted her the interview.

It was allegedly a female sportswriter who came up with a now-classic retort to a flasher. "You know what this is?" he asked.

"It looks like a penis, only smaller," she responded.

But after a while, women don't feel so cheery, so witty. With just twenty or thirty minutes to conduct interviews and write an article, they often don't have time to laugh at young men's antics or deflect potential harassment with jovial repartee. Editors and fans can also be annoying. Michelle Kaufman sometimes finds herself responding with anger. When male fans complain that she shouldn't see naked men in the locker room, Kaufman says, "What about nurses? They see men all the time. They put enemas up their butts. No one complains about that."

Oregonian columnist Julie Vader uses another medical analogy: "What I say to people who gripe about women in the locker room is just two little words: Male gynecologists."

Coaches, commissioners, editors, and athletes can sometimes be helpful. Ailene Voisin, reporter-columnist for the *Atlanta Journal—Constitution,* was interviewing Larry Johnson in the Charlotte Hornets locker room when Hornets rookie Alonzo Mourning suddenly told her, "Would you please leave so I can get dressed?" Voisin, a twenty-year sports writing veteran, refused, citing the NBA equal-access policy. Mourning cursed at Voisin. She suggested he should start acting like a pro rather than a rookie. He walked angrily toward her and Larry Johnson intervened, stepping in front of Mourning and calming him down. By the time she arrived home, Voisin had apologetic messages on her answering machine from both the NBA and the Charlotte Hornets; within a week, Mourning apologized.

Basketball players harass women relatively rarely, reporters say, compared to football players (the worst) or hockey or baseball players. This may be because NBA Commissioner David Stern sets the tone. When women become beat reporters, Stern phones them, offers his home number, and asks them to report any access or harassment problems directly to him.

Editors can also provide important support. *USA Today* sports editor Gene Policinski demanded an apology and a change in policy when

Denise Tom was kept out of the Cincinnati Bengals' locker room in 1990.

When demanding equal access, sports radio pioneer Claudia Polley says, "the most important thing is to stay cool and be insistent. If you lower your voice and look them straight in the eye, that's far more intimidating to a man than screaming and yelling."

"How did you learn that?" I asked.

"Every woman knows that, don't they?" she said. "When you lower your voice, that's when men get scared."

"I've noticed it works with pets," I said.

I hadn't thought of doing that with men. Anthropologist Thomas Kochman, in *Black and White Styles in Conflict,* contends that African-American women (such as Polley) may be better prepared than white women (such as myself) to deal with various forms of harassment. "In the black culture, women are perceived as having power," he writes. "A black woman . . . counters offense with offense."[35]

Though Polley began working in sports more than twenty-five years ago, only about a dozen African-American women now cover sports, most notably ESPN anchor-reporter Robin Roberts, *New York Times* baseball writer Claire Smith, and *Orange County Register* women's sports columnist Miki Turner. So it's hard to know if they're any more assertive than their non-black sisters. But as a group, female reporters seem to be in the process of figuring out that they don't have to take abuse. "I don't see why I should have to," says Kate Callen, who is white. "Men don't have to. Can you imagine men putting up with any of this?"

Former AWSM president Cathy Henkel, one of the country's four female sports editors (for the *Seattle Times*) recalls, "When I began on the sports side of this business, I figured the mooning in the locker room, the swimsuit calendars in the office and the jokes on the road were all part of the initiation fee. I toughened up and desensitized myself . . . so well that I was numb."[36] But after sixteen years, she now counsels other women, including her own staff, "You have to speak up."

Austin American Statesman sports editor Tracy Dodds agrees, conceding, "We've been putting up with too much."[37]

Christine Brennan says she and other women in their thirties and forties eagerly train and support young women entering the business. "These college kids say, 'What should I do about the locker room?' and we all jump in, saying, 'Don't back down, don't accept unequal treatment, stand up for yourself, we'll help you, and here are our phone numbers.' "

• • •

Female reporters are starting to realize that they can't be "one of the guys," and that they don't have to settle for being treated worse than the guys. They're starting to realize they can use their public voices to protest sexism.

In the more than fourteen hundred published newspaper stories regarding the Patriots' harassment case, female response was uniformly supportive of Olson. "We wrote articles, but reluctantly," says Lynn Zinser, a reporter for the *Charlotte Observer.* Like Olson, female sportswriters didn't want to be the focus of attention. Like female athletes, reporters are not necessarily feminist in perspective or interest. Many feel more comfortable writing about home runs and draft picks than women's rights.

But many came forward anyway, trying to reframe the issue as a legal one, not a moral one, and about sexism rather than sex. Women outside the sports writing domain were the most outspoken. *New York Times* columnist Anna Quindlen condemned the men's behavior, calling it "psychological rape."[38]

Back in the twenties, Lorena Hickok deliberately wrote with a different voice. Feigning ignorance, she gently mocked men's sports in a series of tongue-in-cheek newspaper columns for the *Minneapolis Morning Tribune.* Taking on the role of "uninitiated girl reporter" and covering a baseball game between two police teams, she pretended not to understand the word "ringer." Told two men are "out," she asked, "Where?" She argued that when a player "walked," it "wasn't walking at all, but a sort of trot."

In another column Hickok suggested that watching a "good game of checkers" might be more interesting than college football, or "you might just as well put in your time watching a lot of ants running in and out of their hole. That is, if there isn't anything else you'd rather be doing right then."[39]

More recently, *Oregonian* columnist Julie Vader mocked a male sportswriter who informed her that women could never be good sportswriters because they haven't played football or baseball. "He honestly wanted to help me," she wrote. "He was very sincere. He was getting quite worked up and his voice got higher and higher."

She couldn't take him seriously, she said, because of her own athletic history. She was the fastest girl in her eighth grade gym class. In tenth grade, she tackled "Claire Stabler, future homecoming queen, in a powder-puff football game and preserved our team's shutout." And she's a good equestrian. "If the need arose (as it so often does in modern life) to suddenly ride off on horseback," she wrote, she could do it.

As she looked at him, hearing him say "something about the grind of all the travel in a sportswriter's life," she noticed that he had "little bits of hair on the rim of his ears." She found this "charming." She found his concern "adorable." She wanted to tell him that he was beautiful when he was angry, and "not to worry his pretty little head."

Vader's irreverent *Oregonian* sports columns have attracted new readers, mostly women, who previously did not read the sports pages. The columns have also enraged some men, who write her furious letters ("I hope you die of a horrible disease," said a recent one) and who complain about her on the local sports talk radio station. She finds their anger amusing. She refers to them as "the contenda's." She says, "I don't take sports seriously. I think they're for fun. For some reason, this drives people nuts."

Most female reporters do take sports seriously. Perhaps this stems in part from trying so hard to be taken seriously themselves. But though they're not necessarily a feminist bunch—they were not hired for their radical ideas—they are more likely to offer a feminist perspective than men are. They also seem likely to ask different—and perhaps better— questions. Many say they offer a human touch, less encumbered than men with statistics and a know-it-all stance.

Deborah Tannen critiques as masculine a fundamental tenet of journalism—that "objective" reporting means presenting two (and usually only two) sides to each issue. She says male reporters' "preoccupation with controversy grows out of men seeming to find conflict energizing and interesting, and women don't. They find it unappealing and distressing."[40]

Ann Schatz, a broadcaster for KOIN-TV in Portland, confirms, "I don't think in black and white. I allow the players to feel. You get a hell of a lot more out of them that way."

Melissa Ludtke once wrote about the relationship between catchers and home plate umpires. At the time, she says, "I didn't understand why I was so drawn to this particular story and why no one else had written it." Eventually she realized that she didn't have to "try to think and act and sound" like her male colleagues.

After Isiah Thomas and Magic Johnson dissolved a long, close friendship, it was Johnette Howard who investigated the breakup. Male writers focused on Thomas' alleged contention that Johnson was bisexual, an accusation that apparently caused the rift. "Everyone else wanted to know about how Magic got the AIDS virus, about his sex life," recalls Howard. "What I saw is that he lost his best friend."

Baseball writer Linda Gebroe used refreshing common sense to explore the ritual of a beaned batter rushing toward the mound to sock the pitcher. "Why does the batter rush the mound?" she asked in a recent essay. "Why doesn't the pitcher rush the plate? Why doesn't he show concern for the stricken batter? Does he feel bad about what he's done? And why does the batter only show anger instead of hurt? Is this the stuff that men are made of?"

The *Boston Globe*'s Bella English wrote repeated columns criticizing the men who sucked on life-sized blow-up dolls in Fenway Park. She listed the ballpark's phone number, asking readers to complain, which many did. Eventually, the dolls were banned.

When the Atlanta Hawks basketball organization staged halftime "bathing suit fashion shows," starring *Sports Illustrated* and *Sport* magazine models, and hired scantily clad women called "Hot Shots" to serve drinks at court side, *Atlanta Journal-Constitution* reporter-columnist Ailene Voisin repeatedly criticized them. "I was pretty relentless," she recalls. "It was incredibly offensive to many of the women I spoke with and, I would assume, to men with any conscience." Finally, after two years, she called for a boycott, and that got the Hawks' attention. In 1993 they replaced the Hot Shots and the fashion show with female dancers. ("I question whether a basketball game is the place for dancers, but at least they have a pseudo-legitimate purpose of entertaining both male and female fans," says Voisin, "whereas the Hot Shots were strictly there to titillate male fans.") The Hawks also offered any women or men who had boycotted or been offended to say so at the ticket window and receive a free ticket to one game. About 3,000 fans took them up on the offer.

Julie Vader recently wrote a scathing indictment of *Sports Illustrated* editors, her former employers. Noting that managing editor Mark Mulvoy settled out of court after being sued for sexist remarks he made about an employee in a 1987 speech, she implied that sexual harassment was common among the magazine's top editors. Naming "the age-old problem of unattractive, married men who behave as if they are neither," she contended that, "the biggest obstacles women sports journalists face are not a locker room of Neanderthals. No sir, It's the guys wearing suits, who proclaim they are all for fairness, whose smiles are a little too wide, whose handshakes linger a little too long."[41]

Other women take issue with their colleagues' televised commentary. Billie Jean King says it drives her crazy that male tennis commentators often cast women as highly emotional, and that they blame defeats on women's "choking" rather than on an opponent's superior play. In retaliation, she deliberately points out male nervousness when she's covering a match. She smiles when she tells this story, clearly enjoying this subversive act.

It also irks her that male reporters use first names for women and last names for men. So King does the opposite. "I like to call men "Jim" or "Jimmy," she says, laughing.

Put a man and a woman in a broadcasting booth together and the woman will occasionally provide a counterpoint to the man's sexism. This happened during the 1986 New York City Marathon, which Kathrine Switzer broadcast with Jim Lampley. When Lampley made his infamous remark about Grete Waitz—that she "cooks, sews and washes clothes just like most wives," Switzer immediately retorted, "But she also joined the Norwegian Olympic Committee and works in a health clinic in preventative medicine. So that's very outstanding for her."[42]

Kate Callen, a former sports editor, contends, "We do a far better job because we're not dazzled by the stars. Men ask, 'Aren't you glad you won?' If you want tough sports reporting, send a woman in."

Melissa Ludtke says, "I never did think that asking a batter where the pitch he hit for a home run crossed the plate was a very intriguing question—yet it was one I heard asked a thousand times."[43]

The dearth of female and enlightened male editors limits the opportunities for women's sports coverage, but some women, such as Carol Herwig and her colleagues at *USA Today*, consistently report on college sports discrimination. *Orange County Register* writer Miki Turner writes one of the few women's sports columns in the country. Freelance writers Michele Kort, Susanna Levin, Felicia Halpert, and others have successfully convinced mainstream women's magazines to write occasional features about female athletes, and to spend fewer pages on tummy-flattening and more on team sports.

Johnette Howard of the *Washington Post* recently received this letter:

> *Dear Johnette:*
>
> *It should be obvious even to the most stupid dame that men* DO NOT *want female reporters in their locker room. So you should—must—respect privacy* first! *We don't like* any *female ogling our private parts.*
>
> You're weird!
>
> *From a male who is proud of being one.*

Howard, who has received many similar letters, was pleased to notice something missing from the familiar pattern: the writer didn't question her sports knowledge. "Ten years ago, these guys would write that we were creeps and we didn't know what we were talking about," recalls Howard. "Now they just write that we're creeps. Progress!"

• • •

If we make more progress, I think it will be because women are in fact lookers. Having spent years on the sidelines, we have become adept at observation. We are also speakers. We have voices.

Fear has often silenced us, even made us complicit in the manly sports system. But that fear is dissipating as we grow stronger. The more we look, the more we will be able to analyze the misogyny of the manly sports world, beyond the smokescreen of Super Bowls and statistics and league expansions. The closer we look, the better we will understand the "gaze in the locker room" issue. The rape-as-sex issue. And men's desperate struggle to keep women out of manly sports and to control and objectify the women who do play sports.

Sports are a battle, the newspapers tell us daily. Most competitors—skaters, swimmers, long-jumpers, horseback riders, volleyball players—don't see it that way. They play for camaraderie or excellence or the sheer joy of gliding one's body through water, space, or air.

But manly sports *are* a battle against women. While sports define masculinity, they also define male sexuality: aggressive, abusive. Women who refuse to be fans threaten to name the inner game: the dominance game. Women who challenge men's sports verbally, or on paper, or in groups, insinuating themselves into the male locker rooms as athletes, coaches, umpires, or reporters, wrest control from men of female bodies, even female sexuality.

Who's winning? Surely not the nearly nude "lap" dancers, nor the athletes fondled by their own coaches. Nor the women whose fellow Navy officers "team up" against them, nor the women who venture onto previously all-male sports teams only to be taunted as lesbians or bombarded with pornographic palaver. Surely not the women at baseball games who cringe in disgust when men on adjoining bleachers suck on the plastic parts of life-sized blow-up dolls.

"Emotionally dysfunctional, pathetic, fundamentally lonely" men who patronize places like Scores are not winning either. Men who sing rugby songs with their buddies but want to create meaningful relationships with women are not winning. Nor are men who, like misguided patriots, sacrifice their fragile bodies on the bloody football fields.

Along with concerned men, women need to devise sporting experiences in which bodies are not weapons but more like musical instruments to be played joyously, reverently. We need to keep thinking and talking about ways to take the sex and sexism and even gender out of sports, creating models of celebration and challenge that include physical, sensual delights in which everyone wins and no one is exploited.

The more we see, the more we will say, speaking up for female athletes, reporters, umpires, coaches, university presidents, team owners, International Olympic Committee members. We need to keep challenging sexual harassment, rape, statutory rape, college and high school gender discrimination, sex testing, and the myriad ways men try to preserve sports and heroic ideals and physical power for themselves. We need to keep filing lawsuits, writing letters to editors, working as reporters, getting ourselves promoted to the level of editor and producer, and creating our own sports businesses so we can hire more women and begin to tell the truth about women's sports, as well as the truth about men's. We need to keep talking—to each other and to men who will listen—about our own feelings about the men who tackle us in our own kitchens, and the TV idols they adore. We need to protest the production of images of women as men's playthings or rape/sex receptacles. We need to keep saying that no form of sexual abuse or harassment or discrimination is sporting.

It is this voice, I think—these voices—that will split the world open.

• • •

When Vanalyne Green became a baseball fan and became conversant in baseball jargon she found, she says, that "The words gave me something to say to the old Italian men on my street. The words saw me through the feeble gestures of a bad blind date. The words made me feel that I had some shred of America I could call my own without shame or loss." [44]

Many women were taught, when we were teens, to learn to talk about sports because such knowledge might help us converse with boys. Some of us still play this game, trying to gain the respect of colleagues or dates or men on the street by speaking the manly sports language. But as we search for some shred of America we can call our own without shame or loss, I suggest we turn away from sports lingo and discuss instead the myriad ways the manly sports system affects women. I suggest we also spend time discussing female athletes, including ourselves.

We need to look at our own bodies. We need to honestly and optimistically assess our own physical potential and make prudent, daily decisions about how to develop and sustain strength, flexibility, endurance, and teamwork for their own sake, because strength, flexibility, endurance, and teamwork come in handy, not because they bring us closer to the ever-elusive goal of being "lookers" in that other, male-envisioned sense of the word.

We tend to acquire strength fairly easily. By turning our gaze to other women, and to our own mirrors, we will notice our own miraculous capacity to become strong, healthy, wise, and committed to female empowerment. In these ways, I believe, we can begin to understand and change the manly sports culture in which we are all, whether we like it or not, swimming.

Notes

Chapter 1
We Don't Like Football, Do We?

1. Susan Birrell, "The Woman Athlete: Fact or Fiction?" Paper presented at the National Girls and Women in Sport Symposium, Slippery Rock State University, Slippery Rock, Pennsylvania (February 6–9, 1992).

2. Lester Munson, "Against Their Will." *The National Sports Daily* (August 17, 1990), p. 30.

3. Rich Hofman, "Rape and the College Athlete: Part One." *Philadelphia Daily News* (March 17, 1986), p. 104.

4. Mary P. Koss and John A. Gaines, "The Prediction of Sexual Aggression by Alcohol Use, Athletic Participation, and Fraternity Affiliation." *Journal of Interpersonal Violence* 8 (March 1993), pp. 94–108.

5. W. O. Johnson, "Sports and Studs." *Sports Illustrated* (August 8, 1988), p. 70; cited in Myriam Miedzian, *Boys Will Be Boys: Breaking the Link Between Masculinity and Violence* (New York: Doubleday, 1991), p. 188.

6. Joyce Carol Oates, guest, "The Derek McGinty Show." WAMU (Washington, D.C., August 6, 1993).

Chapter 2
Feminism and Football: Then and Now

1. Midge MacKenzie, *Shoulder to Shoulder* (New York: Alfred A. Knopf, 1975), p. 224.

2. For a discussion of what I call the partnership model of sport, see my first book: Mariah Burton Nelson, *Are We Winning Yet? How Women Are Changing Sports and Sports Are Changing Women* (New York: Random House, 1991).

3. Elisabeth Griffith, *In Her Own Right. The Life of Elizabeth Cady Stanton* (Oxford University Press, 1984).

4. Lynne Emery, "The First Intercollegiate Contest for Women: Basketball, April 4, 1896," in Reet Howell, ed., *Her Story in Sport: A Historical Anthology of Women in Sports* (West Point, NJ: Leisure Press, 1982), p. 420.

5. Allen Guttmann, *Women's Sports: A History* (New York: Columbia University Press, 1991), p. 116.

6. Ibid.

7. Ibid.

8. Janet Woolum, *Outstanding Women Athletes* (Phoenix: Oryx Press, 1992), p. 24.

9. Adrianne Blue, *Grace Under Pressure* (London: Sidgwick & Jackson Limited, 1987), p. xi.

10. Sally Fox, *The Sporting Woman Book of Days* (Boston: Bullfinch Press, 1989), photo opposite April 7–12.

11. Guttmann, 1991, p. 110.

12. Ibid., p. 117.

13. Ibid., p. 124.

14. Ibid., p. 134.

15. "The Revolutionary Bicycle." *The Literary Digest* XII (July 20, 1895), p. 334; cited in Sidney H. Aronson, "The Sociology of the Bicycle," in Marcello Truzzi, ed., *Sociology and Everyday Life* (Englewood Cliffs, NJ: Prentice Hall, 1968), p. 298.

16. Lois Banner, *American Beauty* (Chicago: University of Chicago Press, 1983), p. 174.

17. Guttmann, 1991, p. 123.

18. Harvey Green, *Fit for America: Health, Fitness, Sport, and American Society* (New York: Pantheon Books, 1986), p. 231.

19. Banner, 1983, p. 145.

20. Green, 1986, p. 232.

21. Stephanie Twin, *Out of the Bleachers: Writings on Women and Sport* (Old West-bury, New York: The Feminist Press, 1979), p. xxvi.

22. Helen Lenskyj, *Out of Bounds: Women, Sport, and Sexuality* (Toronto: The Women's Press, 1986).

23. Guttmann, 1991, p. 122.

24. Ibid., p. 131.

25. Ibid., p. 111.

26. Kathleen E. McCrone, *Playing the Game: Sport and Physical Emancipation of English Women, 1870–1914* (Lexington: University Press of Kentucky, 1988).

27. Guttmann, 1991, p. 132.

28. Banner, 1983, p. 145.

29. Green, 1986, p. 251.

30. Ibid., p. 258.

31. Guttmann, 1991, p. 117.

32. Green, 1986, p. 257.

33. Banner, 1983, p. 143.

34. Guttmann, 1991, p. 127.

35. Ibid., p. 117.

36. Michael A. Messner, *Power at Play: Sports and the Problem of Masculinity* (Boston: Beacon Press, 1992), pp. 13–17.

37. Michael S. Kimmel, "Baseball and the Reconstruction of American Masculinity 1880–1920," in Michael A. Messner and Donald F. Sabo, eds., *Sport, Men, and the Gender Order: Critical Feminist Perspectives* (Champaign, Illinois: Human Kinetics Books, 1990), p. 57.

38. P. Filene, *Him/Her/Self: Sex Roles in Modern America* (New York: Harcourt Brace Jovanovich, 1975); cited in Messner, 1992, p. 13.

39. Kimmel, 1990, p. 58.

40. Ibid.

41. Michael A. Messner writes of this era, "Sport was a male-created homosocial cultural sphere that provided men with psychological separation from the perceived feminization of society while also providing dramatic symbolic proof of the 'natural superiority' of men over women." In Michael A. Messner, "Sports and Male Domination: The Female Athlete as Contested Ideological Terrain." *Sociology of Sport Journal* 5, no. 3, (1988), pp. 197–211.

42. Michael B. Poliakoff, *Combat Sports in the Ancient World: Competition, Violence, and Culture* (New Haven: Yale University Press, 1987).

43. Green, 1986, pp. 198, 213.

44. Ibid., p. 202.

45. E. Weber, "Pierre de Coubertin and the Introduction of Organized Sport into France." *Journal of Contemporary History* 5, no. 2, (1970), pp. 3–26; cited in David Whitson, "Sport in the Social Construction of Masculinity," in Messner and Sabo, 1990, p. 21.

46. Kenneth Sheard and Eric Dunning, "The Rugby Football Club as a Type of Male Preserve: Some Sociological Notes." *International Review of Sport Sociology* 8 no. 3 (1973), p. 6.

47. Ibid., p. 12.

48. Green, 1986, p. 237.

49. Kimmel, 1990, pp. 60–61.

50. Theodore Roosevelt. Inscription on a memorial monolith at Theodore Roosevelt Island, Washington, D.C.

51. Ben Brown, "This Queen's Court Is Made of Hardwood." *USA Today* (October 18, 1993), p. 2C.

52. "Pompons? No! No!" *Time* (February 19, 1990), p. 67.

53. Steven P. Schacht, "The Sadomasochistic Ritual of Male Rugby Players and the Social Construction of Gender Hierarchies." Paper presented at the annual meeting of the North American Society for the Sociology of Sport (Toledo, Ohio: November 5, 1992), p. 3.

54. Nielsen Media Research, telephone interview, November 23, 1992.

55. Naomi Wolf, *The Beauty Myth: How Images of Beauty Are Used Against Women* (New York: William Morrow and Company, Inc.), p. 184.

56. Messner, 1992, p. 168.

57. Richard Cohen, "Blessed Are the Blessed," *Washington Post* (October 25, 1992), p. 5.

58. Betty Weider and Joe Weider, *The Weider Book of Bodybuilding for Women* (Chicago: Contemporary Books, 1981).

Chapter 3
Stronger Women

1. Don Sabo and Marjorie Snyder, "Miller Lite Report on Sports and Fitness in the Lives of Working Women" (in cooperation with the Women's Sports Foundation and *Working Woman,* March 8, 1993).

2. Susan Greendorfer, professor of kinesiology at the University of Illinois, Urbana-Champaign, asserts that women's sports are inherently a political act. Susan Greendorfer, "Making Connections: Women's Sport Participation as a Political Act." Paper presented at the National Girls and Women in Sports Symposium, Slippery Rock State University, Slippery Rock, Pennsylvania (February 13, 1993).

3. Anne Cameron, *Daughters of Copperwoman* (Vancouver, British Columbia: Press Gang Publishers, 1981), pp. 101–102.

4. Alice Adams, "A Public Pool," *Mother Jones* (November 1984), p. 38.

5. Sabo and Snyder, 1993.

6. Women's Sports Foundation, Eisenhower Park, East Meadow, New York 11554 (1992).

7. Ibid.

8. L. Jaffee and J. Lutter, "A Change in Attitudes? A Report of Melpomene's Third Membership Survey." *Melpomene Journal* 10, no. 2 (1991), pp. 11–16; and L. Jaffee and R. Mantzer, "Girls Perspectives: Physical Activity and Self-esteem," *Melpomene Journal* 11, no. 3, (1992), pp. 14–23.

9. Frances Johnson, "Life on the Fringe: The Experience of Rugby and Ice Hockey Playing Women." Paper presented at the annual meeting of the North American Society for the Sociology of Sport (Toledo, Ohio: November 5, 1992).

10. Audre Lorde, *Sister Outsider: Essays and Speeches* (Freedom, California: Crossing Press, 1984), p. 57.

11. LaFerne Ellis Price, *The Wonder of Motion: A Sense of Life for Woman* (Terre Haute, Indiana: LaFerne Ellis Price, 1970).

12. Adrienne Rich, "Phantasia for Elvira Shatayev," *The Dream of a Common Language* (New York: W. W. Norton & Co., 1978), p. 4.

13. Susan Birrell and Diane M. Richter, "Is a Diamond Forever? Feminist Transformations of Sport." *Women's Studies International Forum* 10 no. 4 (1987), p. 401.

14. Adrienne Rich, "Compulsory Heterosexuality and Lesbian Existence." *Signs* (Summer 1980), pp. 631–60.

15. Ibid., p. 643.

16. Simone de Beauvoir, *The Second Sex* (New York: Vintage Books, 1952), p. 331.

17. NCAA Gender-Equity Study (Overland Park, Kansas: National Collegiate Athletic Association, 1992).

18. R. Vivian Acosta and Linda Carpenter, "Women in Intercollegiate Sport: A Longitudinal Study—1977–1992." Unpublished paper. Department of Physical Education, Brooklyn College, Brooklyn, NY 11210, 718/780-5879.

19. Annelies Knoppers, Barbara Bedker Meyer, Marty Ewing, and Linda Forrest, "The Structure of Athletic Obstacles to Women's Involvement in Coaching." Paper presented at the annual forum of the Council of Collegiate Women Athletic Administrators (Washington, D.C.: September 17–19, 1989).

20. Women's Sports Foundation.

21. Christine Grant and Mary Curtis, "Judicial Action Regarding Gender Equity." Unpublished manuscript (University of Iowa, 1993).

22. Jack Carey, "Sportsline: Cold Cash." *USA Today* (June 25, 1993) p. C1.

23. Sabo and Snyder, 1993.

24. Ibid.

25. Knoppers, Meyer, Ewing, and Forrest, 1989.

26. de Beauvoir, 1952, p. 330.

27. Diana E. H. Russell, *Sexual Exploitation: Rape, Child Sexual Abuse, and Workplace Harassment* (Beverly Hills, California: Sage Publications, 1984).

28. Gloria Steinem, *Revolution from Within* (Boston: Little, Brown and Company, 1992) p. 217.

29. Amelia Brown is a pseudonym, and some of the facts of her life have been changed to protect her identity.

30. Thomas L. Jackson, "A University Athletic Department's Rape and Assault Experiences." *Journal of College Student Development 32* (January 1991), p. 77.

31. Marilyn French, *The War Against Women* (New York: Summit Books, 1992).

32. Merle Hoffman, "Editorial," *On the Issues* (Winter 1991), pp. 2–3.

33. Hannah Alejandro, "Letters," *Ms.* (March/April 1993), pp. 8–9.

Chapter 4
Boys Will Be Boys and Girls Will Not

1. Brian Whipp and Susan Ward, letter to the editor, *Nature,* (January 2, 1992).

2. Amby Burfoot and Marty Post, "Battle of the Sexes," *Runner's World* (April 1992), p. 40.

3. Stephanie Twin, *Out of the Bleachers: Writings on Women and Sport* (Old Westbury, New York: The Feminist Press, 1979), p. xxxvi.

4. Susan Birrell, "The Woman Athlete: Fact or Fiction?" Paper presented at the National Girls and Women in Sport Symposium, Slippery Rock State University, Slippery Rock, Pennsylvania (February 6–9, 1992).

5. Ed Dolnick, "Super Women." *In Health* (July/August 1991), p. 42.

6. Adrianne Blue, *Faster, Higher, Further: Women's Triumphs and Disasters at the Olympics* (London: Virago Press, 1988), pp. 154–55.

7. Paul Willis, "Women in Sport in Ideology," in Jennifer Hargreaves, ed., *Sport, Culture, and Ideology* (London: Routledge and Kegan Paul, 1982), p. 130.

8. Carol Tavris, *The Mismeasure of Woman: Why Women Are Not the Better Sex, the Inferior Sex, or the Opposite Sex* (New York: Simon & Schuster, 1992), p. 24.

9. The Wellesley Center for Research on Women, *How Schools Shortchange Girls.* Report commissioned for the American Association of University Women Educational Foundation (1992), p. 10.

10. Mary A. Boutilier and Lucinda SanGiovanni, *The Sporting Woman* (Champaign, Illinois: Human Kinetics Publishers, 1983), p. 102.

11. Becky Beal, "Skateboarding: Alternative Masculinity and Its Effects on Gender Relations." Paper presented at the North American Society for the Sociology of Sport Conference (Toledo, Ohio: November 4–7, 1992).

12. Beal, 1992, pp. 5–11.

13. Ibid., p. 11.

14. Holly Devor, *Gender Blending: Confronting the Limits of Duality* (Bloomington: Indiana University Press, 1989).

15. J. E. Vader, "Sex Play." *M Magazine* (February 1992), pp. 41–47.

16. D. Stanley Eitzen and Maxine Baca Zinn, "The De-Athleticization of Women: The Naming and Gender Marking of Collegiate Sports Teams." *Sociology of Sport Journal* 6 (1989), pp. 362–70.

17. *Webster's New Collegiate Dictionary* (Springfield, Massachusetts: G. & C. Merriam Company, 1981).

18. Barbara G. Walker, *The Woman's Encyclopedia of Myths and Secrets* (New York: Harper & Row, Publishers, Inc. 1983), pp. 24–25.

19. Charlene Spretnak, ed. *The Politics of Women's Spirituality* (New York: Anchor/ Doubleday, 1982); cited in Walker, 1983, p. 27.

20. Andrea Dworkin, *Pornography: Men Possessing Women* (New York: Plume, 1989), pp. 199–200.

21. Deborah Larned, "The Femininity Test." *womenSports* (July 1976), p. 10.

22. Adrianne Blue, *Grace Under Pressure: The Emergence of Women in Sport* (London: Sidgwick & Jackson, 1987), p. 148.

23. Alison Carlson, "The Athlete's View of Gender Verification in Sports." Paper presented at the International Athletic Foundation Symposium on Gender Verification for International Team Physicians." (London: May 15–16, 1992).

24. Ibid.

25. Larned, 1976, p. 11.

26. Alison Carlson, "When Is a Woman Not a Woman?" *Women's Sports and Fitness* (March 1991), p. 26.

27. Ibid., p. 29.

28. Calling estrogen "female" and testosterone "male" is misleading, since both genders have some of both, and there is considerable overlap; some women have more testosterone than some men.

29. Gina Kolata, "Who Is Female? Science Can't Say." *New York Times* (February 16, 1992).

30. Alison Carlson, "Chromosome Count." *Ms.* (October 1988), p. 43.

31. Carlson, 1991, p. 26.

32. Albert de la Chapelle, "The Use and Misuse of Sex Chromatin Screening for 'Gender Verification' of Female Athletes." *Journal of the American Medical Association* (vol. 256, 1986), pp. 1920–23.

33. Carlson, 1988, p. 43.

34. Carlson, 1991, p. 29.

35. Joe Leigh Simpson, *et al.,* "Gender Verification and the Next Olympic Games." *Journal of the American Medical Association* (January 20, 1993), p. 357.

36. Ibid., p. 357.

37. Prince Alexandre de Merode, in a letter to Albert de la Chapelle (University of Helsinki: July 14, 1987).

38. Susan Birrell and Cheryl L. Cole, "Double Fault: Renee Richards and the Construction and Naturalization of Difference." *Sociology of Sport Journal* 7 (1990), p. 2.

39. "Who's That Girl?" *Baltimore Sun* (October 29, 1990).

40. National Federation of State High School Associations 1989–1990 Handbook (Kansas City, Missouri, 1989), p. 71.

41. Frank Hughes, "Female Football Player Files Suit on Injury." *Washington Post* (October 29, 1992), p. D3.

42. Judy Oppenheimer, *Dreams of Glory: A Mother's Season with Her Son's High School Football Team* (New York: Summit Books, 1991), p. 67.

43. Jerry Kirshenbaum, ed., "Scorecard." *Sports Illustrated* (July 1993), p. 10.

44. Birrell and Cole, 1990, p. 5.

Chapter 5
Scoring: What's Sex Got to Do with It?

1. Jane Gross, "Where 'Boys Will Be Boys,' and Adults Are Befuddled." *New York Times* (March 29, 1993) p. A1.

2. Joan Didion, "Trouble in Lakewood." *The New Yorker* (July 26, 1993), pp. 46–65.

3. Ibid., p. 65.

4. Gross, 1993, p. A1.

5. Didion, 1993, p. 54.

6. Ibid., p. 56.

7. Ibid., p. 55.

8. Gross, 1993, p. A1.

9. Wilt Chamberlain, *A View from Above* (New York: Villard Books, 1991).

10. Pearl Cleage, *Deals with the Devil and Other Reasons to Riot* (New York: Ballantine, 1993), pp. 81–87.

11. Alexander Wolff, "The Fall Roundup." *Sports Illustrated* (August 31, 1987), pp. 47–56.

12. Laura Blumenfeld, "Guys Just Wanna Have Fun." *Washington Post* (November 14, 1992), p. C1.

13. Bella English, "Fenway-Bound? Take a Hatpin." *Boston Globe* (June 19, 1991).

14. Timothy Jon Curry, "Fraternal Bonding in the Locker Room: A Profeminist Analysis of Talk about Competition and Women." *Sociology of Sport Journal* 8 (1991), pp. 127–28.

15. Earvin "Magic" Johnson and Richard Levin, *Magic* (New York: Viking Penguin, 1983), pp. i–ii.

16. Earvin "Magic" Johnson and William Novak, *My Life* (New York: Random House, 1992), pp. 233–34.

17. Donald F. Sabo, "The Myth of the Sexual Athlete," in Michael A. Messner and Donald F. Sabo, eds., *Changing Sports, Changing Men: Stories and Essays on Sex, Violence, and Power* (Freedom, California: Crossing Press, 1994). See also Donald F. Sabo and Ross Runfola, eds., *Jock: Sports and Male Identity* (Englewood Cliffs, New Jersey: Prentice Hall, Inc., 1980).

18. Judy Oppenheimer, *Dreams of Glory: A Mother's Season with Her Son's High School Football Team* (New York: Summit Books, 1991), p. 69.

19. David Whitson, "Sport in the Social Construction of Masculinity," in Michael A.

Messner and Donald F. Sabo, eds., *Sport, Men, and the Gender Order: Critical Feminist Perspectives* (Champaign, Illinois: Human Kinetics Books, 1990) p. 26.

20. Donald F. Sabo and Joe Panepinto, "Football Ritual and the Social Reproduction of Masculinity," in Messner and Sabo, eds., (1990), p. 120.

21. "Outside the Lines: Men and Women, Sex and Sports," ESPN (May 27, 1992).

22. Terry Blount, "You Got the Wrong One, Baby." *Houston Chronicle* (October 18, 1993), p. 1C.

23. "Sounds Like a New Woman." *New Woman* (April 1992), p. 63.

24. Rick Telander, "Not a Shining Knight," *Sports Illustrated* (May 9, 1988), p. 122.

25. Ibid.

26. Steven Goff, "Valvano Fired Allegedly for Buying Alcohol." *Washington Post* (March 17, 1992), p. E5.

27. "Bob Valvano Named at St. Mary's (Maryland)." *The NCAA News* (October 12, 1992), p. 15.

28. Dave Meggessey, *Out of Their League* (Berkeley: Ramparts Press, 1970); cited in Myriam Miedzian, *Boys Will Be Boys: Breaking the Link Between Masculinity and Violence* (New York: Doubleday, 1991), p. 198.

29. Elizabeth Ellen Wheatley, "A Women's Rugby Subculture: Contesting on the 'Wild' Side of the Pitch." Unpublished masters thesis, University of Illinois at Urbana-Champaign, 1988, p. 61.

30. Ibid., pp. 61–63.

31. Eric Dunning, "Sport as a Male Preserve: Notes on the Social Sources of Masculine Identity and Its Transformations." *Theory, Culture and Society* 3(1) p. 84; cited in Nancy Theberge, "A Feminist Analysis of Responses to Sports Violence: Media Coverage of the 1987 World Junior Hockey Championship." *Sociology of Sport Journal* 6, no. 3., (September 1, 1989), pp. 247–56.

32. Steven P. Schacht, "The Sadomasochistic Ritual of Male Rugby Players and the Social Construction of Gender Hierarchies." Paper presented at the annual meeting of the North American Society for the Sociology of Sport (Toledo, Ohio: November 5, 1992), p. 20.

33. Ibid., p. 15.

34. Carol Burke, "Dames at Sea: Life in the Naval Academy." *The New Republic* (August 17, 1992), p. 16.

35. Ibid., p. 18.

36. John Lancaster, "Tailhook Assault Victim: Terror and Frustration." *Washington Post* (June 24, 1992), p. A4.

37. Nick Ravo, "Topless Bars for Crowd in Pin Stripes." *New York Times* (April 15, 1992), p. C1.

38. Ibid., p. C12.

39. Kathy Healy, "The New Strippers." *Allure* (June 1992), pp. 99, 115.

40. Jack Bettridge, "The Million Dollar Beach Bum." *M Magazine* (July 1992), p. 89.

41. Jan Graydon, " 'But It's More than a Game. It's an institution.' Feminist Perspectives on Sport." *Feminist Review* 13 (February 1983), p. 6.

42. Liv-Jorunn Kolnes, "Heterosexuality as an Organizing Principle in Women's Sport." Paper presented at the annual National Girls and Women in Sports Symposium (Slippery Rock, Pennsylvania: February 11 – 14, 1993), p. 17.

43. Tony Kornheiser, "Gymnasts Small, Smaller." *Washington Post* (July 31, 1992), p. D8.

44. David Nakamura, "Barrowman's New Suit Draws Lots of Laughs." *Washington Post* (June 15, 1992), p. B6.

45. Judy Mann, "When Less Is More." *Washington Post* (July 9, 1993) p. E3.

46. Wheatley, 1988, pp. 63 – 64.

47. Ibid., p. 66.

Chapter 6
Men in Tight Pants Embracing

1. Allen Guttmann, *From Ritual to Record: The Nature of Modern Sports* (New York: Columbia University Press, 1978), p. 126.

2. Ibid.

3. Donald F. Sabo and Joe Panepinto, "Football Ritual and the Social Reproduction of Masculinity," in Michael A. Messner and Donald F. Sabo, eds., *Sport, Men, and the Gender Order: Critical Feminist Perspectives* (Champaign, Illinois: Human Kinetics Books, 1990), pp. 115 – 26.

4. Ibid., p. 121.

5. Judy Oppenheimer, *Dreams of Glory: A Mother's Season with Her Son's High School Football Team* (New York: Summit Books, 1991), p. 69.

6. Kathryn Ann Farr, "Dominance Bonding Through the Good Old Boys Sociability Group." *Sex Roles* 18, no. 5/6, (1988), pp. 259 – 78; in Michael S. Kimmel and Michael A. Messner, eds., *Men's Lives* (New York: MacMillan Publishing Company, 1989), pp. 403 – 18.

7. Charles Anzalone, "Hail to the Chiefs." *Buffalo: Magazine of the Buffalo News* (February 15, 1987), pp. 12–13.

8. Frank Deford, National Public Radio's Morning Edition, April 22, 1992.

9. Edward R. Hirt, Dolf Zillmann, Grant A. Erickson, and Chris Kennedy, "Costs and Benefits of Allegiance: Changes in Fans' Self-Ascribed Competencies after Team Victory versus Defeat." *Journal of Personality and Social Psychology* 63, no. 5 (1992), p. 724.

10. Laura Blumenfeld, "Guys Just Wanna Have Fun," *Washington Post* (November 14, 1992), p. C1.

11. Tie Domi, "Tough Tradition of Hockey Fights Should Be Preserved." *USA Today* (October 27, 1992), p. 12C.

12. Steven P. Schacht, "The Sadomasochistic Ritual of Male Rugby Players and the Social Construction of Gender Hierarchies." Paper presented at the annual meeting of the North American Society for the Sociology of Sport (November 5, 1992), p. 16.

13. Ibid., p. 10.

14. Ibid., pp. 16–17.

15. Guttmann, 1978, p. 120.

16. Sabo and Panepinto, 1990, p. 123.

17. Ira Berkow, "Walking Away, While He Still Can." *New York Times* (October 3, 1993), section 8 pp. 1–2.

18. Douglas E. Foley, *Learning Capitalist Culture: Deep in the Heart of Tejas* (Philadelphia: University of Pennsylvania Press, 1990), p. 52–53.

19. Brian Pronger, *The Arena of Masculinity: Sports, Homosexuality, and the Meaning of Sex* (New York: St. Martin's Press, 1990), p. 23.

20. Johnette Howard, "The Making of a Goon," in David Halberstam, ed., *The Best American Sports Writing 1991* (Boston: Houghton Mifflin Co., 1991), pp. 119–20.

21. Coakley, 1990, pp. 140–59.

22. Rick Telander, *Hundred Yard Lie: The Corruption of College Football and What We Can Do to Stop It* (New York: Fireside, 1989), p. 87.

23. Coakley, 1990, pp. 140–59.

24. Deborah Tannen shows a fascinating video of same-sex pairs seated, two at a time, in a room with two chairs. Boys and young men move the chairs so they sit side-by-side. Girls and young women move the chairs so they face each other.

25. Gloria Steinem, *Revolution from Within: A Book of Self-Esteem* (Boston: Little, Brown and Company, 1992), p. 223.

26. Mary A. Boutilier and Lucinda SanGiovanni, *The Sporting Woman* (Champaign, Illinois: Human Kinetics Publishers, 1983), p. 104.

27. Paul Hoch, "School for Sexism," in Donald F. Sabo and Ross Runfola, *Jock: Sports and Male Identity* (Prentice Hall, Inc., New Jersey, Englewood Cliffs, 1980), p. 16.

28. Pronger, 1990, p. 191.

29. Clancy Sigal, "Not Their Finest Hour." *New York Times Book Review* (June 7, 1992), p. 9.

30. Rick Telander, "Headlong and Headstrong." *Sports Illustrated* (October 11, 1993), p. 45.

31. Peter Lyman, "The Fraternal Bond as a Joking Relationship: A Case Study of the Role of Sexist Jokes in Male Group Bonding," in Kimmel and Messner, 1992, p. 149.

32. Margaret Morse, "Sport on Television: Replay and Display," in E. A. Kaplan, ed., *Regarding Television: Critical Approaches* (Los Angeles: University Publications of America, 1983), p. 45.

33. Alan M. Klein, "Little Big Man: Hustling, Gender Narcissism, and the Bodybuilding Subculture," in Messner and Sabo, 1990, p. 131.

34. Michael A. Messner, "When Bodies Are Weapons: Masculinity and Violence in Sport." *International Review for the Sociology of Sport* 25, no. 3, (1990), p. 214.

35. "Crackdown on Pornography: A No-Win Battle." *U.S. News and World Report* (June 4, 1984); cited in Naomi Wolf, *The Beauty Myth* (New York: William Morrow and Company, 1991), p. 17.

36. David Kopay and Perry Deane Young, *The David Kopay Story* (New York: Donald I. Fine, 1977), p. 117.

37. Klein, 1990, p. 135.

38. Ben Brown, "Law Gives Women Their Fair Share." *USA Today* (June 9, 1992), p. C1.

39. Buck Turnbull, "Notre Dame's Joyce Says Future of Game on Line vs. Militant Women." *USA Today* (June 7, 1993), p. 12C.

40. Mitchell H. Raiborn, "Revenues and Expenses of Intercollegiate Athletics Programs: Analysis of Financial Trends and Relationships 1985–89." (Mission, Kansas: National Collegiate Athletic Association, 1990). This data refers to NCAA member institutions, which includes most colleges and universities.

41. Ibid.

42. Woody Anderson, Greg Garber, and Lori Riley, "At Last, Title IX Gets Serious Look." *The Hartford Courant*, p. D4.

43. Pat Dye, quoted in the *Birmingham Post–Herald*, cited in "Fundamentals Apply in Education." *NCAA News* (August 19, 1992), p. 4.

44. Chris Grant, *Chicago Tribune,* cited in "Coaches Question Baseball Use of RPI." *NCAA News* (June 23, 1993), p. 4.

45. National Collegiate Athletic Association, 1993. Cited in Donna Lopiano, "Statement Before the Subcommittee on Commerce, Consumer Protection, and Competitiveness." (Washington, D.C.: U.S. House of Representatives, February 17, 1993).

46. Cardiss Collins, "Opening Statement." Subcommittee on Commerce, Consumer Protection, and Competitiveness (Washington, D.C.: U.S. House of Representatives, February 17, 1993).

47. Mary Jordan, "Only One School Meets Gender Equity Goal." *Washington Post* (June 21, 1992), p. D1.

48. Debra E. Blum, "Officials of Big-Time College Football See Threat in Moves to Cut Costs and Provide Equity for Women." *The Chronicle of Higher Education* (June 16, 1993), p. A35.

49. Brown, 1992, p. C2.

Chapter 7
Sexual Assault as Spectator Sport

1. The names in this rape case have been changed. None of the other facts has been altered.

2. Rich Hofman, "Rape and the College Athlete: Part One." *Philadelphia Daily News* (March 17, 1986), p. 104.

3. Mary P. Koss and John A. Gaines, "The Prediction of Sexual Aggression by Alcohol Use, Athletic Participation, and Fraternity Affiliation." *Journal of Interpersonal Violence* 8 (March 1993), pp. 94–108.

4. Anastasia Toufexis, "Sex and the Sporting Life." *Time* (August 6, 1990), p. 76.

5. A woman identified in court as Victoria C. filed a civil suit accusing twelve members or former members of the Cincinnati Bengals of raping her and another eight of standing by and watching after she agreed to have sex in 1990 with Lynn James, their teammate. In 1993, a federal jury found that Victoria C. was bound by a $30,000 liability-release agreement she signed in 1991. "Bengals Rape Case," *Washington Post* (September 9, 1992), p. B7; "Jurisprudence," *USA Today* (March 30, 1993), p. 90; Gary Mihoces, "Bengals: Disclosure of Names in Lawsuit Erases Team 'Cloud,' " *USA Today* (September 9, 1992), p. 8C.

6. In 1986, a female University of California, Berkeley student claimed that four football players raped her in a large student dormitory called the Clark Kerr Campus. Citing a lack of evidence, prosecutors declined to file charges, but after a separate university investigation, the men received letters of censure, wrote letters of apology

to the woman, moved out of the dorm, and did 40 hours of community service. Robin Warshaw, *I Never Called It Rape* (New York: Harper & Row, 1988), p. 111.

In 1993, a non-student accused two freshman football players and a 15-year-old boy of rape, robbery, and battery in a bathroom of the same dorm. Dan Reed, "Prosecution Urged in Gang Rape," *San Francisco Chronicle* (June 26, 1993). No charges have been filed as this book goes to press.

7. Of the five St. Johns lacrosse players charged with sexually assaulting a 22-year-old student on March 1, 1990, three were acquitted, one was found guilty, and the fifth pled guilty to a misdemeanor of sexual misconduct and unlawful imprisonment and received three years' probation, 500 hours community service, and counseling. All were expelled from school. John Kifner, "Jurors Say Complainant Didn't Seem Believable," *New York Times* (July 24, 1991) p. B4; "Outside the Lines: Men and Women, Sex and Sports," ESPN (May 27, 1992).

8. No criminal charges were filed, but two were suspended from the team for the entire season and three received one-semester suspensions. Warshaw, 1988, p. 112.

9. All were acquitted. Lester Munson, "Under Attack," *The National Sports Daily* (August 17–18, 1990), p. 38; Jill Neimark, "Out of Bounds," *Mademoiselle* (May 1991), p. 245.

10. Two 16-year-olds accused four Portland Trailblazers of having sex with them in Salt Lake City. No charges were filed after police concluded that the girls lied about their ages and consented to the sex. Greg Boeck, "Temptations: 'You Can Find Any Trouble,' " *USA Today* (March 10, 1993), p. 4C.

11. A 17-year-old woman accused four Washington Capitals ice hockey players of gang rape and sodomy in the back of a limousine. She told police that Dino Ciccarelli and Geoff Courtnall forced her to have oral sex, Neil Sheehy demanded intercourse, and Scott Stevens asked the limo driver to act as a lookout. Stevens was cleared and the grand jury declined to file charges against the other three men. Gerald Eskenazi, "Male Athletes and Sexual Assault," *Cosmopolitan* (February 1991), p. 221.

12. Charged with raping a woman in their dorm, three men were acquitted and charges were dropped against the fourth. After the trial, two were expelled from school. Warshaw, 1988, p. 112.

13. Christopher Archer and Kevin Scherzer were convicted on March 16, 1993 on two counts of first-degree aggravated sexual assault, using force and coercion, and assaulting a mentally retarded person. Kyle Scherzer was convicted of one count of aggravated sexual assault. All three men were sentenced to fifteen years in a youth detention center, the minimum term required by New Jersey law. Bryant Grober was convicted of third-degree conspiracy and sentenced to three years probation and 200 hours of community service. Rachel E. Stassen-Berger, "3 Men in Sexual Assault Given 15-Year Sentences," *Washington Post* (April 24, 1993), p. A3.

14. No charges were filed against the four players, who admitted having sex with the woman but claimed she consented. The university suspended the players for a month.

Phil Taylor, "New Day Dawns in Arkansas," *Sports Illustrated* (January 13, 1992), p. 32.

15. No charges were filed against baseball players Dwight Gooden, Daryl Boston, and Vince Coleman, accused of raping a 31-year-old New York City woman in Port St. Lucie, Florida, site of the Mets' spring training camp. State Attorney Bruce Colton said the complaint was "the word of the victim against that of three individuals." Jeff Testerman and Marc Topkin, "Mets Won't Face Rape Charges," *St. Petersburg Times* (April 10, 1992), p. 1A.

16. All three were acquitted on 12 counts of raping a woman in a Madison, Wisconsin hotel room after going to a bar to celebrate victory. The university dismissed all three athletes after the filing of charges. The coach resigned. Warshaw, 1988, p. 112; Eskenazi, 1991, p. 221.

17. Derrick Powell, Weldon Parham, and Marvin Childs were acquitted on all counts of rape. Ken Armstrong and Cheryl L. Reed, "Jury: HU Men Innocent," *Daily Press* (August 5, 1992), p. A1.

18. Two University of Colorado football players were charged with rape and acquitted, then left school. Eskenazi, 1991, p. 221.

19. Former Oklahoma University football players Bernard Hall and Nigel Clay are serving ten-year sentences for rape; they both claim innocence. ESPN, 1992; Munson, 1990, p. 38.

20. Leslie Phillips, "Bill Makes Sex Crimes Violation of Civil Rights," *USA Today* (May 28, 1993), p. 3A.

21. Alice Vachss, *Sex Crimes* (New York: Random House, 1993).

22. Mihoces, 1992, p. 8C; "Bengals Rape Case," 1992, p. B7; "Jurisprudence," March 30, 1993, p. 9C.

23. "Bengals Rape Case," 1992, p. B7; "Jurisprudence," March 30, 1993, p. 9C; Mihoces, 1992, p. 8C.

24. Herbert Paul, "Sexual Harassment Settlement Not Deductible," *Journal of Accountancy* (January 1992), p. 29.

25. Laurie Goodstein, "Mother Defends Reputation of Alleged Sex Assault Victim." *Washington Post* (November 25, 1992), p. A3; Bethany Kandel, "4 Guilty in Rape of Retarded Girl," *USA Today* (March 17, 1993), p. 3A.

26. Laurie Goodstein, "Girl's Low IQ at Issue in Assault Trial." *Washington Post* (October 25, 1992), p. A3.

27. Karen Houppert, "Glen Ridge Rape Trial: A Question of Consent," *Ms. Magazine* (March/April 1993), p. 86.

28. Eskenazi, 1991, p. 222; Laurie Goodstein, "Alleged Victim in Glen Ridge Attack Testifies." *Washington Post* (December 10, 1992), p. A3.

29. Bruce Frankel, "Consent at Crux of Assault Trial," *USA Today* (December 10, 1992), p. 4A; Goodstein, December 10, 1992, p. A3.

30. Goodstein, October 25, 1992, p. A3.

31. Stassen-Berger, 1993, p. A3.

32. "Briefly," *USA Today* (May 18, 1992), p. C2.

33. Tom Callahan, "Sex, Lies, and Sporting Heroes." *Washington Post* (May 27, 1990), p. D3.

34. Gary Myers, "Septien, Cade: Too Hot to Handle," *Dallas Morning News* (November 13, 1988), p. 22b.

35. Callahan, 1990, p. D3.

36. "Polonia Settles," *USA Today* (March 16, 1993), p. C1.

37. "Colleges," *USA Today* (October 27, 1992), p. 13C.

38. ESPN, 1992; Munson, 1990, p. 38.

39. "Jurisprudence," *USA Today* (May 12, 1993), p. 13C.

40. Callahan, 1990, p. D3.

41. Ibid.

42. Ibid.

43. B. G. Gregg, "Incidents, Aftermaths," *USA Today* (June 16, 1992), p. 10C.

44. Ibid.

45. Mike Capuzzo, "Unsportsmanlike Conduct." *Philadelphia Inquirer* (December 7, 1990), pp. 1C, 5C; cited in Carol Graybeal, "A Critical Appraisal of the Role of Certain Aggressive Male Sports in Socializing and Institutionalizing Violence Against Women." Unpublished masters thesis (Pennsylvania State University, 1991), p. 8.

46. Ed Christine and Mike Davis, "Strawberry Gets Things Off His Chest," *USA Today* (March 4, 1992), p. 2C.

47. Mel Antonen, "Canseco's Marriage Ends in Divorce Court," *USA Today* (October 30, 1992), p. 2C.

48. National News Network, "Basketball," *USA Today* (September 10, 1992), p. 15C.

49. Michael Messner and William Solomon, "Sin and Redemption: The Sugar Ray Leonard Wife Abuse Story," in Michael A. Messner and Donald F. Sabo, eds., *Changing Sports, Changing Men: Stories and Essays on Sex, Violence, and Power* (Freedom, California: Crossing Press, 1994).

50. John Strege, "Troubled Daly to Go into Rehab," *Orange County Register* (December 30, 1992), p. D1.

51. Interview with Steve Lee, a chief deputy district attorney for Colorado's 18th Judicial District.

52. Toufexis, 1990, p. 77.

53. Eskenazi, 1991, p. 223.

54. "Around the NFL," *Washington Post* (June 3, 1992), p. D2.

55. National News Network, "Colleges," *USA Today* (September 23, 1992), p. 11C.

56. Capuzzo, 1990.

57. National News Network, "Former Alabama Coach Settles Suit for $275,000," *USA Today* (April 14, 1993), p. 11C.

58. "Sampras Pressures Edberg for Win, Final Spot," *Washington Post* (August 16, 1992), p. D2.

59. Jim Myers, "Besieged Sanderson Decides to Step Down." *USA Today* (May 19, 1992), p. C1.

60. "Fanfare," *Washington Post* (May 15, 1992), p. C2.

61. Rick Telander, *Hundred Yard Lie: The Corruption of College Football and What We Can Do to Stop It* (New York: Fireside, 1989), p. 88.

62. Capuzzo, 1990, p. 28.

63. Gene Ruffini, "The Super Bowl's Real Score," *Ms. Magazine* (November/December 1991), p. 93.

64. Ibid.

65. This story was told to Roberta Hacker, of Women in Transition in Philadelphia, by a battered woman and reported in Capuzzo, 1990.

66. Estimates range from 84 to 90 percent. See Warshaw, 1988; also Diana E. H. Russell, *Sexual Exploitation: Rape, Child Sexual Abuse, and Workplace Harassment* (Beverly Hills, California: Sage Publications, 1984).

67. See Peggy Reeves Sanday, "The Socio-Cultural Context of Rape: A Cross-Cultural Study." *Journal of Social Issues* 37 (1981), pp. 5–27.

68. Chris O'Sullivan, "Acquaintance Gang Rape on Campus," in Andrea Parrot and L. Bechhofer, eds., *Acquaintance Rape: The Hidden Crime* (New York: John Wiley & Sons, 1991), p. 153.

69. Warshaw, 1988, p. 112.

70. Martha Burt, "Rape Myths and Acquaintance Rape," in Parrot and Bechhofer, 1991; cited in Graybeal, 1991.

71. Warshaw, 1988, p. 120.

72. Joe Saraceno, "Judge: 'We're Looking at Two Mike Tysons,' " *USA Today* (March 29, 1992), p. A1.

73. Catharine A. MacKinnon, *Feminism Unmodified: Discourses on Life and Law* (Cambridge, Massachusetts: Harvard University Press, 1987), p. 87.

74. Ibid., p. 88.

75. John Stoltenberg, *Refusing to Be a Man: Essays on Sex and Justice* (Portland, Oregon: Breitenbush Books, Inc., 1989), p. 20.

76. Paul H. Gebhard, John H. Gagnon, Wardell B. Pomeroy, Cornelia V. Christenson, and Paul B. Hoeber, *Sex Offenders: An Analysis of Types* (New York: Harper & Row, Publishers, 1965), p. 6; cited in Andrea Dworkin, *Pornography: Men Possessing Women* (New York: Plume, 1979), p. 53.

77. Dworkin, 1979, p. 53.

78. Research was conducted by Virginia Greendlinger of Williams College and Donn Byrne of the State University of New York, Albany. Cited in Warshaw, 1988, p. 93.

79. Warshaw, 1988, p. 39.

80. Miriam M. Johnson, *Strong Mothers, Weak Wives* (Berkeley: University of California Press, 1988); cited in Michael A. Messner, *Power at Play: Sports and the Problem of Masculinity* (Boston: Beacon Press, 1992), p. 101.

81. Michael Kaufman, "The Construction of Masculinity and the Triad of Men's Violence," in Michael S. Kimmel and Michael A. Messner, eds., *Men's Lives* (New York: MacMillan Publishing Company, 1992), pp. 28–50.

82. Susan Brownmiller, *Against Our Will: Men, Women, and Rape* (New York: Simon and Schuster, 1976).

83. MacKinnon, 1987, p. 121.

84. Michael A. Messner, "When Bodies Are Weapons: Masculinity and Violence in Sport." *International Review for the Sociology of Sport* 25 no. 3, (1990), p. 203.

85. David Whitson, "Sport in the Social Construction of Masculinity," in Michael A. Messner and Donald F. Sabo, eds., *Sport, Men, and the Gender Order: Critical Feminist Perspectives* (Champaign, Illinois: Human Kinetics Books, 1990), p. 23.

86. Warren Fraleigh, in *Right Actions in Sport: Ethics for Contestants* (Champaign, Illinois: Human Kinetics Publishers, 1984), delineates four moral agreements athletes ideally must make: (1) each participant freely chooses to play; (2) arrangements are made to equalize opportunity; (3) each participant strives for victory; and (4) game actions are limited to specified spatial and temporal boundaries.

87. Brenda Jo Bredemeier and David L. Shields, "Athletic Aggression: An Issue of Contextual Morality." *Sociology of Sport Journal* 3 (1986), p. 19.

88. This was first explained to me by Brian Pronger in *The Arena of Masculinity: Sports, Homosexuality, and the Meaning of Sex* (New York: St. Martin's Press, 1990), p. 137. Interesting discussions can also be found in Peggy Reeves Sanday's *Fraternity*

Gang Rape: Sex, Brotherhood, and Privilege on Campus (New York: New York University Press, 1990) and Dworkin, 1979.

89. Stoltenberg, 1989.

90. Ibid., p. 35.

91. Joyce Carol Oates, "Rape and the Boxing Ring." *Newsweek* (February 24, 1992), p. 61.

92. Sanday, 1990, p. 20.

93. O'Sullivan, 1991, p. 146.

94. Sanday, 1990, p. 11.

95. Chris O'Sullivan, *Nice Boys, Dirty Deeds: Gang Rape on Campus,* in progress.

96. Jane Hood, "Let's Get a Girl: Male Bonding Rituals in America," in Kimmel and Messner, 1992, pp. 364–70.

97. Joan Didion, "Trouble in Lakewood." *The New Yorker* (July 26, 1993), p. 49.

98. Munson, 1990, p. 30.

99. Sanday, 1990, p. 13.

100. A. Nicholas Groth and H. Jean Birnbaum, *Men Who Rape: The Psychology of the Offender* (New York: Plenum Press, 1979).

101. ESPN, 1992.

102. Constance Johnson, "When Sex Is the Issue." *US News & World Report* (October 7, 1991), p. 34.

103. Warshaw, 1988, p. 149.

104. Bob McNamanan, "Faulkner Sentenced to Jail." *Arizona Republic* (August 28, 1992), pp. D1, D4.

105. Ibid., p. D1.

106. Richard O'Brien, ed., "Tale of the Tapes." *Sports Illustrated* (April 26, 1993), p. 9.

107. Marcia Ann Gillespie, "What's Good for the Race?" *Ms. Magazine* (January/February 1993), p. 81.

108. Pearl Cleage, *Deals with the Devil, and Other Reasons to Riot* (New York: Ballantine Books, 1993), p. 24.

109. Goodstein, October 25, 1992, p. A3.

110. Daniel Begel, "An Overview of Sport Psychiatry." *American Journal of Psychiatry* 149, no. 5, (May 1992), p. 610.

111. Warshaw, 1988.

112. Joyce Carol Oates, 1992, p. 61.

113. MacKinnon, 1987, p. 88.

114. Ibid.

115. Naomi Wolf, *The Beauty Myth: How Images of Beauty Are Used Against Women* (New York: William Morrow and Company, Inc., 1991).

116. Mary P. Koss and Thomas E. Dinero, "Predictors of Sexual Aggression Among a National Sample of Male College Students," in Robert A. Prentky and Vernon L. Quinsey, eds., *Annals of the New York Academy of Sciences* 528 (1988), pp. 133–46.

117. D. Zillman and J. Bryant, "Pornography, Sexual Callousness, and the Trivialization of Rape." *Journal of Communication* 32 (1982), pp. 10–21; cited in Graybeal, masters, 1991, p. 37.

118. Wendy Melillo, "Can Pornography Lead to Violence?" *Washington Post* (July 21, 1992), p. 10, Health Section.

119. Allen Guttmann, *From Ritual to Record: The Nature of Modern Sports* (New York: Columbia University Press, 1978), pp. 130–32.

120. David Phillips, "The Impact of Mass Media Violence on U.S. Homicides." *American Sociological Review* (August 1983), pp. 560–68; cited in Myriam Miedzian, *Boys Will Be Boys: Breaking the Link Between Masculinity and Violence* (New York: Doubleday, 1991), p. 183.

121. National Victim Center and Crime Victims Research and Treatment Center, Arlington, Virginia, 1992.

122. "New Hampshire Writes Parents About Assault and Disrespect of Women," *About Women on Campus* 2, (Summer 1993), p. 10.

Chapter 8
My Coach Says He Loves Me

1. I first reported on this story in Mariah Burton Nelson, "Oregon State Gets New Coach Following Emotional Episode." *USA Today* (August 14, 1991), p. 2C.

2. Peter Rutter, *Sex in the Forbidden Zone: When Men in Power—Therapists, Doctors, Clergy, Teachers, and Others—Betray Women's Trust* (Los Angeles: Jeremy Tarcher, Inc., 1986).

3. Keith-Speigel Pope and B. G. Tabachnick, "Sexual Attraction to Clients." *American Psychologist* 41, no. 2, (1986), pp. 147–58; cited in Mimi Murray, Carole Oglesby, and Hilary Mathesom, "Dangerous Liaisons: Cross Gender Coaching." Unpublished manuscript (March 25, 1991).

4. Rutter, 1986, p. 34.

5. Cindy Hahn, "When Coaches Try to Get Physical." *Fitness* (October 1992), p. 18.

6. Ibid., p. 20.

7. Ibid., p. 19.

8. Murray, Oglesby, and Mathesom, 1991.

9. Rutter, 1986, p. 88.

10. Ibid., p. 27.

11. Todd Crosset, "Male Coach/Female Athlete Relationships: A Case Study of the Abusive Male Coach." Unpublished manuscript (1985).

12. Rutter, 1986, p. 153.

13. Janet Parker Beck, "Sisters Say Ipsen also Molested Them." *The Times* (September 17, 1992), p. C1.

14. Janet Parker Beck, "$1.1 Million Award in Ipsen Case." *The Times* (October 3, 1992), p. C1.

15. Ibid.

16. Desson Howe, "Military 'Men' in Fine Form," *Washington Post* (December 11, 1992), pp. 49, Weekend section.

17. Having investigated whether this man has molested any other girls in the past twenty years, and having come up with no evidence that he has, I have decided not to reveal his name.

18. Rutter, 1986, p. 186.

19. Daniel Begel, "An Overview of Sport Psychiatry." *American Journal of Psychiatry* 149, no. 5, (May 1992), p. 608.

20. Rutter, 1986, p. 51.

21. Helen Lenskyj, "Sexual Harassment: Female Athletes' Experiences and Coaches' Responsibilities." *Science Periodical on Research and Technology in Sport* 12, no. 6 (1992), p. B2.

22. H. Clark and S. Gwynne-Timothy, *Stroke* (Toronto: Lorimer, 1988); Todd Crosset, "The Abusive Coach." Unpublished manuscript, Brandeis University, 1990; cited in Helen Lenskyj, "Sexual Harassment: Female Athletes Experiences and Coaches' Responsibilities." *Science Periodical on Research and Technology in Sport* 12, no. 6 (1992), p. B2.

23. Christine Grant, "The Future of Girls and Women in Sport." Paper presented at the National Girls and Women in Sport Symposium, Slippery Rock State University, Slippery Rock, Pennsylvania (February 6–9, 1992).

24. Rutter, 1986, p. 11.

25. Fern Shen, "Arundel Teacher Gets 26 Years on Sex Charges," *Washington Post* (October 15, 1993), p. A1.

26. Fern Shen, "Md. Teacher Guilty in School Sex Case," *Washington Post* (September 9, 1993), p. A1.

27. Jane Seaberry and Steve Bates, "Fairfax Woman Guilty of Raping Boy," *Washington Post* (August 12, 1993), p. A1.

28. Mariah Burton Nelson, "Perry Gets to Play Again." *Women's Sports and Fitness* (September 1986), p. 22.

29. Rutter, 1986, p. 20.

30. Justin Blum, "Rape Case Prompts Policy Review." *Washington Post* (August 13, 1993), p. B3.

31. Robert F. Howe, "Child Sex Abuse Case Highlights Law's Defect." *Washington Post* (October 15, 1992), p. VA 1.

32. Veronica T. Jennings, "Ex-Student Alleged Abuse by Coach," *Washington Post* (January 24, 1991), p. D4.

33. "Keeping Youth Sports Safe and Fun" is available from the Minnesota Amateur Sports Commission, 1700 105th Ave., N.E., Blaine, Minnesota 55449.

34. Murray, Oglesby, and Mathesom, 1991.

35. Ibid.

36. Rutter, 1986, p. 150.

37. Bill Workman, "Ex-Runner Wins Ruling on Abuse by Her Coach." *San Francisco Chronicle* (October 3, 1992), p. B1.

Chapter 9
How a Woman Is Supposed to Act

1. Wayne Wilson, ed., "Gender Stereotyping in Televised Sports." (Los Angeles: The Amateur Athletic Foundation of Los Angeles, 1990), p. 2.

2. Wayne Wilson, ed., "Coverage of Women's Sports in Four Daily Newspapers." (Los Angeles: The Amateur Athletic Foundation of Los Angeles, 1991), p. 3.

3. Wilson, 1991, p. 4. Gene Policinski, *USA Today* sports editor, disputes this figure, contending that a different method of calculation would reveal a higher percentage, closer to 15 percent.

4. "Yet Another Study Shows Women Receive Less Coverage." *Women's Sports Pages* 3, no. 4 (1991), p. 5.

5. Margaret Carlisle Duncan and A. Sayaovong, "Photographic Images and Gender in *Sports Illustrated for Kids*." *Play and Culture* 3 (1990), pp. 91–116.

6. Jan Rintala and Susan Birrell, "Fair Treatment for the Active Female: A Content

Analysis of Young Athlete Magazine." *Sociology of Sport Journal* 1 (1984), pp. 231–50.

7. Research conducted by Nye Lavelle Group Inc. Cited in Steve Woodward, "Survey: Sports Landscape Is Shifting," *USA Today* (September 8, 1993), p. C1.

8. "Interest Soars for Women's Basketball Event." *NCAA News* (March 31, 1993), p. 1.

9. Research & Forecasts, Inc., "Miller Lite Report on American Attitudes Toward Sports." (Milwaukee: Miller Brewing Company, 1983), pp. 19, 184.

10. Rita Freedman, *Beauty Bound* (Lexington, Massachusetts: Lexington, 1986); cited in Anne Bolin, "Vandalized Vanity: Feminine Physiques Betrayed and Portrayed," in F. E. Mascia-Lees and P. Sharpe, ed., *Tattoo, Torture, Mutilation, and Adornment* (Albany, New York: SUNY Press, 1992), p. 89. Bolin writes, "Muscles encode agonic power, the power of male strength, while women's power is hedonic, that of display."

11. Margaret Carlisle Duncan, "Sports Photographs and Sexual Difference: Images of Women and Men in the 1984 and 1988 Olympic Games." *Sociology of Sport Journal* 7 (1990), 22–43.

12. Mary A. Boutilier and Lucinda SanGiovanni, *The Sporting Woman* (Champaign, Illinois: Human Kinetics Publishers, 1983), p. 188.

13. Wilson, 1990.

14. Margaret Morse, "Sport on Television: Replay and Display," in E. A. Kaplan, ed., *Regarding Television: Critical Approaches* (Los Angeles: University Publications of America, 1983), pp. 44–66.

15. Michael Hiestand, "Sports Radio Scores with Ardent Fans." *USA Today.* (July 28, 1993), p. C1.

16. Frank Ahrens, "For All-Sports Radio, Fans Are All Ears." *Washington Post* (February 11, 1993), p. B1.

17. For more information contact the Women's Sports Foundation, Eisenhower Park, East Meadow, New York 11554; 516/542-4700 or 800/227-3988.

18. Wilson, 1990.

19. Kelly Whiteside, "Sportspeople: Lauren Wolfe." *Sports Illustrated* (February 22, 1993), p. 156.

20. Margaret Carlisle Duncan and Cynthia A. Hasbrook, "Denial of Power in Televised Women's Sports." *Sociology of Sport Journal* 5, no. 1 (1988), pp. 1–21.

21. Michael A. Messner, Margaret Carlisle Duncan, and Kerry Jensen, "Separating the Men from the Girls: The Gendered Language of Televised Sports." *Gender & Society* 7, (March 1993) pp. 123–37.

22. Ibid., p. 127.

23. Margaret Carlisle Duncan, 1990, pp. 22–43.

24. Messner, Duncan, and Jensen, 1993, pp. 123–37.

25. Margaret Carlisle Duncan, "A Hermeneutic of Spectator Sport: The 1976 and 1984 Olympic Games." *Quest* 38 (1986), pp. 50–77.

26. William Drozdiak, "Leading 6–1, 5–1, Sabatini Crashes at French." *Washington Post* (June 2, 1993), p. D1.

27. Messner, Duncan, and Jensen, 1993, p. 128.

28. Tom Callahan, "The Lesser Games Women Play." *Washington Post* (August 16, 1992), p. D3.

29. Duncan, 1986, pp. 50–77.

30. Duncan, 1990, pp. 22–43.

31. Wilson, 1990, p. 19.

32. Tom Callahan, "Glory Hallelujah!" *Time* (August 13, 1984), p. 38.

33. Felicia Halpert, "You Call This Adorable? An Open Letter to the Producer of NBC Sports." *Ms. Magazine* (October 1988), p. 37.

34. Russ Ewald (writer) and Kurt Markus (photographer), "Return to Form." *Men's Journal* (May–June 1992), pp. 86–90.

35. Duncan, 1990, p. 30.

36. "1991 Women's Sports Foundation Athlete Survey," Women's Sports Foundation, Eisenhower Park, East Meadow, New York, 11554.

37. Liv-Jorunn Kolnes, "Heterosexuality as an Organizing Principle in Women's Sport." Paper presented at the annual National Girls and Women in Sports Symposium, Slippery Rock, Pennsylvania (February 11–14, 1993), pp. 10–12.

38. Ed Kiersh, "Graf's Dash," *Vogue* (April 1990), p. 348.

39. Fanfare, *Washington Post* (December 30, 1992), p. C2.

40. Steve Hershey, "Daly Leaves Tour to Enter Rehab." *USA Today* (December 30, 1992).

41. Michael Messner and William Solomon, "Sin and Redemption: The Sugar Ray Leonard Wife Abuse Story," in Michael A. Messner and Donald F. Sabo, eds., *Changing Sports, Changing Men: Stories and Essays on Sex, Violence, and Power* (Freedom, California: Crossing Press, 1994).

42. Ibid.

43. Jay Coakley, *Sport in Society: Issues and Controversies* (St. Louis: Times Mirror/ Mosby College Publishing, 1990) p. 288.

44. Ibid., pp. 288–289.

45. Wilson, 1990.

46. D. Rosner, "The World Plays Catch-up." *SportsInc: The Sports Business Weekly* 1, No. 1, (1989) pp. 6–13. Cited in Donald Sabo and Sue Curry Jansen, "Images of Men in Sport Media: The Social Reproduction of Gender Order," in Steven Craig, ed., *Men, Masculinity and the Media* (Newbury Park, California: Sage Publications, 1992), pp. 169–84.

47. Ben Brown, "This Sports Poll Has an Attitude." *USA Today* (April 12, 1993), p. 3C. Conducted for British Knights athletic shoe company, by Jerico Promotions, 1993.

48. Ken Ringle, "Debunking the 'Day of Dread' for Women," *Washington Post* (January 3, 1993), p. A1.

49. Duncan and Sayaovong, 1990, p. 103.

50. J. B. Strasser and Laurie Becklund, *Swoosh: The Unauthorized Story of Nike and the Men Who Played There* (New York: Harcourt Brace Jovanovich, 1991), p. 30.

Chapter 10
The Looker Room

1. Louise Bernikow, ed., *The World Split Open: Four Centuries of Women Poets in England and America, 1552–1950* (New York: Vintage Books, 1974).

2. These are estimates by *Washington Post* writer Christine Brennan, former president of the Association for Women in Sports Media (P.O. Box 4205, Mililani, Hawaii 96789). The organization has about six hundred members, including about fifty men.

3. Timothy Jon Curry, "Fraternal Bonding in the Locker Room: A Profeminist Analysis of Talk About Competition and Women." *Sociology of Sport Journal* 8 (1991), pp. 119–135.

4. Mary Jo Kane and Lisa Disch, "Sexual Violence and the Reproduction of Male Power in the Locker Room: A Critical Analysis of the 'Lisa Olson Incident.' " *Sociology of Sport Journal* (December 1994).

5. Christine Brennan, "Jocks, Gender, and Justice: A Woman Sports Reporter's View From the Men's Locker Room." *Washington Post* (September 30, 1990), p. D1.

6. Renée D. Turner, "Black Women Sports Writers and the Locker Room Wars." *Ebony* (February 1991).

7. Roger Angell, *Late Innings: A Baseball Companion* (New York: Ballantine Books, 1982), p. 127.

8. Ibid.

9. Ibid., p. 128.

10. Barbara Reynolds, "Editors Should Repeal 'Sir-tax' on Women." *USA Today* (April 12, 1991), p. 13A.

11. G. Kimball, "Counsel Relief for Everyone." *The Boston Herald* (October 2, 1990), p. 73.; cited in Ellen Staurowsky, "Harassment by Any Other Name: A Feminist Analysis of the Lisa Olson Incident." Paper presented at the American Alliance for Health, Physical Education, Recreation, and Dance Convention (Indianapolis, April 8, 1992).

12. Philip B. Heymann, "Report of Special Counsel to the Commissioner of the National Football League," (November 7, 1990), p. 30; cited in Kane and Disch, 1994.

13. Ann Marie Kerwin, "Harassment in the Locker Room." *Editor & Publisher* (October 6, 1990), p. 10.

14. Rachel Shuster, "Kiam Apologizes for Joke." *USA Today* (February 7, 1991).

15. Dave Butz, "Respect Should Keep Women Out of Men's Locker Rooms." *The Washington Post* (October 7, 1990), p. C5; cited in Staurowsky, 1992, p. 9.

16. J. Hart, "No Matter Athletes Behavior, Women Out of Place." *The Norristown (PA) Times Herald.* (October 22, 1990); cited in Staurowsky, 1992. p. 8.

17. Melvin Durslag, "She Would be Wiser to Forget the Lawsuit." *Los Angeles Times* (April 29, 1991), p. C3; cited in Kane and Disch, 1994.

18. Tony Kornheiser, "A Woman's Place." *Washington Post* (October 9, 1990), p. D1.

19. Frank Dell'Apa, "Patriots Try to Focus on Business." *The Boston Globe* (November 29, 1990), p. 91.

20. Leigh Montville, "Season of Torment." *Sports Illustrated* (May 13, 1991), p. 65.

21. Ibid.

22. Ibid.

23. Ibid., pp. 60–65.

24. Cathy Henkel, "Listen Carefully to Olson's Side." *Association for Women in Sports Media* Newsletter (February 1993), pp. 1–3.

25. Ibid., p. 1.

26. Straight women in the military, interestingly, do not fear lesbians looking at them. Not prone to objectifying other bodies themselves, they do not project onto their lesbian sisters such intrusive stares. Nor, of course, are straight women afraid of female sexual assaults. They know too well that it's straight men, not gay men or women, from whom they have the most to fear.

27. Durslag, 1991, p. C3.

28. Lisa Disch and Mary Jo Kane, "Stripped of Power," unpublished paper in progress, 1994.

29. M. L. Stein, "Female sportswriters and sexual harassment." *Editor & Publisher* (October 26, 1991), p. 8.

30. Melissa Ludtke, "Having It All." Paper presented at the Association for Women in Sports Media conference, New York (May 1992).

31. Vanalyne Green, *A Spy in the House that Ruth Built* (New York: Women Make Movies, 1989).

32. Ibid.

33. Susan Fornoff, *"Lady in the Locker Room": Uncovering the Oakland Athletics* (Champaign, Illinois: Sagamore Publishing, 1993), p. xvi.

34. Brennan, 1990, p. D2.

35. Thomas Kochman, *Black and White Styles in Conflict* (Chicago: University of Chicago Press, 1983).

36. Cathy Henkel, "Have We Come a Long Way in The Year?" *Association for Women in Sports Media* Newsletter (October 1992), p. 2.

37. Tracy Dodds, "It's time to act on harassment ..." *Association for Women in Sports Media* Newsletter (Fall 1991), p. 2.

38. Anna Quindlen, "A Case of Psychological Rape." *Cosmopolitan* (February 1991), p. 223.

39. Lorena Hickok, "Gopher Secrets Perfectly Safe When Girl Writer Sees Practice." *Minneapolis Morning Tribune* (November 5, 1922).

40. Judy Mann, "The Media's Message about Women." *The Washington Post* (April 8, 1992), p. C12.

41. J. E. Vader, "Sometimes Life Really Does Imitate Art." *Association for Women in Sports Media* Newsletter (February 1992), p. 3.

42. Margaret Carlisle Duncan and Cynthia A. Hasbrook, "Denial of Power in Televised Women's Sports." *Sociology of Sport Journal* 5 (1988), p. 16.

43. Ludtke, 1992.

44. Green, 1989.

Index